Praise for *The Pin Drop Principle*

"A great book. At the end of each chapter, I found myself cheering for the concepts and wishing I had been introduced to these ideas years ago!"

—**Dan Hebel**, former senior vice president, claims, Allstate Insurance Company

"Practical, straightforward, sane advice. Anyone who speaks will benefit from applying the concepts in *The Pin Drop Principle* to their communication."

—**Eloise Haverland**, director, training and development, Fort Dearborn Company

"The techniques presented in *The Pin Drop Principle* have proven to be the most effective communication tools that I have acquired as a senior executive. I can only imagine how much more valuable they could be if I had been exposed to them twenty years ago."

—**Gregory J. Rizzo**, former president and CEO, Spectra Energy Partners

"*The Pin Drop Principle* is essential for anyone wanting to improve presentation delivery."

—**Roshan Joseph**, global head, learning and development, Virtusa Corporation

"This insightful book provides everything you need to know to move from being an average speaker to becoming a great speaker."

—**Brendan Noonan**, senior vice president, learning and development, Emirates Airline Group

THE PIN DROP PRINCIPLE

Captivate, Influence, and Communicate Better
Using the Time-Tested Methods of
Professional Performers

David Lewis and G. Riley Mills

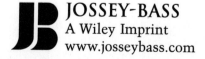

JOSSEY-BASS
A Wiley Imprint
www.josseybass.com

Published by Jossey-Bass
A Wiley Imprint
One Montgomery Street, Suite 1200, San Francisco, CA 94104-4594—www.josseybass.com

Author photos by Ben Newton

Cover image by iStockphoto

Jossey-Bass books and products are available through most bookstores. To contact Jossey-Bass directly call our Customer Care Department within the U.S. at 800-956-7739, outside the U.S. at 317-572-3986, or fax 317-572-4002.

Wiley publishes in a variety of print and electronic formats and by print-on-demand. Some material included with standard print versions of this book may not be included in e-books or in print-on-demand. If this book refers to media such as a CD or DVD that is not included in the version you purchased, you may download this material at http://booksupport.wiley.com. For more information about Wiley products, visit www.wiley.com.

Library of Congress Cataloging-in-Publication Data

Lewis, David
   The pin drop principle : captivate, influence, and communicate better using the time-tested methods of professional performers / David Lewis and G. Riley Mills.—1st ed.
       p. cm.
Includes bibliographical references and index.
   ISBN 978-1-118-28919-8 (hardback); ISBN 978-1-118-31013-7 (ebk);
ISBN 978-1-118-31016-8 (ebk); ISBN 978-1-118-31017-5 (ebk)
   1.   Business communication. 2.   Persuasion (Psychology)
   3.   Communication.   I. Mills, G. Riley. II. Title.
HF5718.L475 2012
658.4'5—dc23

                                        2011050768

Printed in the United States of America
FIRST EDITION
HB Printing   10   9   8   7   6   5   4   3   2

To Celeste, Rider, and Hunter, for their love and inspiration
—DL

For my dad, the greatest teacher and coach of all
—GRM

Contents

THE PIN DROP PRINCIPLE

To be heard so intently that a pin dropping would be a shock ... is, of course, the perfect high C of communication.

—Uta Hagen

Introduction

Communication—the human connection—is the key to
personal and career success.
—Paul J. Meyer

We have been privileged, over the course of our careers, to train thousands of executives around the world. Wherever our travels have taken us, people across all industries consistently bemoan the poor communication skills of the individuals within their organization, from entry-level employees all the way to the C-suite. Complaints include lack of credibility and assertiveness, low levels of enthusiasm, unclear messaging, and more.

This will likely not surprise you. How many times have you attended a meeting, sat through a presentation, or listened to someone's story and thought,

What is the point of this?

Why should I care?

How soon until this is over?

Experts estimate that the average business professional attends a total of 61.8 meetings per month—that's more than three meetings a day.[1] According to the National Statistics Council, 37 percent of employee time is spent in meetings. A full 91 percent of business professionals admit to daydreaming during the meetings they attend, and a shocking 39 percent confess to falling asleep.[2] Judging from these statistics, it is quite apparent that a lot of people out there are not engaging their audiences.

This book, and the methods and techniques we present here, will help you make sure you are never one of those people.

Without engagement—meaning your audience is in a willing state of attentiveness—effective communication is not possible. This is a fact. It doesn't matter who you are or what topic you are discussing, if the arrow that is your message does not hit its intended target, you will have fallen short of the mark as a communicator. Think about it. You can be the most brilliant nuclear physicist in the world, but if the people in the audience you are presenting to have fallen asleep, the theories you are there to explain will not be understood. As a salesperson, you can have the most amazing product on the market, but if your customers aren't clear about what it can do for them, you are not making that sale. As anyone tasked with delivering a message to others knows, you need to penetrate your audience to make an impact on them. You must engage them if you hope to persuade them. We want to teach you the rules of engagement. It's as simple as that.

At the heart of *The Pin Drop Principle* is a conviction that the burden of engagement always lies with the speaker. It is your responsibility, in any communication you deliver—whether you're running a meeting, presenting material, or sharing a story—to engage your audience so fully and completely with what you are saying that, at any given moment, you really could hear a pin drop. As legendary acting teacher Stella Adler puts it, "When you stand on the stage you must have a sense that you are addressing the whole world, and that what you say is so important the whole world must listen."

We all know a great communicator when we see one, that rare individual who captures our attention, rouses our emotions, or compels us to take action. We are drawn to people like this—both in our personal lives and in the public arena—those unique individuals that can project confidence and speak with passion and purpose. In fact, let's try a little experiment. Close your eyes right now and think of the first three people who come to mind when you hear the words *great communicator*. Whose faces do you see? Which voices do you hear? Chances are that some of the names on your list probably include politicians or public figures like Ronald Reagan, Barack Obama, Winston Churchill, or Martin Luther King Jr., individuals generally acknowledged to be great orators. Or you might have gone in a slightly different direction, listing corporate executives like Jack Welch, Steve Jobs, or Meg Whitman, or perhaps you have chosen media figures like Oprah Winfrey, Bill Maher, or Tony Robbins.

All great communicators share five traits in common. When they are speaking—when they're "on"—their speech comes across as clear, concise, confident, credible, and compelling. But they have something extra—some spark that makes them more engaging or dynamic than those who are just good communicators, or even very good ones. What makes them so effective as communicators? Is it simply their self-confidence or their ability to tell a story? The way they use facial expressions or body language? Is it their voice? How does someone attain that mysterious combination of passion and confidence that results in charisma?

In truth, it is never one thing alone that makes a speaker engaging in the eyes of an audience, whether that audience is a boardroom full of investors or a set of in-laws at a dinner party. It is the combination of many skills and qualities all bundled together to support the communicator's secret weapon: the activation of a strong and specific intention in pursuit of a clear and tangible objective.

Many people share a common misconception that great communicators are simply born that way, that they were somehow endowed at birth with the magical ability to move people with their words. Sure, great communicators make it look easy. But like any top athlete or brilliant opera star, this greatness does not happen by chance; it is a result of disciplined practice and hours of hard work. In fact, great speakers refine and perfect their communication skills for precisely that reason: to make it look easy. They want their delivery to appear effortless in the eyes of an audience. But the big secret, as any effective speaker knows, is that great communicators are not born; they are made. The greatest orators in history didn't start out great; they achieved their polish and panache through effort and diligence, through trial and error, and by pushing through mediocrity, never settling for good enough.

In other words, they learned the tools and techniques of great communication, and they never stopped honing them.

In the system of effective communication we teach (it's called the Pinnacle Method, and we talk about it more in a page or two), the secrets to success as a communicator are expressed graphically in what we call the Pinnacle Matrix (Figure I.1).

The matrix is two concentric circles, with the center ring, or bull's-eye, representing what we believe are the heart and soul of great communication: intention and objective. As we begin to discuss in Chapter One, these two concepts are the spark that transforms communication from good to great. Once activated, intention and objective will inform all the other main aspects of your communication—your material, your preparation, and your delivery (or, as we call it in the Pinnacle Method, your *performance*).

As anyone in business knows, countless books and articles have been written on the subject of effective communication: how to appear more likeable, how to influence people, how to make more sales, and so on. *The Pin Drop Principle* is different from those, packed with the effective and accessible tools and techniques for organizing material,

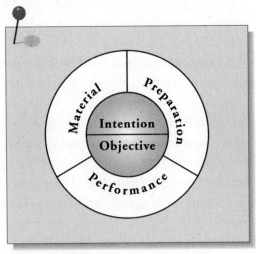

Figure I.1   The Pinnacle Matrix

preparing to communicate, and delivering a message—both time-tested approaches and techniques informed by recent research in psychology and neuropsychology.

But there's a twist—a crucial one. In *The Pin Drop Principle*, every aspect of communication is filtered through a unique lens. We approach the subject of effective communication from a perspective that most people have probably never even considered before, in a methodology we call *Performance-Based Communication*. Specifically, we build on the time-honored delivery techniques that professional actors have used for centuries to deliver credible and compelling performances to their audiences.

That's right. We said *actors*.

What exactly does a professional actor know about effective communication? The answer: just about everything. Think about it. Aside from psychologists and novelists, no one studies human behavior and motivation more thoroughly than the actor. (Christian Bale, who won an Academy Award for playing a crack addict in *The Fighter*, recently remarked that "studying people endlessly without having to apologize" for it was his favorite part of the job.)[3] And then, after studying people's behaviors, emotions, thought processes, motivations, movements, facial expressions, gestures, and voices, the professional actor channels it all, and we receive it in all its power. Together, actor and audience communicate.

In his seminal book *The Presentation of Self in Everyday Life*, sociologist Erving Goffman uses imagery from the theater to discuss human interaction in daily life. Calling every person a "social actor," Goffman makes the case that we all play various roles in our relationships with others, writing, "the part one individual plays is tailored to the parts played by the others present."[4] We behave and present ourselves one way in front of the boss and another way in front of a next-door neighbor. How we behave depends on our circumstances—the person with whom we are communicating and the objective we are pursuing at any given moment.

So what makes actors such great communicators? Ronald Reagan, one of the most popular presidents in U.S. history, was actually dubbed

"The Great Communicator" by the press because of his impressive skills as a speaker and influencer. When asked how his background as an actor served him in his role as a world leader, Reagan responded, "Some of my critics over the years have said that I became president because I was an actor who knew how to give a good speech. I suppose that's not too far wrong. Because an actor knows two important things—to be honest in what he's doing and to be in touch with the audience."[5] When asked how Reagan's years as an actor influenced his presidency, Reagan's Chief of Staff, Kenneth Duberstein, said, "Certainly, it's the communication, the ability to communicate, the ability to find the right words … the right expression or the right anecdote … proving yourself each day … because you have another performance."[6]

Communication, as defined by researchers John Schermerhorn, James Hunt, and Richard Osborn, is "the process of sending and receiving messages with attached meanings."[7] These messages can be delivered verbally and nonverbally, and no one is more of an expert in both verbal and nonverbal communication than an actor. Quite simply, that is what actors do. Professional actors spend years honing their craft—learning how to employ voice, gestures, and body language to influence others. And it is a craft, with techniques, tricks, skills, and practices that can be taught and learned—by anyone.

The premise we operate on is a simple one: that the exact same toolbox of skills that has been used for centuries by professional actors can also be used quite effectively by non-actors. In fact, anyone who desires to appear more confident and compelling in their communication—whether they're trying to reach and influence their boss, a client, or their future in-laws—can take advantage of these methods. And there's more good news: you already have many of these tools in your communication arsenal. What we do over the course of *The Pin Drop Principle* is show you how to use them more effectively, in ways you may never have considered before, to sharpen your communication and deliver your message—any message—with purpose.

In taking cues from actors, you will be in illustrious company. Leaders throughout history have inspired nations with their soaring rhetoric. And for years, many of these powerful leaders have quietly enlisted the help of professional actors and acting coaches to train them in the art of performance-based communication.

In 2011, the Academy Award for Best Picture went to a film called *The King's Speech*. The movie was based on the little-known but true story of King George VI, who, racked with stage fright and an uncontrollable stutter, in 1926 secretly employed an Australian actor named Lionel Logue to help him overcome his fear of public speaking. Using the very same training methods of speaking and breathing employed by actors in the theater, Logue was not only able to help the king overcome his devastating stammer, he was also able to transform the shy and timid leader into a confident and credible orator who was eventually able to lead and inspire his countrymen through the trials and tribulations of World War II.

Of course, up until recently, very few people knew anything about King George studying acting techniques to help him project a strength and confidence he did not actually possess. Imagine the reaction at the time if word about this had gotten out—the king of England being trained by ... an actor! As it happened, Logue had taken great pains to keep their relationship a secret as a gesture of respect for the king and his privacy. It was only decades later, long after both men had passed away, when Logue's grandson discovered his grandfather's diaries detailing what had taken place, that this amazing story finally came to light.

But King George was not the only great leader who has borrowed from the performer's toolbox to sharpen and shape their personal communication. Other individuals of passion and influence have also achieved success at least in part due to these methods—people like Abraham Lincoln, Bill Clinton, Winston Churchill, Bob Dole, Jimmy Carter, Menachem Begin, Hu Jintao, Rahm Emanuel, Hillary Clinton, John F. Kennedy, Oprah Winfrey, and Robert F. Kennedy, to name just a few. Sadly, even Adolf Hitler is said to have secretly studied with an acting coach to teach him to use his voice and body more effectively in his communication. Of course, the origins of these techniques don't simply go back decades, but centuries, all the way back to ancient Athens, where Demosthenes—arguably the greatest orator of all time—was inspired by the actor Satyrus to perfect his delivery.

There is an adage in the theater that all you need to create drama is a plank and a passion. In the years before television and radio, actors would travel from city to city performing on makeshift stages wherever crowds would gather. This same principle of a plank and a passion is often referenced in the business world, since the concept is equally applicable for someone communicating in a corporate setting. As the actor John Lithgow pointed out in an interview on *The Colbert Report*, in the end "All business is show business."[8]

Think for a moment, and strip away the flashy PowerPoint slides and glossy handouts. It doesn't matter whether you are selling a product, delivering a performance review, or starting a neighborhood book club, at its very essence, every communication consists of three simple elements: you, your message, and your audience.

In many ways, the relationship between speaker and audience in a corporate setting is the same as the relationship between actor and audience in the theater. Both operate under an unwritten contract: an audience will willingly offer time and attention if, in return, the speaker will provide that audience with information or content that is worth the value of their time. A communion of sorts takes place in this exchange, a flow of give-and-take between speaker and audience. Whether it is Hamlet delivering his "to be or not to be" monologue, Mark Zuckerberg pitching the concept of Facebook to a group of potential investors, or a young man asking his girlfriend to marry him, it all comes down to the same formula—one formulated for the ages by the Greek philosopher Aristotle. Aristotle wrote eloquently about such subjects as oratory, politics, and theater (three things that have a lot in common). In his famous treatise *Rhetoric*, Aristotle discussed the art of persuasion, recognizing that any speech or communication basically consisted of three things: speaker, subject, and audience.

We all present ourselves on a daily basis; we all perform. As author Ken Howard writes in his book *Act Natural*, "Every day in our life and work, we play many different roles—as friends, lovers, spouses, parents, students, teachers, employees, managers, CEOs. . . . The key to genuine communication, whether you're playing Hamlet, a top job candidate, or a VP of marketing, is getting your authentic self before the people in the room."[9] While most people think of a presentation as a formal event involving standing up in front of a crowd, in reality, every time you interact with another person you are presenting ideas or information for the benefit of another person or group. And just as every interaction can be considered a presentation, you can take it a step further and think of it as a performance as well—a chance for you to consciously and skillfully put your best self forward and deliver your message effectively and engagingly. With *The Pin Drop Principle*, we invite you to think of every communication you do as a performance. Not acting. Not theatricality for theatricality's sake but as a performance to an audience, even if that audience is only one person.

ABOUT THE PINNACLE METHOD AND *THE PIN DROP PRINCIPLE*

The birth of *The Pin Drop Principle* dates back to the creation of our performance-based communication skills firm, Pinnacle Performance Company. What began as a unique and experimental approach to training communication and presentation skills has evolved into a proven, innovative learning system that has empowered thousands of executives around the world, at companies such as Apple, GE, Oracle, Capgemini, Walgreens, Allstate, Barclays, and Emirates—not just in their business interactions, but their social communication as well. This year, Pinnacle was proud to accept the 2011 Award for Vendor Innovation in Learning & Talent Management from the World Human Resources Development Congress at a ceremony in Mumbai, India.

To understand what makes *The Pin Drop Principle*'s approach to effective communication different, you first need to understand our individual backgrounds as the book's authors. Aside from our years of corporate experience running companies, managing sales teams, and facilitating learning, we share one other trait in common: we both have extensive training and experience as professional actors. And it is precisely the meshing of these two skill sets that led to the creation of this book.

One of us graduated from Cornell University, majoring in business and communication before ultimately focusing on acting; the other studied acting at the Theatre School, DePaul University, before shifting over to the world of business. After completing our respective studies, we both embarked on dual career tracks, working in business while also continuing to appear professionally onstage and onscreen, in film and on television, working with the likes of Ewan McGregor, Milos Forman, Lois Smith, Zack Snyder, Jason Alexander, Tom McCarthy, Juliana Margulies, Patrick Wilson, Michael Jordan, Neil McDonough, John Heard, Kyle Chandler, and Penelope Milford.

Prior to launching Pinnacle, we worked in various corporate leadership roles, where we were often tasked with bringing in vendors to provide workshops and seminars for our teams: leadership training, sales training, or communication skills training. And while some of these workshops had value, we quickly discovered that virtually every company we hired (and every book we purchased) came up short, failing to cover in any significant detail the two most important aspects of communication—the ones we had mastered as professional actors: the concept of intention and the application of a person's *physical delivery* to achieve their given objective, whether that objective was making more sales, motivating a team, or creating a more streamlined workforce. Time after time, these so-called experts focused on theory and structure, while barely mentioning the actual delivery and outward communication of the people we had sent to the training!

We quickly realized that while our team members were generally prepared with their content and knew their material, too many times when they actually delivered that material, their physical and verbal messaging—their *performance*—failed to put the information across; it was a serious blind spot, and sometimes a fatal one. The disconnect in their communication between material and delivery often meant losing a million-dollar deal, angering a loyal customer, or inadequately training a new employee—costly, damaging situations that could have been avoided if their message had been delivered properly the first time.

And that's when the light went on.

We realized that we basically had two options. We could continue to pour our limited training dollars into workshops and seminars that were disappointing, cookie-cutter, or simply a waste of time, or we could create a brand new curriculum ourselves—one that originated from the invaluable tools and techniques we had mastered as professional actors. And with that, the Pinnacle Method was born.

After piloting our initial series of programs and curricula with a select group of Fortune 500 companies, we instantly knew that we were onto something: that the exact same methods and techniques used by professional actors could be transferred, quite easily, to any environment to make anyone's communication more effective and compelling. It is precisely these methods that we have decided to share with you in the pages of *The Pin Drop Principle*. A note: this book is not about acting. And it will not teach you how to be a great actor. Acting is a craft, and like any craft, it takes years to study and perfect. What we have done in *The Pin Drop Principle* is take the time-honored performance delivery techniques you would have learned in an acting conservatory and mesh them with the essential communication skills needed to thrive and succeed not only in your personal life but at every level of the corporate world.

This book is a toolbox and each chapter provides you with new tools—or with new ways of looking at tools you already possess. Each chapter deals with various aspects of communication preparation or performance—storytelling, managing anxiety, controlling your audience, and much more. We encourage you to read the first chapter, which unlocks the secret of pairing objective with intention—an approach that informs everything else in the book. Then read through from beginning to end, or start with the chapters that interest you the most. Chapter Two teaches storytelling skills, while Chapter Three deals with structuring your overall presentation and teaches rhetorical techniques that will keep your audience with you. Chapter Four disposes of the myth that there is such a thing as over-preparation, showing you how to prepare effectively and how to minimize anxiety and error.

Chapters Five and Six are full of the sorts of insights into and methods of using your body and your voice that actors all learn—and that few businesspeople have even heard of. Chapter Seven deals with listening from two perspectives: how understanding how an audience listens helps you maximize their listening; and how improving your own listening will improve your communication. Chapter Eight uses the lessons of theatrical improvisation to empower your impromptu speaking, and also gives you the tools to handle one of the most common and important impromptu speaking opportunities in the business world: the "What do you do?" question. Chapter Nine is packed with tools to use while delivering a presentation in tough circumstances—when you're facing a distracted or hostile audience, or a challenging question-and-answer situation. And Chapter Ten helps you assert yourself to get what you want in challenging or high-stakes situations—closing a deal, getting buy-in from senior leadership, giving critical feedback, or delivering bad news.

Take the tools and techniques here for a spin. Try them out. Explore. Experiment. Practice.

Knowing is not enough; we must apply. Being willing is not enough; we must do.

—LEONARDO DA VINCI

One of the underlying tenets of the Pinnacle Method is that, whether you are delivering a presentation, running a meeting, or telling a story, if your audience is bored during your communication, it is your fault. It is not the audience's responsibility to be engaged, it is your responsibility to engage them. If you are not able to get through to your audience and move them with what you are saying, your communication will have fallen short of its mark.

By learning and applying the methods and techniques detailed in this book, you will be able to engage your audience in every communication you deliver: whether running a meeting, telling a story, or simply presenting information. These tools and techniques will allow you to become more present in your daily communication, more confident in your abilities, and more engaging in your delivery. The end result: the ability to get your audience to react the way you want, in any situation, simply by mastering the delivery of your message.

Let's get to it, shall we?

CHAPTER 1

Understand the Secrets of Persuasion

Communicating with Intention and Objective

The starting point of all achievement is desire.
—NAPOLEON HILL

We've all seen or heard persuasive speakers—people who engage us with their communication effectively, whatever its subject may be. And because they are able to capture our attention (and perhaps our imagination), the chances are good that they will also be able to move us emotionally or change the way we think about a topic or issue. But how exactly do they do it? What makes someone persuasive as a communicator?

The story of one of history's most famously persuasive speakers gives us some insight.

Often regarded as the greatest of Greek orators, Demosthenes, the Athenian statesman and rhetorician, rallied the citizens of Athens against the military power of Philip of Macedon and Philip's son, Alexander the Great, for almost thirty years. So powerful was Demosthenes in his ability to rouse the passions of his audiences that Cicero (perhaps the greatest Roman orator) called him "the perfect orator."

But Demosthenes, who was the son of a wealthy sword maker and was orphaned at age seven, was not always celebrated for his abilities—in fact, his early attempts at speaking were met with ridicule.

In ancient Greece, public speaking was a vital aspect of everyday life, and skilled orators or rhetoricians were valued very highly. When he was still a boy, Demosthenes saw some of the great rhetoricians of the day speaking in court or in the assembly—a regular meeting of the citizenry, where they would deliberate and vote on all aspects of Athenian life. He was captivated by their power and popularity, and set about to study their methods and become a great orator himself.

He had some early success in court, bringing suit against his guardians for mishandling his estate. But his first efforts in the assembly were met with jeers and derision—his style was stilted, his sentences tortuously long, his voice weak and breathy. People hated listening to him. Crushed by this public humiliation, Demosthenes fled the assembly in shame.

On another day, when Demosthenes had not been allowed to speak before the assembly at all, he came upon an acquaintance—an actor named Satyrus. *It's not fair*, Demosthenes said. *I work hard on my speeches; I'm far better prepared than any of those idiots they let speak, and they won't even listen to a word*. Satyrus, as a professional actor, perfectly understood the cause of Demosthenes' failure in the assembly: the problem was not his message—it was the poor *delivery* of his message. Demosthenes' speeches failed to connect with his audience because they lacked something vital—they lacked *intention*. The young orator took no care in how he came across to his audience—he didn't even seem to know he should—and as a result he thoroughly alienated the people he meant to persuade.

To demonstrate the problem, Satyrus had Demosthenes read a passage from the classics, and then he read it himself, using his voice and body with all his skill. Demosthenes was thunderstruck—the passage seemed like an entirely different text when the actor read it—and from that day he began to believe that if a speaker neglected his presentation, he might as well not speak at all. He saw that a speaker's *intention*—the choice to act and speak persuasively—was imperative and essential to his *objective*—to persuade.

Demosthenes took to the actor's teaching with a vengeance. He built an underground chamber—a sort of cave—and he practiced his gestures and intonation there every single day. He picked apart speeches—his own and others'—rephrasing what was said more gracefully and practicing it aloud in his chamber. He trained his breathing by reciting a speech while running or climbing. He put pebbles in his mouth to improve his enunciation. He rehearsed in front of a mirror to check how his posture, gestures, and other body language would come across to his audience.

When it was time for Demosthenes to speak in front of the assembly again, all of Athens took notice. His fiery speeches about the political, social, and economic issues of the day riveted, persuaded, and roused the Greek citizenry. Neither his subject matter nor his audience had changed, nor had his objective—to compel his listeners to action. But once he began delivering his speeches with intention—and with an actor's techniques—the results could not have been more different.

INTENTION AND OBJECTIVE

The Pinnacle Method, adapting the actor's approach to a wide range of communications, is based on the simple premise that whether you are making a customer service call, delivering a large presentation, running a team meeting, or having dinner with your family, the success of your communication depends upon two things. First, you must identify an *objective*—something you want or need from your audience. And second, you must choose an *intention* that will assist you in the pursuit of that objective. Think of the objective and intention in your communication like this:

- Objective = What You Want
- Intention = How You Are Going to Get It

Actors, by training, know the secrets of objective and intention and how to make them work together for effective communication.

It's a common misconception that actors pretend to be other people. In reality that's not what we do at all. Rather, we are trained to put ourselves—our *true* selves—into imaginary circumstances and deliver our message (in this case, our lines) with a specific *intention* to generate a desired reaction from our audience (whether that audience is our scene partner or the audience who paid to come and see us). We need our audience to believe what we are saying as the character in that moment. If they don't believe what we say, the credibility of our character comes into question, and the success of our performance is compromised.

The same can be said for any person's communication. If we don't believe what someone is saying—whether that person is a salesman, a mayoral candidate, or our teenage daughter—they end up communicating to us something different from what they intended—for example, we come to believe that this product is actually not a good fit for our needs; that these policies don't sound very effective; or that perhaps we should check to see if her homework is really done.

All of these people in the examples above want something that depends on us, their audience—a sale, a win, a trip to the mall—and they want to compel us to do something—buy the product, vote for them, give them permission to go. If their objective and intention are not well aligned, we'll remain unconvinced, their communication will have failed, and they won't get what they wanted.

Thus an objective, if properly aligned with intention, should result in a successful communication—one that changes your audience's knowledge, attitude, or action with regard to the topic being discussed or presented. As a communicator, you must have a specific objective in mind—*something you need to accomplish*—if you hope to impact and move your audience. In the end, without an activated intention behind your delivery—and one that is specifically in line with your objective—the best your message will be is ambiguous. A strong intention behind your words will literally fuel the emotion of your delivery.

In the rest of this chapter, we show you how to clearly identify a specific objective for your communication—to understand exactly what you want to have happen as a result of your message. We also guide you in the process of pinpointing and choosing the most effective intention to accomplish it.

For your communication to achieve its objective, all aspects of your delivery must be supported and driven by the chosen intention. It is the ability to combine these two elements working in tandem that separates engaging communicators from those who fail to engage an audience in any meaningful way.

Defining Your Objective

As Demosthenes discovered, effective communication never consists of words alone. There must be a purpose behind those words that calls an audience to action. The result of this action is, ideally, identical to what we call a communicator's *objective*. Simply put, your objective is the goal or purpose you hope to achieve with your audience as a result of the delivery of your message. A computer sales rep wants to sell a computer, a teacher wants the students to learn their state capitals, and a safety manager wants the workers to avoid injury.

Constantin Stanislavski, the founder of the Moscow Art Theatre in the late nineteenth century and the father of modern acting, wrote extensively on the concept of objective in his groundbreaking book *An Actor Prepares*.[1] In his books and methods, Stanislavski developed an approach to realistic acting that is still used to this day. One of the major precepts of the Stanislavski system was the importance of a particular kind of preparation. An actor was to begin by studying the script and identifying goals and objectives for every scene, seeking answers to the following questions:

1. What do I want?
2. What is in the way of what I want?
3. How am I going to get what I want?

By carefully and thoroughly answering these three questions, actors gain a much clearer idea of what they want to accomplish in a particular scene. The questions are so effective that they have come to represent a sort of "holy trinity" for actors.

But they can just as easily be applied to communication in any setting—whether you're managing a team, hoping to influence a stakeholder, or asking someone out on a date. As Stanislavski explains, "Life, people, circumstances . . . constantly put up barriers . . . Each of these barriers presents us with the objective of getting through it. . . .[2] Every one of the objectives you have chosen . . . calls for some degree of action."[3]

But not all objectives are created equal, and most communication doesn't consist of just one objective; instead, it comprises numerous objectives—smaller goals that need to be achieved in order to accomplish the main one. Your most important objective, the one that best describes your overall goal, Stanislavski called a *super-objective*. For example, a teacher's super-objective might be to teach the students geometry, but first they must be induced to take their seats and be quiet.

Before delivering any message, you need to understand what you want at the end of your communication. What is your super-objective? Is it buy-in from the other party, or commitment for more funding, or additional personnel? Is it a signature on a contract or the adoption of a new policy? Whatever the goal is for your communication, you need to clearly understand it for yourself. Otherwise you risk being like a marathoner who runs and runs but has no idea where the finish line is. Write it down, using concrete language. If you have more than one objective, express each clearly and concretely.

Once you know your objective you have half of what you need to communicate effectively. The other half is the communicator's secret weapon and most invaluable tool—*intention*.

Choosing an Intention

Often when we develop a message, we focus primarily on the words and content we are delivering. We usually also have an objective in mind, of course, even if we have not defined it carefully and precisely. What we often fail to ask ourselves is *why that overall message should be important to our audience*. Why should they care? What would make them care? We neglect to pair intention with objective. This very common mistake is usually fatal to effective communication.

Before delivering their messages, communicators *must* understand with great clarity how they want their audience to react to each message. How do they want their audience to *feel* as a result of their communication? The answer to this question is the speaker's intention; according to the dictionary, *intention* is "an aim that guides action."

Understanding the importance of intention and deploying it effectively is the cornerstone of brilliant acting, often separating a memorable performance from a forgettable one. Actors use intention in every aspect of their performance, breaking down each moment of a scene to understand their objective and help them identify the specific intentions they will use to deliver their lines. Actors always have an objective in a scene, something they want (to get the money, to sleep with the girl, to convince the bully to stop picking on them) and they always pair that objective with a complementary intention. They use their intentions to threaten, seduce, or intimidate to accomplish the objective. While actors focus their intention and objective on their partner in a scene, there is always another audience at play in the theater: the people sitting in the dark watching the action on stage. The director's job is to make sure that the intentions of the actors on stage are strong and specific so they have the effect of bringing the other (theatrical) audience along, ensuring that they feel the appropriate emotions at the appropriate times. And as circumstances in a scene change, an actor's objectives and intentions will change as well. As a communicator, you'll find intention the most powerful tool in your arsenal too. It will not only bring passion and purpose to your message, it is the most critical component in the pursuit of your objective—the rocket fuel that will launch you toward the eventual accomplishment of your goal.

In *Tell to Win*, Hollywood producer and former chairman of Sony Pictures Peter Guber writes that capturing your audience's attention "involves focusing your whole being on your intent to achieve your purpose.... Your *intention* is actually what signals listeners to pay *attention*."[4] In other words, without a strong intention supporting your delivery, your audience is less likely to give you their attention in the first place. And that's just the first benefit a strong intention brings to your attempts to communicate. It also *holds* the audience's attention, and the passion and purpose it conveys actually bring the audience members into sympathy with your point, so that they are connecting both emotionally and intellectually with your message.

Dan Siegel, a UCLA neuroscientist and author of *The Mindful Brain*, has discovered that a listener's mirror neurons only switch on when they sense another person is acting with passion and purpose. Everything people do with their voice or their body communicates information to a listener or audience. For this reason, Siegel states that people such as teachers or instructors "need to be aware of their intentions ... to make the experience of learning as meaningful and as engaging as possible.... In return, [the students or audience] will feel inspired and engaged in the passion of the work."[5] Humans begin reading each other's intention cues as soon as they are physically close enough to see, hear, or smell them. Says Siegel, "With the attention to intention we develop an integrated state of coherence."[6] This is precisely why all aspects of a person's communication and delivery must be in sync. The cues your face, voice, and body send are so powerful that your audience will pay attention to them before anything else; thus an intention that's out of sync with the content of your message or your desired objective will torpedo your communication.

When you're identifying your intention, express it as a verb—a strong action word that can activate and inform your delivery. For example, your intention might be to *inspire* your employees to act in a certain way, or to *reassure* a colleague that a decision was correct. Here are a few examples of different intentions commonly used during the average person's daily communication:

Clarify	Demand	Dazzle	Inspire	Encourage	Tease
Excite	Criticize	Manipulate	Challenge	Unnerve	Patronize
Urge	Cajole	Rattle	Soothe	Reprimand	Calm
Inform	Enlighten	Frighten	Caution	Involve	Motivate
Reassure	Empower	Engage	Commend	Intimidate	Persuade
Enchant	Soothe	Irritate	Provoke	Ridicule	Champion

Think of a recent interaction with someone where you tried to convey one of the intentions in the list. Did your physical and vocal delivery support your intention so effectively that your listeners knew exactly how you wanted them to feel? A strong intention, activated properly, will inform all aspects of one's communication—body language, facial expressions, vocal dynamics, and all the rest. To experience how this works, try this: using the list of intentions provided previously, say the phrase, "Can I see you in my office?" five different times, each time reflecting a different intention. You will notice how the delivery of the words changes as your intention does.

PUTTING INTENTION AND OBJECTIVE INTO PRACTICE

The famous acting teacher Uta Hagen writes in her seminal book *Respect for Acting*, "The action of the words, how I will send them, for what purpose and to whom, under what circumstances, hinges solely on what I want or need at the moment."[7] What she is speaking about here is the combination of *intention* and *objective*. When identifying the intention and objective, you should be able to describe the purpose of your message in a single sentence:

Purpose of Message

I want to _____ my audience so that my audience will_____.
        (Intention)   (Objective)

Here are a few examples of different communication scenarios to illustrate the point:

Scenario #1: A manager in a warehouse calls a staff meeting after discovering that the workers have not been following the required safety procedures while operating the trash compactor.
Intention and Objective: *I want to* warn *my employees about their unsafe behavior so they* comply with safety policies and avoid injuries.

Scenario #2: As the polls close after a long and difficult political battle, a winning politician gathers the campaign committee for a private meeting before going on television for the acceptance speech.
Intention and Objective: *I want to* commend *my staff and volunteers for their great work in this campaign so they* feel appreciated and validated.

Scenario #3: When a young girl receives an "F" on her report card, her father sits down with her to explain why achieving good grades in school can contribute to her future success and happiness in life.
Intention and Objective: *I want to* motivate *my daughter so she* applies herself and studies harder.

Scenario #4: A loss prevention manager in an orientation meeting with newly hired cashiers recounts the story of five former employees at the store who were caught stealing money from the register and eventually ended up in jail.
Intention and Objective: *I want to* caution *these new cashiers about their personal conduct so they* understand company policy and don't commit employee theft.

Scenario #5: A vacuum cleaner sales rep demonstrates the difference between a homemaker's twenty-year-old vacuum cleaner and the new state-of-the-art model.
Intention and Objective: *I want to* persuade *this homemaker about the superiority of this vacuum cleaner so she* places an order for purchase.

In any communication, it is helpful to imagine that your intention is connected to a human emotion you hope to access in your audience. Imagine how you want your audience to *feel* as a result of hearing the words you will be saying. Remember, it is always about your audience and how you want them to feel about your material or message; it is never about how you feel. You might find the material boring. You might not feel connected to or enthusiastic about your company's product or offering. In fact, you may not even agree with the program you are required to speak about or the subject you are assigned to teach. In the end, the fact that *you* are not engaged with your material is irrelevant because, as a communicator, it is never about you: it is always about your audience. You must choose an intention that makes your audience react the way you need them to react (we discuss using your voice effectively in Chapter Six). For example, if you want new employees to feel welcome, smile when you are introducing them to the team and use the various aspects of your voice (something else discussed in later chapters) to express your enthusiasm. If you are disciplining a child for breaking a vase, use stern facial expressions and direct eye contact to communicate the seriousness of the situation.

We all know what it means to truly have an objective. To get him or her into bed, to get the job, to get out of mowing the lawn, to borrow the family car. We know what we want, and, therefore, we know whether we're getting closer to it or not, and we alter our plans accordingly. This is what makes a person with an objective alive: they have to take their attention off themselves and put it on the person they want something from.

—DAVID MAMET

Often we are tasked with presenting material or a message that might be dry or dull. This is a case when intention and objective are particularly valuable tools in your communication arsenal. Even though you may not personally find the topic or content interesting or exciting, you still need to understand why that information is important to your audience, and you still have to deliver the information with meaning. (Delivering financial numbers or technical data can be especially challenging, both from your perspective as the speaker and from your audience's perspective. This is a case where it becomes vital to clearly understand why the information you are providing is important to the audience and what you hope to achieve by conveying it to them.)

Regardless of the content of your message, you want your listeners to be emotionally engaged, and you want their investment in what you are saying. You may or may not be emotionally engaged or invested in your message; that's not the point. You can still communicate effectively if you choose your intentions wisely. Let's see how that works in practice.

Intention Cues

So, to review: for your communication to have impact, you first must decide how you want your audience to act upon your message (your objective); then you need to pinpoint an intention to deliver that message in order to best achieve that action. Finally, you must activate what are known as your *intention cues*—the vocal and physical manifestations of your intention—to ensure the words and delivery match up and the message achieves the desired result with your audience.

As mentioned previously and as we return to in later chapters, everything you do with your voice and body must support your intention. When all of your vocal and physical cues are in sync with your chosen intention, this is called *congruence*. When you offer mixed signals, or there is a disconnect between what you are saying and how you are saying it, your audience can become confused or distracted. This is called *incongruence* and it is the enemy of effective communication.

For instance, if a doctor's intention is to *convince* a patient to eat a healthier diet, his intention cues would have to reflect that. Depending on the patient, cues might include a serious facial expression, direct eye contact, and a warm but serious tone of voice. Other signals such as rushed speech, flickering eye contact, or attention to the file or the clock rather than the patient can convey a lack of seriousness or concern and lead the patient to tune out the message.

Let's try another example. The stereotype of a used car salesman is of someone who communicates in a pushy or dishonest way. Of course, in reality, there are good used car salesmen and bad used car salesmen. Any used car salesman has an objective: he wants to sell you a car. But his intention cannot be the same as his objective. If his intention is to *sell*, then everything he does with his body language and vocal cues would signal "selling," and this would be a turn-off for a potential customer. For the salesman to sell that car effectively, he needs to think not about selling but about the feelings he wants to elicit in his audience—trust, reassurance, and excitement. That's his message: "I see what you want in a car; this is a good car that I feel proud to have in inventory; you'll feel good owning it." Not "I want to sell you this car"—never that. He has to convey his intention through the way he uses his body and voice—a smile and open posture, attentive facial expression when the buyer is talking, quiet excitement in his voice and gestures when he is showing off the car's features. The buyer needs to feel persuaded or excited about purchasing that car for the salesman to achieve his objective and, in the end, make that sale. But the way the salesman achieves his objective is to turn his back on it, so to speak, and immerse himself in his intention—how he wants to make his audience feel.

In whatever position you find yourself, determine first your objective.

—FERDINAND FOCH

Once you understand your objective and intention, you can become aware of how your intention cues get your audience to react the way you want. By shouting, you will get a room of children to be quiet; by waving your arms wildly you will get the attention of the lifeguard; by smiling at your coworkers you will let them know you are happy to see them. In Chapters Five and Six we talk more about intention cues and how to best deliver your message, both vocally and physically.

Primary and Secondary Intentions

Just as an actor might identify various intentions throughout a scene, someone presenting in a corporate environment will most likely move through different intentions over the course of a speech or presentation. We call these *primary* and *secondary* intentions. The primary intention will be your main intention and the one that connects most directly to your super-objective, while secondary intentions are no less important but shift according to the smaller objectives you move through in the course of the presentation. You might think of the primary intention and the super-objective in terms of strategy, while your secondary intentions and objectives are tactics in support of that strategy.

As a speaker moves from one intention to the next, noticeable changes should take place in eye contact, facial expressions, vocal aspects, and body language to help signify and communicate that change to the audience. Each of these transitions from one intention to the next must be clear. For example, the intention at the opening of your presentation might be to *welcome* your audience, but could shift to *reassure* as you begin presenting industry trends, and then to *excite* as you unveil the new product you will be launching. Actors call these transitions that move you from moment to moment *beats*, the term used by Stanislavski at the Moscow Art Theatre, where actors were trained to break up their scenes into smaller sections.

Every communication you deliver will include various intentions and objectives. Understanding what you want and how you are going to get it is important whether the communication is in a formal business setting or happens more informally over drinks with friends. If the message you are delivering is in the form of a speech or presentation, you may take advantage of the format (which is prepared in advance to the point of written notes or talking points, an outline, or a full manuscript) to practice breaking your message down into beats. Actors do this when they mark up their scripts, physically marking or *coding* each section by intention and objective.

Take a look at the speech in Figure 1.1 as an example. As you can see, the speaker has coded the text of the speech by identifying the intentions to be applied throughout, paired with their corresponding objectives.

Each of the first four paired intentions and objectives works in the service of the final set of primary intention (excite) and objective (make the listeners feel good about the organization and their work).

The How of Intention Cues

As the speaker who codes beats in advance will clearly understand, identifying the objective and activating the proper intention in each section of the message will help the audience understand how they should feel about the material or information they are receiving.

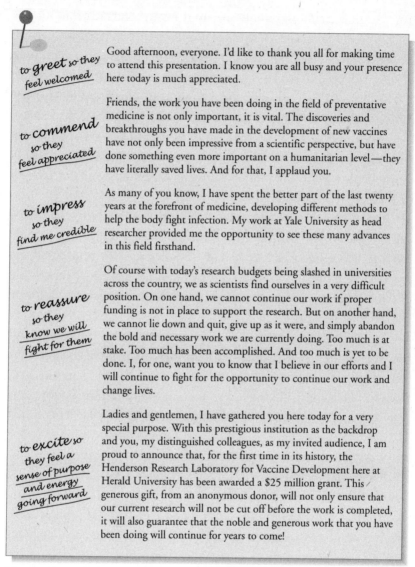

to greet so they feel welcomed

Good afternoon, everyone. I'd like to thank you all for making time to attend this presentation. I know you are all busy and your presence here today is much appreciated.

to commend so they feel appreciated

Friends, the work you have been doing in the field of preventative medicine is not only important, it is vital. The discoveries and breakthroughs you have made in the development of new vaccines have not only been impressive from a scientific perspective, but have done something even more important on a humanitarian level—they have literally saved lives. And for that, I applaud you.

to impress so they find me credible

As many of you know, I have spent the better part of the last twenty years at the forefront of medicine, developing different methods to help the body fight infection. My work at Yale University as head researcher provided me the opportunity to see these many advances in this field firsthand.

to reassure so they know we will fight for them

Of course with today's research budgets being slashed in universities across the country, we as scientists find ourselves in a very difficult position. On one hand, we cannot continue our work if proper funding is not in place to support the research. But on another hand, we cannot lie down and quit, give up as it were, and simply abandon the bold and necessary work we are currently doing. Too much is at stake. Too much has been accomplished. And too much is yet to be done. I, for one, want you to know that I believe in our efforts and I will continue to fight for the opportunity to continue our work and change lives.

to excite so they feel a sense of purpose and energy going forward

Ladies and gentlemen, I have gathered you here today for a very special purpose. With this prestigious institution as the backdrop and you, my distinguished colleagues, as my invited audience, I am proud to announce that, for the first time in its history, the Henderson Research Laboratory for Vaccine Development here at Herald University has been awarded a $25 million grant. This generous gift, from an anonymous donor, will not only ensure that our current research will not be cut off before the work is completed, it will also guarantee that the noble and generous work that you have been doing will continue for years to come!

Figure 1.1   Speech Markup.

So how would someone delivering the speech in Figure 1.1 activate the intention cues throughout the actual delivery? Simple: by playing the circumstances and intentions of only one section at a time. For example, the first section (to greet) will require a smile to support the message and appear genuine. The next section (to commend) would probably benefit from continued smiling, enthusiasm in the voice, and the prompting of applause from the audience to make people feel appreciated and valued. The next sections (to impress and reassure) get more serious, so the tone of voice will need to reflect this as well. And seriousness doesn't require a smile here, so that can fade for the moment. Finally, as the speaker moves to the main point of the message and the big finish (to excite), the task would be to build the energy of the delivery by modulating volume, pace, gesture, and facial expression so that the audience clearly understands what this new information means to them and exactly how they should feel about it.

It may all seem a lot to consider, and it is. But the ability to identify super-objective and primary intention, the process of breaking a whole message down into beats of paired objective and intention, and the practice of simply concentrating on one beat at a time, makes the effective delivery of even the most complex communication not only possible but even easy.

As you begin to consider your own individual communication and how you can start to incorporate an awareness of intention and objective into it, understand this: once your objective and intention are engaged, these two elements will often do your communication work for you. If you can generate a genuine feeling or emotion inside, it will be reflected in what others see and hear. But this cannot happen without your choosing and activating a specific intention and objective.

To impact or influence your audience you must have clarity and purpose in your message, and this can only happen through identifying an objective for your communication and then activating the specific intention (or intentions) that will move you toward it and result in your audience reacting the way you want them to react.

CHAPTER 2

Tell a Good Story

Using Personal Experiences to Inspire and Persuade

Storytelling is the most powerful way to put ideas into the world today.
—Robert McAfee Brown

All great leaders are great storytellers. And all great communicators understand the power of narrative. The ability to tell a good story is a crucial tool for anyone who wants to impact an audience or make a point in a compelling way. A good story will not only make your messages more memorable, it will also help you clarify meaning and illustrate a concept or idea. According to Jerome Bruner, one of the fathers of modern cognitive psychology, an audience is *twenty times more likely* to remember a fact if it is presented as part of a story that touches them emotionally.[1] Stories allow you to share personal experiences, helping you connect with your audience by building trust and establishing credibility.

Telling good stories, however, is often perceived to be a skill that only a few can master. This is not the case. As with all other aspects of communication, good storytellers are not born; they are made. Anyone can develop the ability to tell a compelling story, and in this chapter, we provide the tools to do it. We explain why storytelling is important, present a simple formula that screenwriters and playwrights have used for centuries to create compelling stories, and show you how to make the power of story work to your advantage. A real-life example:

Magdy El-Damarawy, an HR professional from Egypt, had always understood the power of personal storytelling. Magdy grew up in Cairo, and his father and grandfather loved telling stories. He could recall instances where they had shared their experiences or told tales meant to teach him a lesson as a young boy. As an adult and professional, Magdy had adopted a career path that had taken him around the Arab world, from Egypt to Oman to Abu Dhabi to Qatar, and he also used storytelling—jokes, illustrations, examples, and anecdotes from his life experiences—as he managed his various teams over the years. But there was one story that stood out above all others, a personal story from Magdy's life that had shaped and defined him as a person. It was this particular story that he shared with his team members or business associates whenever he had the chance and whenever it served his message.

It all began on a sunny October morning in 1977 when Magdy was a young cadet at the military academy. A notice had gone up recently looking for candidates interested in rappelling out of a helicopter as part of a demonstration during an upcoming graduation ceremony at the academy. A judo champion as well as an artillery cadet, Magdy was never one to shrink from an opportunity to impress his peers and superiors. He registered and was eventually chosen as one of three jumpers (from a pool of a hundred who had signed up). Thrilled at the opportunity, Magdy began training for the jump. He soon grew so confident in his skills that he ended up missing a portion of the training—specifically most of the sessions that included jumping from an actual helicopter.

As he stepped out onto the tarmac for the final training session before the graduation ceremony, the blades of the military chopper thundered overhead. Young Magdy's heart raced with excitement. He understood that the routine itself—simulating an enemy ambush by jumping out of the chopper—was a difficult exercise and one with very little margin for error. The truth was that he had never performed this exercise before. In fact, because he had missed the training sessions, he had never even been in a helicopter before and now here he was, about to rappel down from nearly seventy-five feet in the air for the very first time.

As they reached the designated height for the jump, Magdy sucked in a couple of breaths to calm his heart rate. The reality of the moment was starting to settle in. The sounds inside the helicopter were deafening as the first jumper gave the signal and slipped down his rope, disappearing out of sight. The second jumper followed suit, leaving Magdy standing there by himself, the lone jumper left in the copter. It was his turn. Signaling to the two pilots, Magdy grabbed his rope and jumped. A rush of wind hit him in the face as he slid down the rope toward the tarmac below. Using a building in the distance as a marker, he tried to gauge when to begin slowing his descent speed, but as he glanced down he realized the building was farther away than he thought; he had miscalculated the distance. As the black tarmac rushed toward him, Magdy made the split-second decision to kick his legs out in a desperate attempt to break his fall.

Then everything went black.

When he awoke, Magdy found himself lying on the tarmac, surrounded by people—fellow soldiers, officers, and medical personnel. He had survived the fall, but both of his legs had snapped like twigs, broken in twelve places. A sharp section of bone in his left leg had torn through the skin and was now protruding through the thick fabric of his military uniform, and blood spurted from his wounds. Magdy was rushed to the nearby military hospital.

He would spend the next three months in surgery and the next year and a half in and out of military hospitals, slowly recovering from his injuries. Gradually he learned to walk again through intensive sessions of physical therapy. During that time, he met many other soldiers in those military hospitals. Some had lost limbs, some had been paralyzed, but they all had a story. As he listened to story after story shared by each of these wounded warriors, Magdy realized that to go forward in his life he would need to summon the same courage as these other injured soldiers. They all had a journey that started right here and right now. His accident was simply another obstacle in his life that he would need to face and overcome. He had to start his new life from scratch.

Wherever his career has taken him over the years, Magdy has never let what happened that day in the helicopter stop him from pursuing his goals and dreams. He carried with him the importance of proper preparation every day of his life. When his employees or team members have struggled in their roles he has used the story to inspire them; when they are aimless and unmotivated, he has used the story to focus them; and when they are afraid of the future he uses it to show them that there is virtually no challenge in our lives that cannot be surmounted. This one story has been a powerful source of inspiration, motivation, and wisdom for Magdy and for others in his orbit for many years now.

THE POWER OF STORYTELLING

Storytelling is an art form as old as man. Prior to the invention of writing, storytelling (or the *oral tradition*) served as the sole means of cultural continuity: stories were handed down through the centuries, telling each new generation of the wisdom and the deeds of their ancestors. Many epic texts such as the *Iliad*, the *Odyssey*, *Beowulf*, and the *Epic of Gilgamesh* originated as oral tradition. Stories were so prized that good storytellers could always find a willing audience. In fact, in the past, the ability to tell a good story often meant respect and acceptance, a hot meal, and a warm place to sleep.

Traditional storytelling often took place, as it still does today, wherever small groups of people gathered to work or socialize. Whether around a campfire, at the barbershop, or in a break room at the office, people have always had an appetite for stories—those shared experiences that bind us together as human beings. Good stories have the ability to create mutuality and social cohesion within a society. They can define cultures and chart paths to the future. Often, specific stories are passed down within families, and they become an important part of what defines the group as a family. In business, stories are frequently told and retold over the years until they eventually become corporate lore, a part of the organization itself.

So what is a story? Simply put, a story is a narrative account of an event or a series of events. Or, as author Robert Maxwell has written, "A story is a fact, wrapped in an emotion that compels us to take an action."[2] A story can be true or it can be fictional. The difference between telling a story and simply providing information to someone is that a story adds emotion and sensory elements to the telling. Stories include many things—details, locations, characters, action, lessons—but a story is always more than the sum of its parts.

When delivered effectively, a story should resonate emotionally with its listeners and impact the way they think or feel about a subject; it should also connect to what they already feel is important to them—what they want or need. Stories can take a listener by surprise and make a point with a single image, sometimes a single word. A story can simplify the complicated, articulate the confusing, and illuminate the elusive.

By sharing personal stories or experiences, you can build trust with a listener quickly and effectively. When you tell a story, you reveal parts of yourself and your personality and make yourself vulnerable—and in turn, you invite the listener to do the same. We humans have the same basic wants and needs, fears and aspirations. No matter where we come from, how we were brought up, or what political or religious affiliations we hold, in

People will forget what you said, people will forget what you did, but people will never forget how you made them feel.

—MAYA ANGELOU

the end, we share more similarities than differences. We are all imperfect, and the acknowledgment of those imperfections is precisely the reason we are drawn to stories. As the Nigerian poet Ben Okri has written, "Storytelling hints at a fundamental human unease, hints at human imperfection. Where there is perfection there is no story to tell."[3]

Unlike any other tool in your communication arsenal, a good story has the power to transport an audience to places they may never have even thought of going before or considering things they have never previously considered. A compelling story should take an audience on a journey—beginning in one place (emotionally speaking) and ending in a different place altogether. An effective storyteller should be able to lead an audience away from the specific content, make a point, and then return them *back* to the content in a way that changes how they think about the content itself.

If a speaker can affect a listener through storytelling, that listener will often attribute the feelings experienced during the telling of the story to the storyteller. For example, if your story is exciting, you will create excitement in your audience and they may think of you as exciting. If your story contains a strong moral lesson, they may (consciously or unconsciously) connect the attribute of strong morals with you as a result of your communication. Consequently, when the story is later recalled, the positive emotions the listeners experienced listening to it will be remembered as well, and your objective will benefit as a result.

Anyone working in today's business environment can benefit from using storytelling as a communication tool. And yet, businesspeople rarely think of doing so. Why? According to Lou Hoffman of the public relations firm The Hoffman Agency, "There's a fair amount of science supporting the theory that the human mind from an early age is wired for stories. It's a more interesting and compelling way of communicating, which in turn increases the listening quotient of the audience and ultimately makes what you say more memorable. Somewhere along the line, people got the idea that business communication needed to be different—vanilla, stiff, jargon-filled, etc.—than [communications] in personal life. As a result, the vast majority of business communications is deadly dull."[4] Business communication does not have to be dull and different—in fact, it *should not* be, if it is to be effective.

In a business context, stories can serve as springboards to communicate new strategies, structures, policies, identities, and goals. A quick anecdote that establishes common ground between you and a colleague can forge a bond that might have taken weeks to accomplish otherwise. A good story can help you personalize the information you are trying to convey. It turns out that facts and numbers on their own don't have the power to influence. Only when facts are given *context*—when listeners clearly understand *what's in it for them* and *what it all means*—do facts have the ability to carry emotional weight (and the power to persuade) for a speaker. (Or as comedian Mitch Hedberg put it, "I find a duck's opinion of me is very much influenced by whether or not I have bread.") Information must have relevance in the eyes of the audience, and a good story is the ideal vehicle for providing such context, making your content more accessible to a listener.

WHY IS STORYTELLING SO EFFECTIVE?

Stories can be a powerful lever for persuading or affecting a listener. For starters, people remember stories, especially if they pack an emotional wallop. A well-told story will not only help your audience retain your message more effectively, it will also help them understand it more clearly. When one person tells a story and another listens, a bond is formed between the sender and the receiver. In one study, researchers from Princeton University found that the brains of storytellers and their listeners actually sync up during the telling of a story, activating the same regions of the brain in the very same ways.[5]

Unfortunately, oftentimes when we present material to others, we are under the impression that we can simply let information—facts, statistics, data—speak for itself. Subject matter experts such as scientists or engineers, in particular, tend to feel that the actual delivery of their message is irrelevant, and that the data or information is all that really matters. If they are boring presenters, so what? After all, they are subject matter experts! The data is all the audience really cares about.

This is not the case. If your audience is not engaged by your delivery—*how* you are saying something—they will be less likely to retain *what* you are saying and less likely to understand it. That's because numbers or facts on their own don't create emotional resonance in an audience. Numbers are inert. Only when they are placed in a specific context or framework do they take on meaning and relevance in the ears of a listener.

Employing storytelling in your business communications and presentations has one other advantage. Audiences don't like to be hit over the head with the point you are trying to make. When they are hit over the head, they feel manipulated and often disengage from the speaker. By tucking data or other important parts of your message subtly into a good story, you are more likely to gently persuade your audience.

Storytelling allows the teller to put forward certain values while letting an audience think for themselves. Whereas overt selling or persuading during communication are *push* strategies, stories involve more of a *pull* strategy. A story starts slowly, drawing the listener in before building, bit by bit, to the big payoff. Listening to a good story, an audience is more likely to arrive at the hoped-for conclusion on their own, as opposed to passively accepting the message that is served up to them. This is an important point, as people generally value their own conclusions more highly than those of others. To play off an old phrase, you can lead your audience to water but let them take the drink. If you let the message of your story—the "aha!" moment—sneak up on the listener, it will ultimately have much greater resonance.

HOW TO CRAFT A GOOD STORY

Listeners are drawn to passion. Passion can unify an audience and create an immediate bond between a listener and a storyteller. Passion is palpable; it is the energy behind your words that makes you want or *need* to tell the story in the first place. It can ignite a fire in the hearts of your listeners, making them actually *feel* what you are feeling.

Say you are a sales manager and you need your sales force to sell more. This is a specific and clear objective: you want them to drive more sales. A story might provide just the spark needed to motivate your team to be more productive. In this case, maybe choosing a story where you (or someone else) had to overcome an obstacle or objection would be an effective way to make your point. Consider what specific emotions you want your team to experience as a result of hearing your story. What do you want them to *feel*? Does the story you have in mind convey that feeling? Next you'll select an intention—a strong verb—to help you access in yourself the emotions you want to arouse in your audience. In this example, the appropriate intention might be to *excite* or *motivate*. If your sales team feels *excited* about overcoming their current challenges or *motivated* to put in the extra effort necessary to succeed, you will be well on your way toward achieving the objective you hoped to accomplish by telling the story—in this case, driving more sales.

EXERCISE
Choosing the Right Story

For each of the following scenarios, come up with one or more different stories based on your own life experiences.

- A devastated employee has just admitted to making a huge mistake. You need a story that shows how mistakes happen to everyone and we can all learn from past errors. What story do you use?
- A child who is attempting to learn how to play the piano gets frustrated and decides to give up. You need a story that demonstrates how hard work and dedication can pay off in the end. What story do you use?
- A friend just got assigned the task of delivering a keynote address in front of the entire company, including the CEO, and is absolutely terrified about having to do it. You need a story about overcoming fears and persevering against all odds. What story do you use?

As with any communication, for a story to come across effectively, you must first identify your objective and then choose the correct intention. When you take the time to do this, your intention will inform how you tell the story, giving it power and persuasiveness.

Structuring Your Story

Storytelling is a skill that most people can master with a little work. It helps to understand the elements that create the framework for any story. Playwrights, screenwriters, and novelists nearly all use variations on a model of storytelling—a particular *dramatic structure*. Based on his analysis of classical Greek and Shakespearean drama, Gustav Freytag, a nineteenth-century German novelist, delineated a theory of dramatic structure that is still very much in use. Freytag argued that for a story to be compelling, it had to include several distinctive elements, placed in a specific order. Most good stories—including plays, movies, and novels—follow a variation of Freytag's model.[6]

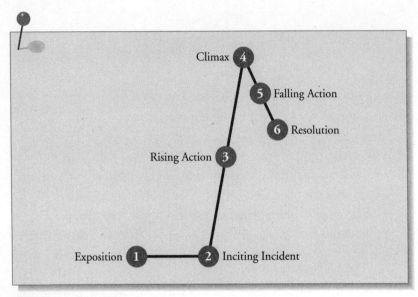

Figure 2.1   Story Map.

Think of the diagram for dramatic structure in Figure 2.1 as a *story map*—a framework on which you can hang the details of your story. Use it to outline your story by identifying what details correspond with each of the six points on the map. As you progress from one point to the next, your story should flow and build in an effective and compelling way.

1. Exposition. The part of your story where you introduce the setting, characters, and any background information your audience will need is called the *exposition*. It often (though by no means always) comes at the beginning of the story. This is where we meet the protagonist (hero) of the story. Is the hero a young man who lived once upon a time in a kingdom far away? A new product your company is developing? A ragtag team of female volleyball players? Exposition answers the who, what, when, and where of the story you are telling, giving you a foundation to build on.

2. Inciting Incident. The *inciting incident* is the initial trigger or event that gets the story started, and without which nothing happens. It may also set up a conflict between opposing forces and define the antagonist (villain) of the story—the person or obstacle standing in

the way of the hero's efforts to reach a goal. The villain kidnaps the princess. The prototype for your new product is finally complete. A losing volleyball team suddenly gets a brash new coach.

3. Rising Action. With the action of the story under way, events are set in motion through a series of cycles that build the story's dramatic tension. Most of your story takes place here. The plot develops and a major dramatic question is asked that will eventually need to be answered by the end of the story. Will the princess be saved? Will the new product be successful? Can the dedicated young coach turn this losing volleyball team into winners?

4. Climax. This is the highest point of tension in the story, the turning point where everything suddenly changes. The hero pushes the villain over the edge of the cliff and into the lava. The new product is—at last—unveiled to great public fanfare. The volleyball players beat the rival team and win the state championship. A good story must build to a climax to drive home the main message or theme of the story itself.

5. Falling Action. Once the climax has been reached, the action takes a breath. Any loose ends are tied up and the story winds down. The hero saves the princess and they get married. The new product gets rave reviews from the public. The volleyball players thank their coach for believing in them even when they didn't believe in themselves.

6. Resolution. This is the conclusion of the story where the main conflict gets resolved and the major dramatic question finally gets answered. The hero and princess live happily ever after. The new product transforms the industry. The volleyball players learn the value of teamwork and discipline.

EXERCISE
Using the Storytelling Formula

To put this formula into practice, think of an important incident in your life—your wedding, the birth of your first child, the day you got hired at your present job. Using the storytelling formula in Figure 2.1, sketch out how you would tell that particular story. What exposition would you need to set up at the outset? What is the inciting incident; what circumstances drive the rising action; what is the climax? After creating your outline, practice telling the story to someone who may not have heard it before. Get their feedback. Did they find it interesting? Which sections dragged on too long or seemed confusing? Taking their comments into consideration, refine the story and practice telling it to someone new.

The Power of Surprise

Once you get comfortable with the story map, feel free to experiment. For example, you don't need to start every story with the first element, exposition. Instead, you can start a story in the middle of the action, with events already in motion, plunging the listener into a crucial situation, the circumstances of which will be developed and explained later in the story, often through flashbacks. Think of the opening scene of a James Bond movie or the beginning of *Jaws*, *The Godfather*, or *Raging Bull*. Each of these films uses this device to great effect. This is an ancient narrative technique, used by Homer in the *Iliad* and the *Odyssey*, and it is called *in medias res* (which means "in the midst of things"). Imagine someone starting a story with the line, "I was eight years old, sitting in the back seat of my family's station wagon, when I saw the grizzly bear attack our car . . ." Opening a story in this way will almost certainly capture an audience's attention.

When director Mel Stuart first offered Gene Wilder the lead role in his film adaptation of Roald Dahl's classic children's book, *Charlie and the Chocolate Factory*, Wilder accepted the role under one condition: he wanted to completely change the way his character, Willy Wonka, made his initial entrance at the start of the movie.

"When I make my first entrance," explained Wilder, "I'd like to come out of the door carrying a cane and then walk toward the crowd with a limp. . . . As I walk toward them, my cane sinks into one of the cobblestones . . . but I keep on walking, until I realize that I no longer have my cane. I start to fall forward, and just before I hit the ground, I do a beautiful forward somersault and bounce back up, to great applause." When Stuart asked Wilder why it was so important to him that his character make such an odd and puzzling entrance, Wilder replied, "Because from that time on, no one will know if I'm lying or telling the truth."[7]

Never underestimate the power of surprise.

According to cognitive psychologist Jerome Bruner, good stories always arise out of the unexpected.[8] As listeners of stories, we want to be surprised—we *need* to be surprised. For a storyteller, the use of surprise is essential if you hope to keep an audience engaged, from the opening moments of your story to the final conclusion. A good storyteller should provide details to the audience, bit by bit, on a need-to-know basis. Just as Gene Wilder did in his portrayal of Willy Wonka, a storyteller should keep the audience off-balance by solving the puzzle that is the story one piece at a time. By doing this, you will create questions in the minds of the listeners that can only be answered by you. Share the details of the story in a way that allows you to build suspense and heighten the dramatic tension of the story itself.

As David Ball reminds us in *Backwards and Forwards*, "Often the core of dramatic tension resides in *keeping information from* the audience. Don't negate the tension by premature revelation."[9] In other words, don't give away the best parts of the story all at once. And never give away the ending before you get there. Think of how great movies such as *Raiders of the Lost Ark*, *The Usual Suspects*, or *Chinatown* deploy the element of surprise. Stories that include unexpected revelations or shocking twists have a very powerful impact on an audience. The more you can keep an audience on the edge of their seats, the more emotionally invested they will be in the story and, ultimately, in the story's message itself.

Director J. J. Abrams frequently leverages mystery and the withholding of information in his movies and television shows with the precise goal of capturing and keeping an audience's attention. "I believe in anything that will engage an audience and make the story more effective," he says, but cautions, "Withholding things in a story is no good if you aren't building to something substantial. It becomes foreplay without the main event, and no one wants that."[10]

Using Humor

People like to laugh, and laughter is contagious. In fact, the average adult laughs seventeen times a day.[11] Laughter connects people and breaks down barriers, crossing all communities and cultures. Think about it. It is nearly impossible for two people to maintain an emotional distance while they're laughing together. And because laughter is so *universal*, the strategic use of humor in communications can connect you with others, sharing common experiences.

And laughter is good for us. Studies have shown that laughter is not only an effective tool to minimize stress and relieve tension, it can actually boost a person's immune system. When we laugh, it triggers chemical changes in our bodies that make us more calm and relaxed, releasing endorphins and bringing more oxygen into the body as a result of deeper inhalations.[12] Laughter can soothe and laughter can heal. In India, the health benefits of laughter are so valued that over six hundred groups called Laughter Clubs have sprung up in recent years, organizations whose sole purpose is to gather as a community and . . . laugh. As the great silent film actor Charlie Chaplin once said, Humor "heightens our sense of survival and preserves our sanity."[13]

> *The duty of comedy is to correct men by amusing them.*
>
> —MOLIÈRE

The use of humor in storytelling goes at least all the way back to the Greeks, who used comedy and satire in their plays and poetry with the intention of informing and influencing the masses. That same method of using comedy to persuade and educate audiences can be seen today on programs like *The Daily Show* and *The Colbert Report*. And while not everyone is comfortable using humor, those who are can use it to great benefit. Humor, if used effectively, can lighten the mood, break down barriers, and add meaning or depth to a message.

Of course, using jokes or humor is not always appropriate. If you do choose to do so, proceed thoughtfully. As with any mode of storytelling, for a joke to work, it must elicit the specific emotion in your audience that will move them toward your objective. If the joke does not accomplish this, it is probably best to avoid it. For instance, if you are calling someone in to your office to terminate their employment, it is absolutely not the time to trot out your latest gut-buster. When humor backfires, it can harm relationships, erode trust, and damage credibility, so use it carefully and judiciously.

FINDING YOUR VOICE AS A STORYTELLER

Stories define us. They provide a snapshot of how we think, how we make decisions, and how we interact with the world around us. Think of how the stories we know and tell about famous people help us understand them as human beings: Michael Jordan failing to make his varsity basketball team in high school; John McCain being shot down in Vietnam and spending five and a half years as a POW; Bill Clinton growing up poor, the son of a single mother.

One of the reasons that people avoid telling stories is they feel they don't have a story to tell. Not true, says Sarah Kay, founder of Project V.O.I.C.E. "Too often . . . people don't have the courage or confidence to believe in their own stories. They fear it is boring, or irrelevant, or that somebody else could tell it better."[14] But we all have stories we can access to leverage the power of story in our daily communication.

EXERCISE
Crafting a Story

Tell a story—one that you might use in a speech or presentation. Choose one that you enjoy telling. Chances are, if you are excited to tell it, your audience will be excited to hear it. Think about how you can structure it for the most drama and impact: where do you start? How can you reveal and withhold information to build suspense, or build toward a funny punch line? What highly descriptive words can you use that will make your story more vivid and memorable? Avoid generalizations as much as possible—the more clear and specific you make the important details, the more impact your words will have on your listeners. Finally, practice it until you are comfortable telling it without notes. Have someone you trust serve as a test audience for you—a friend or spouse.

Here are five essential types of a story that an effective communicator should be prepared to share.

- *The Essence Story*. This story will offer a window into you as a person so the listener will better understand your background, your upbringing, your values, your passions, and your outlook on life. It will also allow the listener to more fully understand how you make decisions and how you operate as a person. Examples might include family stories, childhood experiences, or anecdotes about parenthood.
- *The Crucible Story*. This story is about a moment in your life when you had to step out of your comfort zone and summon the courage needed to succeed or fight. By relating how you rose to the challenge, it shows how you changed or grew as a person, possibly through a near-death experience, personal loss, or other dramatic event.
- *The Leadership Story*. This story relates how you were able to lead others through a challenging set of circumstances. It allows you to show that you can exhibit drive, focus, and the ability to inspire others as a boss, parent, or manager.
- *The Helper Story*. This story shows an instance where you displayed selflessness or reached out to assist someone in need, exhibiting empathy and compassion in the process. It could also be a story where you worked with others as part of a team for the betterment of the entire group. Helper stories might involve your personal experiences as an athlete, anecdotes about helping someone less fortunate, or stories where you reached out to a person and shared knowledge or wisdom.
- *The Pie-in-the-Face Story*. This story proves that you are fallible and human, with a sense of humor, by detailing how you made a mistake or failed in some way. It could be a funny story displaying self-deprecating humor or even an embarrassing incident from

his type of story, you share a personal failing or
ıat helped shape you, as well as the lessons you
of having gone through it.

ı the experiences of your life and try to pinpoint
ıe categories listed here. Then create an outline
formula discussed earlier and practice telling
co-worker. Once you've told your story, solicit
ur listener. Each of us has countless stories
be told, including every person you come in
ıan, your accountant, your son's teacher, your
ss a unique reservoir of stories from which to
grow as individuals and learn about the world
to experience aspects of the story as though
experiences, teaching us compassion by allowing us
to walk in someone else's shoes or feel someone else's pain.

Seek stories out. Comb your past for stories you may have forgotten. Ask your family members to share theirs. Write them down and file them away. Boil each story down to its essence and consider how you might use it at some point in the future. Ask yourself: What is the story's main message? What point does it make? What feeling does it convey?

Stories are out there. Go find them. Become a story collector; it will make you a better storyteller.

CHAPTER 3

Craft a Compelling Narrative

Building the Framework to Support Your Message

Architecture starts when you carefully put two bricks together.
There it begins.

—LUDWIG MIES VAN DER ROHE

Just as architects must start by first constructing a solid foundation for a building, communicators must begin by creating solid material—the architecture—for their message: the words, facts, and other content that will support their intention and allow them to accomplish their objective. Whether speaking to an audience of one or a crowd of thousands, the first step in the process is gathering and compiling all the pertinent information, creating smooth and logical transitions, and making sure that the material to be delivered will fit into the allotted time.

As any actor knows, you are nothing without strong material. In the theater, the script is the foundation of the performance. And for anyone who thinks a good script isn't important, go watch Robert De Niro in *Raging Bull* and then watch a clip of him doing an interview while promoting a movie; same brilliant actor, two very different performances—one the result of having strong material and being comfortable and prepared while delivering it, the other out of character and off the cuff. The same is true in a corporate setting: an effective message begins with strong material that not only is well-organized but also supports your intention and objective.

• • •

In July 1863, during the height of the American Civil War, General Robert E. Lee's Confederate Army clashed with Union forces near Harrisburg, Pennsylvania, in the battle of Gettysburg. The fighting—the bloodiest of the war—lasted three days and resulted in more than 43,000 casualties. When Lee's army finally retreated, more than 7,600 Americans (some as young as sixteen) lay dead on the blood-soaked battlefield; the scene was horrific. Because of the sheer volume of bodies, most of the dead were simply covered with dirt in the exact spot where they fell.

Weeks later, when Andrew Gregg Curtin, the governor of Pennsylvania, toured the battlefield, the rains had washed away much of the dirt that had covered the bodies. The governor was appalled, believing these brave men deserved a more honorable resting place. He immediately planned for a military cemetery to be constructed on the site to serve as a memorial to the lives lost that terrible day. In four months, the cemetery was finished and a dedication ceremony was planned. The governor needed a powerful figure to deliver the main dedication speech that day so he invited the man who was widely thought of as the best orator in America to deliver the memorial: a man named Edward Everett, a former governor and senator of Massachusetts. Almost as an afterthought, Curtin also extended an invitation to the White House for President Lincoln to say a few words at the event. Lincoln accepted and planned a trip by train to Gettysburg. The president hoped that his presence at the memorial could help ease the pain of his divided country and raise the spirits of the American people. Lincoln, like Everett, was known to give a good speech. An actor himself, Lincoln had refined his oratorical techniques by performing the speeches of Shakespeare for any willing (or unwilling) audience who would listen.[1] He also knew how to use his voice and inflection to engage and influence a crowd.

In the weeks before the trip, Lincoln did not get much time to prepare his remarks, though he had an overall idea about what he wanted to say and how he wanted his audience to react. After a sixteen-hour train ride, Lincoln arrived in Gettysburg as the sun was going down. He ate dinner and went to his room to finalize the words he would deliver the following day.

The next morning, a slow parade of men on horseback made its way to the military cemetery where a huge crowd had gathered. A military band played patriotic music and soldiers stood at attention, saluting, as President Lincoln and the procession passed, making their way to the stage. After an opening prayer, Edward Everett took the stage to deliver his dedication address. He spoke of the causes of the war, the war itself, the effect the war had on cities, the soldiers who perished in the fighting, and his hopes for a speedy resolution to the fighting. He spoke of many things . . . in fact, his speech went on for over *two hours*—a whopping 13,607 words!

When Everett finished, he took a seat and President Lincoln took his place before the crowd of thousands. He looked out over the battlefield, the very place where those thousands of brave men lost their lives. He saw the faces of those in the crowd as they waited for him to speak, to offer them hope and inspiration. Taking out a paper containing the message that he had carefully crafted, he took a breath and spoke the words that would become so famous: "Four score and seven years ago . . ."

And in less than three minutes, he was done.

Lincoln's Gettysburg Address would go on to be widely acknowledged as one of the greatest speeches of all time, something *Harper's Weekly* described as "the most perfect piece of American eloquence." The day after the dedication, Edward Everett, recalling the reaction Lincoln had generated in the crowd that day, wrote to the president, saying, "I wish that I could flatter myself that I had come as near to the central idea of the occasion, in two hours, as you did in two minutes." At only 272 words—a mere three paragraphs—Lincoln's Gettysburg Address is an exercise in economy. His use of powerful word choices, alliteration, and metaphor showed how a simple, well-crafted message with a clear purpose can move the masses and resonate in a nation's collective consciousness for centuries.

COMPOSING YOUR MESSAGE: AN OVERVIEW

For most people who have to deliver a speech, facilitate a training session, or present material of any kind, there is nothing more unnerving than the blank sheet of paper. The process of beginning can be daunting and even overwhelming, filling one with anxious questions. But unfortunately, thinking is not doing. Eventually you have to put pen to paper (or fingers to keyboard) and begin. As the writer Jack London once remarked, "You can't wait for inspiration; you have to go after it with a club."

A good place to start?

The two most important factors to focus on when crafting your material are content (what you'll say) and organization (how you'll make the pieces of content fit together into a cohesive and compelling whole). Content comes first. Make a list. What points do you want to cover? What can you read about the subject in preparation? What supporting material will you need? Actually putting your thoughts or ideas onto paper—in any order to start with, you'll organize it later—provides you with clay to start molding.

Once you have your clay—your raw content—you can begin creating a structure for your message. The classic outline structure is unbeatable for organizing not only the order of material but also the relative importance of your points and the relationships among topics and subtopics. An effective presentation, like any good play or movie, needs to have a solid, well-built structure and move smoothly from one topic or section to the next in a logical way. Each point should build upon the point that came before it, and there should be clear transitions between points. Content that is meandering, disjointed, or difficult to follow can frustrate or confuse an audience.

Once you have a rough outline, decide how much time should be allotted for each topic or section, based upon the total amount of time you have for your presentation. Begin fleshing out the outline accordingly, paying attention to both your points and the spaces between them—your introductions, transitions, planned pauses or breaks, and so forth. Over the course of several drafts, you should strive to create a narrative that reflects your personality and feels comfortable and appropriate to both your message and your audience. Above all, bring yourself to the content.

The written word and the spoken word work in different ways; practice reading the material out loud to make sure it is easy to speak. If sentences are too long to be read in one breath, you may need to rewrite them to make them simpler to speak out loud. Read the material through, taking the audience's perspective. Is it clearly organized in a way that will be accessible and interesting to your listeners? While you are the expert when it comes to the content itself, it's crucial that it be organized with your audience in mind. Well-organized material will not only flow more smoothly and make a speaker sound more confident and credible, it will be easier for an audience to follow, easier for them to understand, and ultimately easier for them to remember. With any message you deliver—whether it is a speech to thousands, a meeting with your boss, or a status update to stakeholders—think of yourself as a tour guide, navigating your audience through the information you are there to deliver.

In the next page or two we discuss audience and theme. Basically, these are lenses through which to view your content as you're drafting your presentation. Each will help you focus your material and target your presentation.

ASSESSING YOUR AUDIENCE

One of the basic rules of effective communication is *always know your audience*. An audience, whether it consists of one person or one hundred, is a living, breathing entity with specific expectations it is looking to have met. In life and business—just as in the theater—without an audience, communication is impossible. The audience completes the act—as the great Broadway composer and lyricist Stephen Sondheim put it, "When the audience comes in, it changes the temperature of what you've written."[2] Without someone *listening* to what you are saying, you will have no one to buy your products, implement your programs, or pass along your message.

The best way to ensure that your audience listens to you is to first pay attention to them, starting when you are putting the presentation together. What needs are they looking to have met? What do they want? By understanding the expectations of your listeners, you will be prepared to meet or exceed those expectations. And this can only happen with content that both

Listen, wait, and be patient. Every shaman knows you have to deal with the fire that's in your audience's eye.

—KEN KESEY

supports your intention and offers a clear benefit to your listeners. When preparing to address a particular audience, answer the following questions, as applicable:

- Who is my audience?
- What is the size of my audience?
- What are the demographics of my audience (age, gender, educational background, religious views, and so on)?
- What is my audience's level of familiarity with my content and topic?
- What are my audience's feelings about my content and topic?
- What are my audience's feelings about me as a speaker?
- What are my audience's goals and expectations?
- What benefit can I offer to my audience?

Every proposal you pitch, every sales call you make, and every meeting you facilitate should be thought of in dramatic terms—like a story. And, like any good story, the message you are communicating should have a hero and a villain. The problem that needs to be solved—that's your villain. (For our organization, Pinnacle Performance Company, boring meetings, forgettable presentations, and ineffective communications are the villains; hence, the tools and techniques taught in our workshops are the heroes.) When approaching your material, ask yourself how you or your company will facilitate positive change for your customer or their organization. How will your product save them time? How will your service make their life easier? Once you identify how you are going to help them, you can use your intention and objective to vanquish the villain (the underlying problem or need) and make yourself (that is, your product or proposal) the hero.

FINDING YOUR CORE THEME

What is your presentation about? While assembling your content, it is helpful to identify a *core theme* for your message and let it serve as a touchstone. Think of your core theme as a distillation of your communication down to its essence, expressed in the form of a headline—a short, compact summary that puts across the main thrust of your message in a single phrase. The core theme you decide upon will guide you to what content you choose to include and how you choose to include it. (Your intention and objective will guide you as well—ask yourself what material you need to include in order for your audience to react the way you want them to react.)

As Dwight D. Eisenhower believed, the core theme of a speaker's message should fit on the inside of a matchbook.[3] Most memorable speeches or presentations throughout history can be simplified to a single theme or idea. For example, Steve Jobs unveiling the iPhone ("Apple Reinvents the Phone"), Barack Obama campaigning for president ("Change Is Coming to America"), and George W. Bush launching the war on terrorism ("Either You're with Us or with the Terrorists"). Once chosen, your core theme can serve as a framing device, allowing you to shape and form the intention behind your communication—whether you are a parent reprimanding your child ("Follow the Rules or No Ice Cream"), a human resources director detailing company policies ("Sexual Harassment Will Not Be Tolerated"), or a software sales rep pitching a new product ("Protect Your Data in Three Easy Steps").

Identifying a core theme can also be helpful when you are presenting or facilitating with others. With your fellow presenters, collectively decide on a core theme: it will inform all aspects of the content and ensure that everyone is telling the same story, employing the same intention, and pursuing the same objective. And since communication is always about providing a benefit to an audience, your core theme should be written from the perspective of the listener, indicating *what is in it for them*.

THE PRIMACY–RECENCY EFFECT

You want your audience to retain the main points of your communication. How you structure it can make a difference to retention. One effective way to do this is to work with what is called the *serial position effect*, a term coined by the German psychologist Hermann Ebbinghaus in the late nineteenth century (see Figure 3.1).

Ebbinghaus found that when people take in information, they tend to remember the first and last things they hear, with the content in the middle being the least likely to be recalled. This phenomenon is known in psychological circles as the *primacy-recency effect*, and it presents a unique challenge for anyone communicating a message, since the meat of a message usually falls smack dab in that middle section.[4] But since the ideas or information that stick best for people are what they hear at the beginning and at the end, it is essential that you carefully place your most important content where it is most likely to be remembered

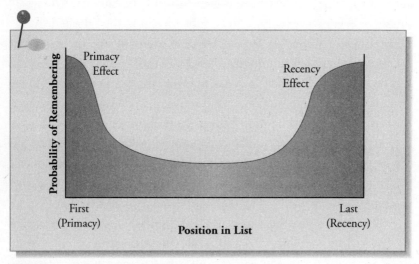

Figure 3.1   Primacy and Recency.
Source: David A. Sousa, *How the Brain Learns*, 4th ed. (London: Corwin Press, 2011), p. 95.

(to support this, we discuss the importance of Master Introductions and Master Closings in a few pages). Using a three-part structure of an opening, a main body, and a closing can assist you in doing this—a structure we discuss later in the chapter.

THE RULE OF THREE

The *rule of three* is a concept in writing that suggests that content or messages delivered in threes is generally more satisfying and effective than content delivered in other numbers. A series of three parallel words, phrases, or clauses—called a *tricolon*—is a rhetorical device that has been used for centuries by world leaders and great communicators. Three is the smallest number of elements required to create a pattern and it is precisely the combination of pattern and brevity that allows content structured in threes to carry such a punch. It is not by accident that most Hollywood movies employ a classic three-act structure or that some of the most memorable quotes throughout history also follow this simple organizing principle. In fact, the Latin expression *omne trium perfectum* literally means "everything that comes in three is perfect."

In *Writing Tools*, author Roy Peter Clark discusses the rule of three: "The mojo of three offers a greater sense of completeness than four or more."[5] He goes on to explain how and when to use other sets of points for greatest effect: "Use one for power. Use two for comparison, contrast. Use three for completeness, wholeness, roundness. Use four or more to list, inventory, compile, and expand." In truth, we've all been exposed to the rule of three since we were children. Fairy tales employ the rule of three to teach lessons (think of "Three Blind Mice," "Three Little Pigs," and "Goldilocks and the Three Bears"). Good jokes use it as well.

Governor Jon Huntsman, the U.S. Ambassador to China from 2009 to 2011, often uses the rule of three to help simplify his message when negotiating. Asked in an interview why speaking in triplicate was a device he employed so frequently, Huntsman replied: "It's easy to manage, easy to stay on top of, and easy to do."[6] Barack Obama used the progression of three to great effect during his 2009 inaugural address when he said, "We must pick ourselves up, dust ourselves off, and begin again the work of remaking America."

Using the rule of three can be especially helpful to gain commitment or buy-in from an audience. Concluding your message with a call to action that embodies the rule of three leaves no ambiguity about what you seek or what you want from that audience. A group of energy executives whom we trained recently presented a proposal to senior leadership that ended by asking for a significant commitment: an investment of $20 million. To be crystal clear about what they sought at the end of their presentation, these executives used a one-two-three punch in their call to action, concluding, "Gentlemen, we need your buy-in. We need your support. We need your endorsement."

Repetition is another tool that can be used to help drive your most important points home. By stating a figure or fact more than once, you are signaling to your audience that it is significant and should be given special attention. Winston Churchill, one of the most persuasive communicators in history, praised the value of the rule of three as it related to repetition when he said, "If you have an important point to make, don't try to be subtle or clever. Use a pile driver. Hit the point once. Then come back and hit it again. Then hit it a third time—a tremendous whack."

MASTERING YOUR TRANSITIONS

One of the most common reasons that presentations or meetings fail to achieve their desired outcome is that the facilitator or presenter does not have clear and specific transitions; this is usually a result of inadequate preparation. Consequently, everything just blends together in one long blur of data. When crafting your message, it is important to give special attention to how you move from one topic to the next. Think of transitions as little openings and closings—the connective tissue that links the different sections of your content together. The tighter and more efficiently you are able to move from one point to the next, the easier it will be for your audience to stay with you. Without seamless transitions, your message will likely seem choppy or disjointed. Transitions should be clear, smooth, and logical, effortlessly moving your audience from one point or topic to the next.

Try to build every section to a mini climax by using any of the transitional tools described in this section as a *button* to signal to your audience that one topic is ending and a new one is about to begin. Conversely, once you have buttoned up one section, you then have to start the next session off by capturing your audience's attention through a *hook*, another device discussed shortly. Effective transitions are often done verbally with words or phrases such as "Moving on..." "Additionally," and "Turning to..." but can also be signaled nonverbally, through the use of the voice or body. Here are some examples of nonverbal transitions that can be used effectively:

- Movement
- A change in facial expression
- Silence or dramatic pause
- A change in pace
- Variance in pitch
- A change in body posture
- Use of a prop
- Adjustment in volume
- A new visual aid
- Variance in gestures

STRUCTURING YOUR MESSAGE

Certain types of presentations or messages will require more structure than others, for example, when you are teaching a class or demonstrating a process. As you begin to gather and organize your material, don't think of yourself as *writing* a speech or presentation; think of yourself as *preparing* one. Once your core theme is set, select material that will support your intention and then assemble it all in a logical order. Just like a good story, almost any message you deliver can be divided into three parts:

- The Opening
- The Main Body
- The Closing

Whether you are asking your boss for a raise, presenting a status update to a team, or seeking commitment from a group of stakeholders, the three-part structure can help you frame your message in a way that

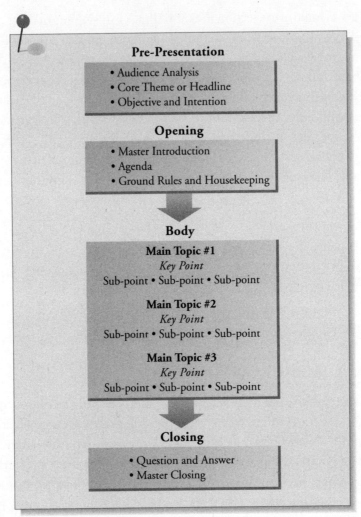

Figure 3.2   Presentation Flow.

is clear and concise. Think of how prosecutors or defense attorneys in court present their case to a jury—both follow a similar three-part structure: an opening statement, the trial itself, then a closing statement. Each of the three sections serves a purpose and helps move your audience in the direction of your intended objective. The flow chart in Figure 3.2 maps a typical business presentation, from the preparatory work to the close.

The Opening

The opening of your presentation is where it all begins. This is your chance to make a strong first impression in the eyes of your audience, establish your credibility, and set up what points or topics you will be discussing and what your goals are at the end. The opening is also your opportunity to cover any housekeeping details (frequency of breaks, start and end times, location of rest rooms, and so on), set up your agenda, and establish any ground rules that will need to be followed.

Establishing Your Credibility If your audience is not aware of your qualifications, the opening would be the place to establish your credibility. If appropriate, include mention of any pertinent degrees, awards, accomplishments, education, experiences, titles, or affiliations that might help establish your bona fides in the eyes of your audience. Unless there's a program for your presentation that contains your biographical information, don't assume that your listeners are aware of your history or accomplishments. Establishing your credibility at the outset compels your audience to listen to what you have to say and give you their full attention.

Using a Hook In 2003, actor Will Ferrell was invited to give the commencement address at Harvard University, perhaps the most prestigious school in America. As he was introduced, Ferrell entered, dressed in a blue and white yachtsman's uniform (complete with a captain's hat and ascot), dancing to "Celebration" by Kool and the Gang. After a few moments, Ferrell stopped, apparently confused. Feigning embarrassment that he had shown up at the wrong event, he spoke into the microphone. "This is not the Wooster Mass. Boat Show, is it? I'm sorry. I have made a terrible mistake . . ." This is what we call an effective *hook*.

A hook is any attention-grabbing device used to capture an audience's interest and compel them to continue listening. As Lyndon Johnson once said, "If they're with you at the takeoff, they'll be with you in the landing."[7] Because of this, try to position a hook as close to the beginning as possible. When considering a hook to include, be creative. People respond to emotion, so you might try to craft an opening that appeals to an audience's heart as well as their head. Surprise them; challenge them; intrigue them. Or as Will Ferrell did, make them laugh.

When the poet Maya Angelou spoke at the funeral of Coretta Scott King, before she uttered a single word, she began by singing the first few lines of a gospel song: *I open my mouth to the Lord and I won't turn back, no. I will go, I shall go. I'll see what the end is gonna be.* This attention-grabbing opening was so unexpected and moving that the audience in the New Birth Missionary Baptist Church erupted in cheers and applause. At a *funeral*. Any time you can take your audience by surprise with an opening hook, you increase the odds that they will stick with you for the rest of your message. Examples of potential hooks:

- Stating a problem
- Making a provocative statement
- Sharing an impressive statistic
- Reciting a famous quote
- Asking a thought-provoking question
- Telling a relevant story
- Utilizing a meaningful prop
- Referencing a previous speaker
- Using humor

A warning: Hooks are not all created equal, so be careful when developing yours. A poorly chosen hook can confuse an audience and detract from the message you are attempting to communicate. Test your hook out on others ahead of time and gauge their reaction. Ask yourself: How will it be received by my audience? Does it serve as an appropriate springboard for the message that will follow? Does it logically tie in to the core theme of the material itself?

Presenting a Master Introduction The purpose of your Master Introduction is to establish the core theme of the message in a way that engages the audience and compels them to listen to you. It should also establish you as a credible messenger and summarize your main points in a way that compellingly introduces the benefit you'll provide the audience. These are the five points that need to be established in an effective Master Introduction:

- Hook or attention grabber
- Name, role, and credibility
- Reason we are here
- Benefit to audience
- Goal at the end of the presentation

Chris Epperly is the director of strategic partnerships with the Country Music Association in Nashville. As part of Chris's role, he frequently has to speak to potential advertisers and promote the CMA brand. His intention and objective are clear: he wants to excite these sponsors so they forge a partnership with the CMA. One of his potential clients was NASCAR. During his preparation for his presentation to NASCAR executives, Chris knew that in order to capture their attention, he would need to begin by crafting an effective Master Introduction. Using the guidelines just provided as a road map, he put together the following Master Introduction:

Thirty-eight NASCAR events over the course of ten months in any given year. Forty-seven million fans. That's a lot, right? Now double that. Ninety-four million—that's how many country music fans there are out there. My name is Chris Epperly and for the past ten years, I have had the privilege of creating strategic partnerships with a lot of corporate American brands, bringing these brands to the Country Music Association. So why are we here? I am here to tell you about our core assets at the CMA as well as why you should be involved in the things we have to offer. What's the benefit to you? Well, that's easy: I want to increase your brand awareness. I want to drive consumer insight and enlighten people as to why your brand is so unique and why the consumer should consider using it. The goal for this presentation is pretty simple: I want to provide you with a unique partnership opportunity with CMA as a whole and then, once we've become partners, I want to drive consumer traffic to your business.

As you can see, Epperly hits all five points of the Master Introduction. He hooks us at the outset with an exciting stat

("Thirty-eight NASCAR events over the course of ten months in any one given year. Forty-seven million fans. That's a lot, right? Now double that. Ninety-four million—that's how many country music fans there are out there"). After his initial hook, Epperly introduces himself, setting up his role and why he should be taken seriously ("My name is Chris Epperly, and for the past ten years I have had the privilege of creating strategic partnerships with a lot of corporate American brands"), before outlining very clearly the overall purpose of the presentation ("I am here to tell you about our core assets at the CMA as well as why you should be involved in the things we have to offer"). Epperly then lays out, in clear terms, exactly what the benefit is to the customer ("I want to increase your brand awareness. I want to drive consumer insight and enlighten people as to why your brand is so unique") before spelling out his goal at the end of the exchange ("I want to provide you with a unique partnership opportunity...I want to drive consumer traffic to your business"). Because Epperly has included all five points in his Master Introduction, his audience knows exactly who he is, why they should listen, and what's in it for them.

Main Body

Once your opening is completed and you have delivered your Master Introduction, it's time to get into the meat of your presentation. The main body will be the largest section of your presentation. This is your chance to lay out your main points in detail and supply supporting material that backs up your arguments or helps illustrate your points. What are the three or four main topics you will be covering? Once you identify them, you need to expound upon those main topics through key points and sub-points that can illustrate or illuminate what you are attempting to communicate. This can be done through explanations, examples, and facts. Without the inclusion of data and information that support your core theme and explain your main topics, your presentation runs the risk of being nothing more than a series of assertions. There are countless places from which to gather information—books, periodicals, industry surveys, studies, encyclopedias, interviews, video recordings, and organizational websites are just a few examples, as well as internal company documents that are relevant to your topic and appropriate to share. It is also important to give examples or share anecdotes that link to your listeners' experiences; this will help them understand and retain the information you are discussing.

This is the part of your presentation where you might choose to use supporting material to help clarify, justify, or emphasize the points you are trying to make. This could include data, statistics, charts, graphs, quotes, video or audio clips, photographs, testimony, or anecdotes. As you consider specific supporting material to include, ask yourself the following questions, and only use the material if the answers are all yes.

- Are your statistics accurate?
- Are your sources reliable?
- Are you using the statistics correctly?
- Do your statistics support your points and intention?

Oral presentations are not the same as written presentations. As you create the text for your content, write in a tone that is conversational, as if you are speaking to a friend. Try to avoid long, run-on sentences. These are hard to speak and difficult for an audience to follow and comprehend. Keep your phrasing simple. A good way to test out your text is to read it out loud. Are your phrases and sentences easy to say? Do you use words likely to show up in an informal conversation? If you find yourself tripping or stumbling over words or running out of breath before you reach the end of a sentence or phrase, these are the sections you might want to go back and rewrite.

The information you *don't* include in your content is often just as important as the information you *do* include. A good speech or presentation cannot just be a data dump. Less is almost always more, so thoughtfully restrict the information you choose to include. Leonardo da Vinci once said, "Simplicity is the ultimate sophistication." Or, as Steve Jobs put it in an interview with *Businessweek*, "Simple can be harder than complex: You have to work hard to get your thinking clean to make it simple. But it's worth it in the end because once you get there, you can move mountains."[8]

William Henry Harrison, the ninth president of the United States, learned this lesson the hard way. On March 4,1841, while standing outside in the freezing cold, Harrison gave the longest inaugural address of any president in U.S. history—lasting 105 minutes! As a result of the speech being so long (and because Harrison was sick and refused to dress appropriately for the event), he ended up coming down with pneumonia and died a few weeks later, making him the shortest serving president in history and the first president to die while in office. Perhaps President Harrison could have benefited from the advice of actor and comedian George Burns, who often joked that the secret to a good speech was "to have a good beginning and a good ending, then having the two as close together as possible."[9]

Too often, presenters don't take the time to properly edit their material and, as a result, they waste their audience's time with redundant or unnecessary content. Honor your audience by reducing your content to only the essential information needed to make your points and achieve your objective. Editing is the art of synthesizing your material down to the minimum needed to communicate your message. Winston Churchill understood the importance of honing and refining content. After delivering one rather lengthy address, he was reported to have remarked: "I must apologize for making a rather long speech this morning. I didn't have time to prepare a short one." Another reason to limit the amount of content you attempt to communicate is that the human short-term memory can only process so much information. Including too much can be overwhelming to an audience and can result in their missing the main points you are trying to make.

In 1956, psychologist George A. Miller published a paper titled "The Magical Number Seven, Plus or Minus Two" in *The Psychological Review*.[10] The paper presented the concept of "chunking" as it related to the average person's ability to process and remember data, facts, or information. What Miller found in his studies was that people are only able to hold between five and nine separate pieces or "chunks" of information in any meaningful way—with the "magic number" being seven. (A good example of this is the "I'm going on a camping trip" game we played as children. Seldom does the game progress much past nine items before people start to get eliminated.) As Miller's study suggested, working memory can only retain so much information, so it is helpful to limit the main points of your message to around seven, and then illustrate those points through the use of supporting material. By limiting your content to seven points or fewer, you help your audience more clearly understand how each point links to your overall theme. A person of few words needs to make those words count, so choose carefully.

Miller's theory should extend to any PowerPoint slides you choose to create as well. For slides, we recommend you follow what we call the "statute of six," meaning no more than six word slides in a row (break them up with a graph, diagram, or photo), no more than six bullets per slide, no more than six words per bullet, and (most important), the main message or essence of your slide should be easily understood in six seconds or less. For excellent examples of visual aid use, watch Al Gore in *An Inconvenient Truth* or any product launch by Steve Jobs.

Closing

After completing the main body of your presentation and taking questions, it is time to wrap things up. The goal is to end your presentation with impact so the audience is able to walk away remembering exactly what you wanted them to remember. Make sure that you take time to summarize what you have previously told them and drive home your key points one last time.

Creating a Master Closing Just as your Master Introduction framed your message at the outset, you need a Master Closing to revisit those points and reframe the message for your listeners at the end. Here are the five points that should be included with your Master Closing:

- Summary of main points
- Review of benefit to audience
- Reintroduce the goal and ask for action
- Closing hook or challenge
- Thank-you to audience for time

We used the example earlier in this chapter of a Master Introduction done by Chris Epperly from the Country Music Association to the NASCAR executives. At the end of his presentation, Epperly's Master Closing might look something like this:

> So I've provided quite a bit of detail today about the CMA brand as a whole and all of the exciting assets we could make available to you if you choose to join with us as a strategic partner. If you do decide to align yourself with all that the CMA has to offer, I am confident that we will be able to increase your brand awareness and, ultimately, drive consumer insight, showing people exactly why your brand is so unique. To put it plainly: it will increase your business. The goal I laid out at the top of this presentation was to provide you with a unique partnership opportunity. I've detailed why I believe a partnership with the CMA would drive consumer traffic to your business. The ball is in your court now. As Henry Ford once said, "Coming together is a beginning; keeping together is progress; working together is success." Thank you very much for your time. I look forward to your decision.

Again, following the road map of an effective Master Closing, Epperly summarizes his main points ("I've provided quite a bit of detail today about the CMA brand as a whole and all of the exciting assets we could make available to you") and then reminds the audience of the benefit ("increase your brand awareness and, ultimately, drive consumer insight"). He tells them again what he wants to come from the presentation ("provide you with a unique partnership opportunity . . . drive consumer traffic to your business") and before thanking them, ends with a closing hook (Ford quote) and challenge ("The ball is in your court"). Because Epperly made sure to incorporate all five points in his Master Closing, the conclusion of his presentation and the purpose of his overall message are clear and unequivocal.

RHETORICAL TOOLS AND TECHNIQUES

This section presents a number of rhetorical tools that can help you keep your audience engaged, illustrate a point or idea, and make the information you are providing stick in their memory. Try to think of times when you have used these in your own communication and try to recognize how others—politicians, coaches, broadcasters, or executives—have used them effectively when delivering their message.

Signposts

Signposts are brief previews, usually in the form of a short list, that let your audience know where you are headed and help them organize the ideas or concepts you are discussing. Think of each signpost as a little road sign for your audience as they travel down the highway that is your presentation. Since your audience will rarely have a hard copy of your presentation, signposting helps them organize your points mentally for better comprehension and retention—simply put, signposts can help your listeners stay with you by providing them a road map. Examples of signposting:

"There are three things you should do to reduce your risk of diabetes . . ."
"Our founder built this company based on four distinct principles . . ."
"There are five characteristics that are consistently exhibited by highly motivated people . . ."

Spotlights

Spotlights are used to give special focus to a specific fact or detail in your presentation. Think of this technique as suddenly shining a bright light on a particular piece of information that you want your audience to remember or give special attention to. Examples of spotlighting:

"If you remember only one thing that I have told you today . . ."
"My next point is one that saved my company over one million dollars last year . . ."
"The true secret to more efficient productivity and higher profits for your division is . . ."

Another way to use spotlighting effectively is to repeat a specific word or phrase to give it emphasis in the eyes of your audience. For example:

"Last year we doubled our profits in the first three months of the
    year—you heard me right—we literally *doubled our profits!*"

When tasked with presenting slides or other visual aids that contain
too much content or overly technical information, spotlighting can be
used effectively to boil the content down to something the audience can
absorb. For example:

"I realize this slide contains a lot of data, but the main point you should
    take away from it is this . . ."

Teasers

Teasers are used to give your audience a peek into something—a topic
or subject—that will be coming up later in your presentation. This will
serve to pique their interest enough that they will stay with you as you
take them along on the journey that is your presentation. Be careful
not to give them too much information. Make sure it is just enough
to whet their appetite so they want to hear more and stay with you
all the way. Think of movie trailers and how they show you just a few
exciting scenes from a movie. If the trailer is good, it will show just
enough to hook people so that they will want to see the entire movie.
In fact, according to world-renowned anthropologist Dr. Helen Fisher,
when we are teased with some information and left with a bit of mystery
it actually triggers the flow of dopamine, a chemical in the brain that
provides a natural high.[11]
    Examples of teasers:

"Does anyone know the #1 complaint customers have when speaking
    on the phone? I'll tell you what it is after lunch . . ."
"There is one thing you can do to reduce your nervousness by up to 75
    percent. We'll talk about that first thing tomorrow . . ."
"Can anyone name the highest-paid athlete of all time? Write down
    your guess and I'll reveal the answer at the end of class . . ."

At a recent conference in San Diego one speaker used a teaser quite
effectively. The main topic of his particular session was "The Ten Secrets

of Effective Time Management." Over the course of his one-hour session, this polished and compelling speaker discussed the first five secrets to an audience that was clearly engaged with his content and delivery. As the one-hour mark approached, the speaker smiled and remarked, "As you might have noticed, I have only given you five of the ten secrets and we are, unfortunately, out of time." The audience groaned with disappointment. "Well, fear not, friends," smiled the presenter. "It is not my intention to leave you hanging here. What we have done, is we have placed a secret link on the homepage of our website." He then flashed a slide containing his company's website and instructions for accessing the secret link. "Go to our website and click on that secret link. It will take you to a page containing the final five secrets to effective time management." Do you think the vast majority of that audience went to the secret link to get those remaining five tips? Of course they did! Not only did this speaker surprise his audience with the secret link, he created a teaser that actually drove traffic to his company's website!

Callbacks

This is a technique often used by comedians—they "call back" to a joke they told earlier in the set, often in a different context. Presenters can use them too, mentioning something from earlier in the presentation to reiterate a point or draw a comparison. Not only does it help create familiarity and rapport with an audience, it also helps to reinforce any important points that you want your audience to take away and remember. Examples of callbacks:

"How many of you remember yesterday when we discussed the spread of malaria in Africa . . . ?"

"On Monday we spoke about the average rainfall in southern Sri Lanka . . ."

"If you remember, this morning I asked you: what's the one thing you dislike most about visiting the dentist . . ."

Metaphor and Simile

A *metaphor* is a figure of speech that uses one thing to mean another in order to make a comparison between the two, often unrelated, things.

Examples would be Shakespeare's "All the world's a stage"; "The torch has been passed" in John F. Kennedy's inaugural address; or simply referring to someone who does well at something as having "hit a home run." A *simile* is a form of metaphor that uses the words "like" or "as" to compare two different things to create a new meaning. "They fought like cats and dogs," "A ruby as red as blood," and "She laughs like a hyena" are all examples of simile. Sprinkled strategically throughout your delivery, metaphors and similes can be powerful tools to connect with an audience and communicate points quickly and effectively. Of course, the various parts of your metaphor must be drawn from the same realm of experience. "Hit a home run" is clear, but "hit a home run right through the goal posts" is confusing and thus ineffective.

When crafting and organizing the content for your meeting or presentation, return frequently to the structure elements and rhetorical tools discussed in this chapter. Try to include as many of them as possible. Experiment with some you use less frequently. Surprise yourself. Creating solid material takes time and effort. By putting in the necessary hours and carefully constructing your content with an eye toward your overall intention and objective, you not only demonstrate a respect and appreciation for your audience, you also give yourself a launching pad from which to begin preparing your delivery.

CHAPTER 4

Be Prepared

Managing Nerves and Controlling Anxiety

Good fortune is what happens when opportunity meets with planning.
—Thomas Edison

Great performances, whether given by an actor on a stage or a CEO in a boardroom, don't just happen; they take time, effort, and commitment. Preparation is the key to projecting a confident presence and delivering a message that accomplishes the objective you've set out to achieve. As the Roman statesman Cato the Elder recommended more than two thousand years ago, "Grasp the subject; the words will follow." The more confident you are in your intention and your message, the more effective you will be in its delivery, and the better the result will be when it is received by your client, your boss, or your customer.

Over the course of this chapter we share the methods that actors have used for centuries to properly prepare themselves *mentally and physically* for what Shakespeare called "the readiness," and we discuss how they can also help you deliver confident and compelling performances in any environment, in front of any audience. We also break down the most common causes of stage fright and provide a series of exercises and techniques that actors have used for centuries to overcome anxiety and manage nerves when going before an audience.

Jerry Seinfeld is one of the most recognizable people on the planet. A successful stand-up comedian, he also created and starred in *Seinfeld*, one of the most popular television shows of all time. However, his ascension to celebrity status was not something that happened without difficulties. The first time he stepped in front of an audience to perform . . . he bombed. Badly. In *Seinfeld: Much Ado About Nothing*, Josh Levine describes the way Seinfeld recounts this painful early experience and what he learned from it to help him properly prepare for subsequent ones.

The day he graduated from Queens College in New York, Seinfeld headed downtown and eventually talked his way into a slot during an open mic night at the famous comedy club Catch a Rising Star. He had always loved comedy and was determined to pursue his dream of working as a stand-up comedian. With little preparation and no prior experience, the twenty-two-year-old Seinfeld stepped in front of the crowd, excited to make his debut. However, he had never performed a comedy act in front of an audience before and as soon as he took the stage . . . trouble. He found himself so paralyzed with fear that he couldn't speak a word. "I got up there, the bright lights hit my face, I'd never touched a microphone, and I froze solid." Despite this disastrous first experience, Seinfeld didn't give up. He wrote new material, practiced, studied the acts of other comedians, and continued to audition and perform at various comedy clubs around the city. Soon, the practice and preparation paid off. He got into his groove as a comedian, found his style, and began to win over his audiences.[1]

The rest, as they say, is television history.

Professional actors and performers like Jerry Seinfeld spend a great deal of time preparing, shaping, and refining the delivery of their content until they are ready to present it in front of an audience. Because people are paying for the privilege of seeing them perform, they know they have to deliver a professional product; they want to honor their audience's time by truly giving them something of value. The same principle holds true for anyone running a meeting or delivering a presentation. Life is short. Time is money. Every moment is a gift. People have busy lives and packed workdays. If someone sacrifices an hour out of their day to attend your meeting, take your call, or consider your proposal you should make sure your message offers them something of value. Professional actors are expected to bring their whole self to their performance—their talent, their passion, their commitment—and the same standard should hold true for anyone tasked with communicating a specific message to others.

Of course, you say. Preparation is important. But how should I prepare? And how much time should I actually spend preparing? For professional actors the formula is simple: for every one minute of performance time, an actor spends around one hour preparing. While that may sound like a lot, this trial-and-error period is essential for an actor to be able to understand what works and what doesn't work in a performance and make adjustments accordingly. When delivering a message during a meeting or presentation, you need to put in the time required to ensure the delivery of your message is polished and ready. If the formula for a professional actor is one hour of prep time for every one minute of performance, how much time is recommended for someone presenting material in a business environment? In *Free Yourself from Fears*, Joseph O'Connor recommends five minutes of preparation for every one minute of presentation.[2] While this is considerably less time than an actor puts in, the underlying lesson is the same: the more time you put into preparing your message, the better the chances your audience will walk away satisfied once you finally deliver it. In the end, you should only run a meeting or deliver a presentation that you would want to attend yourself.

Apple CEO Steve Jobs, one of the most engaging executives of his generation, knew how to deliver an engaging presentation. Jobs was almost obsessive with the level of preparation he put in before a new product launch at Apple, making sure he was involved with every aspect of the process, from the staging to the lighting to the visual aids themselves. He prepared for days and sometimes weeks beforehand, all for a presentation that lasted less than two hours. By preparing thoroughly, Jobs made it look natural, effortless. But that did not come without his putting in the time and hours behind the scenes to ensure he was properly prepared. He spent decades at the forefront of creating innovative products and giving his customers what they wanted, and he had it down to a science.

In *Outliers*, Malcolm Gladwell talks about the value of preparation as it relates to becoming a master in any given field—be it sports, science, music, or business. Gladwell discovered that for people to become expert in any field, they needed to put in at least 10,000 hours of preparation honing their skills. He quotes neurologist Daniel Levitin, who explains: "In study after study, of composers, basketball players, fiction writers, ice skaters, concert pianists, chess players, master criminals, and what have you, this number comes up again and again.... It seems that it takes the brain this long to assimilate all that it needs to know to achieve true mastery."[3] *Ten thousand hours.* If you're doing the math, that's around three hours of practice every day . . . *for a decade.*

PREPARING LIKE A PRO

The audience is king—and the speakers' responsibility to their audience is always greater than their responsibility to themselves. Your communication is always about the other person—the audience, the customer, or the client—and about delivering a message that is not only engaging but provides a benefit. This means proper preparation is required to ensure that the message is delivered as clearly and concisely as possible. Think about the countless hours you have wasted in your life attending poorly planned meetings or presentations that dragged on and on because the speaker had neglected to properly prepare. Respect your audience by being prepared and giving them nothing short of your best. Remember, in almost every instance, you and your audience have the same goal: for your message to be informative and interesting. An audience is not something to be feared; the people listening to you are on your side and want you to succeed. They *want* to be persuaded by your argument or empowered by your data. They *want* the message you are delivering to provide them with value. Otherwise they are simply wasting their time listening to you. Even if you are there to deliver unpleasant news—a pay freeze or an increase in workload—your audience wants you to deliver that message clearly, concisely, and confidently. In nearly every instance, an audience will give you the benefit of the doubt—up until the moment you open your mouth. After that, it all rests on you.

Actors use the rehearsal process to continually repeat a scene or action, sharpening their intention with each reading until it accomplishes the objective they have set out to achieve. It is this method of drilling and repeating that allows actors to refine and polish their delivery. Without preparation, an actor would never be capable of delivering any performance of merit. Preparation will help you lock in your *muscle memory*—the consolidation of a specific activity or motor task into memory through the use of repetition (think of how you learned to ride a bike). Practice really does make perfect (or close to it), so the more you have prepared your message, the more comfortable you will be when delivering it. Most actors love the rehearsal process and look at it as an opportunity to try things and experiment with various choices to see what works and what doesn't.

> *He who rehearsed his speeches was a true man of the people: for such preparation was a mark of deference to the people.*
>
> —DEMOSTHENES

Proper preparation takes planning. Start by developing a time line for the writing and organization of your material. Give yourself a schedule with deadlines and try to stick to them so you have plenty of time to work on the delivery of the material. Most people make the mistake of spending all their time on preparing their material and none on preparing the *delivery* of that material. Work backward from the actual presentation date itself and give yourself plenty of time to complete the research, outlining, drafting, and refining steps discussed in the last chapter. Be realistic but err on the side of giving yourself extra time as a buffer in case something comes up or goes wrong during the process.

In the HBO documentary *Talking Funny*, some of the most successful comedians working today spoke about how they prepare before their routines. Chris Rock goes to the theater where he will be performing and does a sound check before *every show*. By personally checking his equipment and familiarizing himself with the room, he can relax knowing everything is in order. Says Rock, "I want to know where the stage is . . . I want to know the acoustics . . . I don't like being surprised."[4]

Before your presentation begins, inspect your equipment to make sure you have everything you need and it is all in working order. Before a performance, actors will follow a routine known in theatrical circles as "checking your props" to make sure that everything they will need for a successful performance is in place. If you are playing Hamlet, the last thing you want is to reach for your sword to kill Polonius only to discover that your blade is nowhere to be found. Follow the actor's lead and check to make sure all your equipment and material is in place. Eliminate surprises by counting your handouts, testing your markers, and making sure your projector is in proper working order.

The Three Phases of Preparation

When an actor gets cast in a part, three specific phases of preparation occur during the rehearsal process. Each step is important and builds upon the step that came before it. This very same process can benefit you by providing a structure and building-block approach to your personal preparation:

1. The read-through
2. The stumble-through
3. The dress rehearsal

Phase One: The Read-Through The read-through is the first step in the rehearsal process. Here, the cast gathers around a table with their scripts. It is very informal, with all the actors simply reading the words out loud. No great acting happens here and no Oscars are awarded; you can expect lots of mistakes and inelegant line readings as actors experiment with their delivery. Which is precisely the point of this phase of preparation—for the actors to get comfortable with the material and make it their own. Actors need to hear the script out loud and get an understanding of how each section flows from one point to the next. Anyone delivering a speech or presentation should do the same. Once your content is complete, get a friend or coworker to sit across from you as you simply talk through the material and become familiar with the words and flow.

Phase Two: The Stumble-Through Once you have taken your material through the initial read-through phase of the preparation process, your content should begin to feel familiar and you should have a slightly clearer idea as to how it all fits together. It won't be perfect, but it will be better. The second phase of preparation for actors happens here: the stumble-through. Since you will eventually be delivering this material on your feet, you've got to start getting comfortable delivering it that way. To do this, actors start to practice the delivery of their content standing, perhaps including movement. Just as in the first phase, this should be done in front of a team member or spouse so you have someone you can deliver it to and who can provide you with feedback on what is working and what is not. Actors might still have their notes or script in their hands during this phase of preparation, but they will be working to be able to deliver it empty-handed by the time it is complete.

Phase Three: The Dress Rehearsal The third and final phase of preparation that actors go through in the process is the most important one: the dress rehearsal. This is your last chance to experiment with the delivery to identify any problem areas that need to be addressed before delivering it for real in front of the intended audience. In the dress rehearsal, you are practicing it one final time for a simulated audience, doing it exactly how you will do it on the actual day. No stopping. No fixing slides. Just go, running it from the beginning to the end. Again, the dress rehearsal should be done out loud in front of an audience who can provide feedback. If possible, do your dress rehearsal in the actual room you will be delivering the presentation in, using the same equipment and wearing the same clothes you will have to deal with on the day. If possible, have someone videotape the dress rehearsal so you can watch it back and make any final adjustments.

Contingency Plans

Even the best-laid plans can go awry based on circumstances out of your control. Luggage gets lost. Projectors break down. Materials don't get delivered. Ask yourself what could go wrong and plan accordingly—have a contingency plan. Check your equipment ahead of time. Make a list of problems that could arise and devise solutions ahead of time. By anticipating these worst-case scenarios and having a backup option ready to go, you will be better prepared to keep your message on track and retain control of your communication, no matter what curve balls are thrown at you. The more you practice and prepare your message ahead of time, the closer you will be to making it goof-proof when you finally deliver it on the actual day.

Another point to remember is that, in most cases, your audience will be listening to you, not following along on the page. Because the content is yours, you are under no obligation to deliver it exactly as written. Use your preparation time to get comfortable with your content and its flow. Practice your transitions but don't get hung up on memorizing your content word for word. The secret to an effective delivery is to memorize the *outline* of the content—the journey from point A to point B—and then use that road map to give you the freedom to simply *speak*.

The Myth of Over-Preparing

Every so often in a workshop or training, when we discuss the importance of proper preparation, someone will say, "I don't like to rehearse because I don't want to be over-prepared." Let's take a moment to dispel this myth right now: there is no such thing as being over-prepared to deliver your message. You are either prepared or you are not prepared; you are ready or you are not. There are a few different reasons a person would dismiss proper preparation before a speech or presentation. For the most part, a person who is expressing this concern

- Is too lazy to put in the time needed to properly prepare
- Is perfectly satisfied delivering a presentation that is "good enough"
- Is comfortable relying on charm to get them through
- Lacks the necessary time to prepare
- Is not clear on the proper way to prepare

In short, you cannot know your material too well and you cannot be over-prepared. You would never hear a brain surgeon say, "Gee, I feel like I'm over-prepared for this upcoming surgery."

What people who mention over-preparing may be worried about is that their delivery will sound robotic or rehearsed because they have practiced so many times. Of course, this is a legitimate concern. Sounding like you just put a tape in and pressed play during your delivery is not something you ever want. Your communication should sound fresh and spontaneous to each audience, as if they are the first people ever to hear you say those words. To combat a robotic delivery, Stanislavski recommended "a constant supply of spontaneity," saying that being present and "in the moment" is essential for a communicator. Stanislavski also believed that dedicated and focused preparation needed to be part of a communicator's process to avoid laziness or bad habits becoming part of a person's communication style. "Habit is a two-edged sword," he said. "The unfortunate and dangerous part . . . is that habits can be developed in the wrong direction." In his championing of thorough and focused practice and repetition, Stanislavski was often fond of quoting the Russian prince S. M. Volkonski, who once said about proper preparation: "The difficult should become habitual, the habitual easy, the easy, beautiful."[5]

THE ANXIETY OF PERFORMANCE

Stage fright is also known as speech anxiety or *glossophobia*. Its symptoms take various forms and happen at various times—the night before a big interview, while waiting backstage, or on the walk down the hall to your boss's office. Here are some of the most common symptoms of speech anxiety. See if you are able to identify which ones you frequently experience when nerves get the best of you.

- Trembling hands
- Shallow breathing
- Dry mouth
- Loss of concentration
- Rambling speech
- Increased heart rate
- Increased pace
- Monotone in speech
- Flushed face
- Ineffective gestures
- Nervous laughter or smiling
- Stammering
- Trembling or low voice
- Sweaty palms

- Weak knees
- Increased muscle tension
- Nausea
- Butterflies

It is probably a safe bet that you have experienced some of these symptoms in the past, either when communicating a difficult message or dealing with a challenging audience. But there's some good news. If you take another look, you'll notice that many of these symptoms are internal and thus can be controlled by you and masked from your audience. Remember, your audience can only perceive what they see or hear. If you don't telegraph or signal to your listeners through your words or body language that you are less than confident, your audience will have no idea. For this reason, it is never a good idea to apologize to your audience for being nervous (a common mistake speakers make). Doing this will only draw attention to the problem and take the focus off your message or material.

But why do we get nervous in the first place? As it turns out, people can have many different reasons to get nervous when they are tasked with communicating a message to others. Once we understand the *reasons* people get nervous, we can start to offer remedies to manage that anxiety and project confidence instead. Here are a number of reasons why people get nervous when delivering a message to others. Can you think of additional ones? Try to pinpoint for yourself which ones commonly cause anxiety for you.

- Presenting to experts
- Being unsure of the audience
- Bad previous experience
- High stakes
- VIP in attendance
- Technology concerns
- Personal insecurities
- Fear of failure
- Fear of judgment
- Lack of confidence in material

As discussed, the best method to combat speech anxiety is to become extremely familiar with your material. To put it plainly: *make your unknowns known*. This eliminates the fear that you are going to get lost or forget what comes next. As Lybi Ma, deputy editor of *Psychology Today*, writes, "Being prepared is your first line of attack. You should be anxious if you haven't done your homework."[6]

With any type of high-stakes communication, whether it be running a staff meeting or engaging your boss in a social conversation, you are stepping out of your safety zone and exposing yourself and your ideas to the judgment of others. This type of self-presentation can cause a person to feel vulnerable and anxious. Stanislavski called the feeling of communicating in front of an audience "solitude in public." For most people, the idea of having to speak in front of others resides somewhere between a terror and a thrill. The feeling of not being ready or being unable to perform a given task or activity fills us with anxiousness and self-doubt. In 2011, when Derek Jeter, the star shortstop for the New York Yankees, was asked by a reporter what his greatest fear in life was, he answered, "Being unprepared."[7]

We've all seen the lists of famous actors (Lawrence Olivier, Kim Basinger, Peter O'Toole, Jennifer Aniston) and musicians (Barbara Streisand, Glenn Gould, Rod Stewart) who have waged their own personal battles with nerves and speech anxiety. No one knows more about this subject than the professional actor. According to one British medical study, the stress that an actor feels on the opening night of a play is "equivalent to [that of] a car-accident victim."[8] But performers know the big secret about stage fright—something that non-actors may not realize: *nearly everyone experiences it*, even heads of state. Lyndon Johnson was haunted by a recurring nightmare during some of the more challenging periods of his term as president. In this dream, Johnson found himself standing, alone, in the middle of a stampede of cattle, frozen and unable to speak or move, while just within earshot he could hear the members of his cabinet discussing how to replace him and divide power among themselves.

Uta Hagen discusses stage fright in *Respect for Acting*, acknowledging that even veteran actors such as herself are not immune to nervousness before and during a performance. The key, she advises, is to be able to *control* that nervous energy so that it does not control you. "At best, they [nerves] will heighten my energy and make me more alert. They should not make for fear. Above all, I try to control them by focusing on my main objects and intentions."[9] The same idea works for someone presenting information to a corporate audience or communicating with another person; regardless of what distractions arise while you are delivering your message, it is your job to remain committed to the moment. When nerves creep in and you start to feel yourself losing control, put the focus back on your intention and the objective you are there to accomplish. This will allow you to stay grounded. "Just remember," Hagen concludes, "that the better your technique becomes, the more you should be able to concentrate, to eliminate distractions and shed concerns."

In other words—again, practice makes (almost) perfect.

Aristotle defined courage not as the absence of fear but as just the right balance between timidity and overconfidence. He was also a vocal champion of proper preparation. "We are what we repeatedly do," he said. "Excellence then, is not an act, but a habit." As we discussed earlier, good speakers are not born; they are made. Plutarch captured this when he wrote about the considerable accomplishments of Demosthenes: "It was thought that he was not a man of good natural parts, but that his ability and power were a product of toil." In other words, it was *practice* that made him great—not some natural-born gift. The more you prepare, the more proficient you will become, and the more proficient you are, the more relaxed you will be in front of your audience. This is something all professional speakers and performers understand. The actress and comedian Sandra Bernhard once remarked to a young protégé who boasted to never suffer from stage fright, "Don't worry. It comes with talent."[10]

As Bernhard was attempting to point out, not all anxiety needs to be battled or feared. Sally Winston, co-director of the Anxiety & Stress Disorders Institute of Maryland, explains it this way: "Anxiety itself is neither helpful nor hurtful. It's your *response* to anxiety that is helpful or hurtful."[11] Physiologically, when a healthy heart reaches about 120 beats a minute, the body begins to secrete adrenaline, which causes a flight-or-fight reaction that makes it nearly impossible to concentrate or listen.[12] It generates consistent effects: shortness of breath, loss of concentration, rapid heartbeat, dry mouth, and the rest.

It was in the late 1700s that studies of anxiety involving work on phobias, including the fear of public speaking, came into prominence.[13] The concept of stress in a biological context was first developed by

Hungarian-born endocrinologist Hans Selye in the 1930s. Through his research, Selye created a model that divided stress into two different types: positive stress or *challenge* stress (something he called *eustress*) and negative stress or *threat* stress (something he called *distress*). He categorized eustress as any stress that was healthy or provided positive feelings in a person (riding a roller coaster, getting married, lifting weights) while distress created the opposite effect and feelings of pain, trouble, or discomfort (being robbed, getting a speeding ticket, suffering from asthma). Selye found that whether you experience eustress or distress in a given situation was determined by various factors such as the experience itself, personal expectations, and resources available to cope with the stress.[14]

Certainly anyone who has ever had to deliver a keynote address, discipline an employee, or interview for a job has experienced the rush of adrenaline associated with nervousness. As it relates to effective communication, adrenaline can be a positive or a negative influence. Positive adrenaline for a speaker often shows up as passion, enthusiasm, and excitement, while negative adrenaline manifests itself as fear, nervousness, and anxiety.

I am always doing that which I cannot do, in order that I may learn how to do it.

—PABLO PICASSO

The key to managing speech anxiety involves the ability to move a particular experience from distress to eustress. Through proper preparation and relaxation, make it an experience you look forward to instead of an experience you dread. This is something that athletes and actors do quite effectively. They welcome that powerful surge of adrenaline that accompanies a big game or performance and, through the use of concentration and focus, use it to their benefit.

A recent study at Hebrew University in Jerusalem found that certain people actually *cultivate* anxiety before an important event such as a test or presentation.[15] Though these feelings of anxiety and stress are often developed subconsciously, those who thrive on this type of anxiousness were actually found to perform better as a result. The anxiety becomes a familiar feeling and provides them with a boost for cognitive performance, much like that experienced by someone who enjoys extreme sports. Says psychiatrist Harris Stratyner of Mount Sinai School of Medicine in New York, "Some people get addicted to feeling anxious because that's the state they've always known. If they feel a sense of calm, they get bored; they feel empty inside. They *want* to feel anxious."[16]

The key for you as a communicator is to employ the adrenaline as fuel to energize your performance and support the intention behind your message. Of course, nervous energy tends to show up in different ways for each person, often putting them into one of two extreme categories: what actors refer to as *bottlers* and *burners*. A bottler is someone whose nervous energy gets bottled up inside them and manifests itself in stiffness or a rigid appearance; a burner tends to shift or move continuously during their communication, unable to stand in one spot for more than a few seconds at a time.

Techniques to Combat Speech Anxiety

As noted, nearly everyone experiences stage fright or speech anxiety when they find themselves communicating in front of a new audience or in an unfamiliar environment. Stage fright is a completely natural and understandable phenomenon. But it must be managed so that the anxiety you are feeling on the *inside* does not get communicated to your audience through what they are seeing or hearing on the *outside*. Actors, who must perform in front of a completely new audience every night, learn to combat their speech anxiety and handle nerves using a handful of effective techniques.

Tackle Cognitive Nervousness Cognitive nervousness involves those tiny mental voices we all have, the ones that tell us we are going to fail: *You moron! Why did you say that? Idiot! You are really going to screw this up! Why would anyone want to listen to you?* These negative thoughts are a result of an internalized critic we all possess, something professionals call our *critical inner voice. You're boring! You've gained so much weight! You don't know what you are talking about!* We all have them, these nagging, poisonous thoughts that erode our confidence and undermine our delivery. Even the most successful actors are not immune to this type of nagging self-doubt.

Actress Helena Bonham Carter, who has starred in dozens of Hollywood films and played the Queen Mother in *The King's Speech*, talked about how personal insecurities still plague her after working professionally for over thirty years. "It's every time you start a job. 'What am I doing here? I can't actually act. Someone employed me again?'"[17]

Negative thoughts such as these, called *internal noise*, can distract you, clouding your thought process and interfering with the effective delivery of your message. The key to silencing those negative voices is to replace them with more positive ones. Timothy Gallwey, who has studied the mental side of succeeding, recently told *Newsweek*, "Winners get in their own way less. They interfere with the raw expression of talent less. And to do that, first they win the war against fear, against doubt, against insecurity—which are no minor victories."[18]

Focus on Your Intention When nerves start to creep in on you during your communication and you feel like a red-hot spotlight is shining on you, remember that your communication is not about you, it is about your audience and the message you are there to provide them. Put your focus back on the intention and the objective you are trying to achieve, and that will shine the spotlight on the audience and not you.

Breathe from Your Core Actors understand that everything begins with the breath. By breathing properly and slowly, the body is able to relax and prepare for optimal functioning. The lower you breathe, the deeper the breath you get. When you speak, your words have a starting point, an energy, and a final destination where they are being sent. To achieve this you need to employ proper breath control. A resting adult's average rate of breath is apt to be around twelve to fifteen breaths per minute while the optimal rate of breath for that same individual is more like six breaths per minute.[19] As babies, we come into the world with full and complete breathing skills, but over time, stress and other life challenges contribute to poor breathing. Because of this, most people breathe inefficiently, using less than a third of their available lung capacity.[20] When it comes to effective communication, you can take advantage of proper breathing for two distinct purposes: for relaxation, and for projection.

As the sixteenth-century yoga master Svatmarama once said, "When the breath wanders the mind also is unsteady; but when the breath is calmed the mind too will be still." Proper breath control used as a preparation tool can help you approach your communication in a calm and confident manner. Proper breathing can also alleviate other roadblocks that prevent effective communication, such as stress from travel, impulsiveness, low stamina, and moodiness. Breathing incompletely will bring unwanted tension into the body. If you are not breathing properly, you won't have enough breath to project your voice to the back of the room where that very important client may well be sitting.

EXERCISE
Finding Your Core Breath

Proper breathing—what we call *core breathing*—should be slow, regular, and controlled. Breathe deeply from the diaphragm (the muscle separating the chest and abdominal cavities) by following these steps.

1. Begin by relaxing your body and making sure your posture is straight.
2. Place your hand on your stomach, just below the navel.
3. Inhale gently through your nose for a count of five. Notice how your hand rises as your diaphragm expands.
4. Hold the breath for a count of five.
5. Exhale through your mouth for a count of five while gently pressing on the stomach.
6. Repeat the entire process from the beginning, this time adding in an audible sigh when you exhale.

Warm Up Your Body It is important that you properly warm up your body before communicating an important message; this will help you release any unwanted tension. Physical activities such as jogging, walking, or swimming can help you shake off nervous jitters as well. In one study, British researchers found that six out of ten people said their management skills, mental performance, and ability to meet deadlines improved on days that they exercised compared to days they did not, and they were about 15 percent more productive in their work.[21] Exercise is also believed to help improve memory, fuel creativity, and improve a person's mood.[22]

It is important to get your blood flowing prior to a presentation or meeting. As actors learn early on in their training, there is no information in tension. In other words, when you are delivering a message, your body is the canvas on which you will be creating so you need it free and available. Just as athletes would never go on the field without doing proper warm-up exercises or opera singers would never go onstage without warming up their voices, you must prepare yourself physically. To do this, use the actor-based warm-up exercises that follow.

EXERCISE
Five-Minute Physical Warm-Up

Shortly before you go before your audience, take five minutes to loosen and warm up your body.

1. Neck: Let your head fall forward and stretch the neck muscles. Next, rotate your left ear to your left shoulder and your right ear to your right shoulder.
2. Eyes: Alternate from a squinting (little eyes) to wide-eyed (big eyes).
3. Face: Alternate between your biggest expression (surprise) to your smallest expression (sour) to engage the muscles of the face.
4. Tongue: Stretch your tongue to your nose, your chin, and your cheeks.
5. Lips: Blow air through your lips to make a motorboat sound.

6. Jaw: Mimic chewing a very large piece of bubblegum to stretch the jaw muscles.

7. Shoulders: Roll shoulders in a circular motion. Then reverse the direction. Shrug and release.

8. Arms: Extend your arms and rotate them in a circular motion. Reverse.

9. Wrists: Rotate your wrists in a circular motion. Reverse.

10. Fingers: As if your fingers are dripping with water, vigorously shake them dry.

11. Back: Mimic the motion of hugging a tree to stretch out the back muscles.

12. Chest: Mimic the motion of crushing an orange between your shoulder blades to stretch out your chest.

13. Legs: Shake out any tension in your legs. Follow with deep knee bends.

14. Ankles: Standing on one foot, rotate your opposite ankle in a circular motion. Repeat on the other foot.

Stay Hydrated Water is the body's principal component, comprising around 60 percent of your body weight. To avoid dry mouth during your communication, stay hydrated. Water that is room temperature is best for your vocal chords; avoid water that is too hot or too cold before a big speech or presentation. Keep a glass of water handy backstage and take a drink before you go on to speak. Other tricks actors use to combat dry mouth include sucking on a lemon drop backstage or biting the inside of their cheek. Both techniques encourage salivation. Also, try to avoid anything with caffeine starting an hour before your speech, and limit milk and dairy products for twelve hours before as they both encourage phlegm.

Employ Creative Visualization Actors often use a technique called *creative visualization* when they need to imagine circumstances that will help them access specific feelings or emotions required for a scene or role. You can use this technique as well to manage nerves. Here's how: As you prepare to deliver your message, remember back to a time when you felt powerful and successful in your communication. Think back to a previous positive experience and how that made you feel. Put yourself in that mind frame. Develop a positive mental image to help center yourself. Picture an environment where you feel confident, powerful, and relaxed and begin your communication from there. And finally, remember this: you are the expert on the content you are prepared to present to this audience. You've done your homework and are ready to deliver the goods. Reminding yourself of this fact should help calm your nerves and ease your fears.

Create a Ritual Many actors have a specific routine that they go through before a performance to help them relax and focus. Some listen to music, some light a candle, some lift weights, while others simply find a quiet place to meditate. Each person has an individual specific ritual, so find one that works for you. Try to choose clothing that is comfortable and makes you feel confident and self-assured. Get up the morning of your presentation early enough to do something for yourself, such as enjoy a cup of coffee, exercise, or read the newspaper. Develop a "day-of" strategy that is familiar and constant. This will help you relax and feel in control before your speech or presentation. Think of George Clooney in the movie *Up in the Air:* his character devised a system for passing through airport security that became a ritual, making him feel comfortable and confident and making his constant travel less stressful. Find the rituals that work for you and use them to help you stay grounded and relaxed before your communication.

Find a Friendly Face As you take the stage and make initial eye contact with your audience, seek out a friendly face. Look for someone giving you some positive nonverbal feedback—a friend, a coworker, or your spouse. Use this person as an anchor to help you stay relaxed and calm. If you feel nervousness start to creep back into your communication during your delivery, direct your message to this person until you feel comfortable enough to move back to the other members of the audience again. Don't neglect the rest of your audience in the process, but go to your anchor whenever you start to feel anxious or uncertain.

Commit to the Moment Once your communication begins, focus on delivering it to the best of your ability. Don't give up and don't telegraph to your audience (verbally or nonverbally) that you are unhappy with your delivery. Don't comment on your performance while you are delivering it. Your focus should be on your intention and your objective—as well as the benefit you are there to provide to your listeners. You've done the preparation and put in the time getting ready. As the playwright and lawyer Eugene Ware said, "All glory comes from daring to begin."[23] Now is your moment to shine. Enjoy it.

CHAPTER 5

Project Confidence

Expressing Your Intention Nonverbally

Confidence is contagious. So is lack of confidence.
—Vince Lombardi

John F. Kennedy, like many great politicians, understood the power of nonverbal communication. He knew the importance of shaping and controlling an audience's perception through visual messages, and he used this knowledge to his advantage as a communicator. When it came time to prepare for his watershed 1960 presidential debate with Richard Nixon—the first televised debate in history—Kennedy took a vastly different approach to preparation than Nixon did. Television was a relatively new medium at that time and Kennedy understood that he needed to make it work for him.

Nixon, who was the favorite going into the debate, chose not to work with a debate coach. Kennedy, however, not only gathered his inner circle of advisers and political consultants to help him prepare, he also secretly enlisted one other person to help him get ready: Tony Award–winning stage director Arthur Penn. Penn, the acclaimed director of such Broadway productions as *The Miracle Worker* and *Wait Until Dark*, was renowned at the time for his ability to coax brilliant performances out of novice actors. Kennedy believed Penn would be able to help him with his delivery and presentation in front of that television audience—specifically to help him project an aura of credibility and confidence to the millions of people who would be watching that night. They were looking for a man who was solid and serious, someone who had the gravitas to be president of the United States.

Arthur Penn, applying his experience working in the theater, may have changed history with the direction and advice he gave Kennedy. Quite cleverly, he instructed Kennedy to look directly into the camera when he was speaking, not at Nixon, who was standing right next to him. This made the candidate appear as if he were talking directly to the viewers at home in their living rooms. Penn told Kennedy to keep his answers short and pithy and coached him to remain relaxed and still with his body language, even while seated. These physical cues allowed Kennedy to project an aura of steadiness and calm, a vivid contrast to Nixon who appeared fidgety, sweaty, and uncomfortable. Other intention cues supported Kennedy's main goal of projecting confidence: he spoke slowly, closed the debate with a provocative question, and wore a base of makeup to make his skin appear tanned and healthy under the bright studio lights. Nixon, on the other hand, leaned against the lectern and gripped it tightly. He appeared pale and sickly, a result of his decision to forgo the use of stage makeup. To many, Nixon's performance was a disaster—after watching the debate on television, Nixon's vice-presidential running mate, Henry Cabot Lodge Jr., reportedly remarked, "That son of a bitch just cost us the election."[1] To this day, political experts still debate the impact Nixon's poor delivery had on his candidacy and how many millions of votes it potentially cost him.

Kennedy's intention cues—his solid and precise body language, combined with his smooth and steady delivery—helped project the image of a confident and poised leader to the millions of viewers who tuned in that night. Kennedy understood the stakes and used his physical delivery to help shape his audience's perception, enlisting the help of Arthur Penn. It just might have tipped the election in his favor.

· · ·

Everything we do while communicating says and means something to other people. And our words are like the tip of an iceberg. Allan and Barbara Pease, authors of *The Definitive Book of Body Language*, estimate that, in business encounters, body language accounts for 60 percent to 80 percent of the impact made around a negotiating table.[2]

Our bodies are billboards sending messages out into the world, and these messages are constantly read and interpreted by others, for better or for worse. By controlling these signals—which we call *intention cues*—we control the message being communicated to our audience. As we discussed in the first chapter, intention is the tool by which you can connect your body and voice to your message. If used effectively, your intention will fuel the emotion of your delivery. But to do that, your intention must be supported through the physical actions that constitute your *nonverbal communication*.

These actions can be a glance, a movement, a gesture—anything that is not speech but that communicates meaning and creates awareness or understanding in another person.

Some kinds of nonverbal communication are very obvious and familiar. Imagine you are traveling in a country where you don't speak the language—how would you ask for directions to your hotel in Guangzhou? Or request a haircut in Yokohama? Or describe to a doctor in Hyderabad the pains you are experiencing? In these circumstances, your body language is intended to take the place of the language you don't share with the person you wish to communicate with.

But in fact, we use nonverbal communication hundreds of times every day in ways that we might not even be aware of, or intend. Nonverbal communication is a complex aspect of human behavior and its impact can be easily underappreciated and even misunderstood. Actors understand its power and use it deliberately, in the form of intention cues, to enhance the delivery of the words they speak. And you can do the same. Through the controlled and focused use of facial expressions, gestures, posture, and movement, you will be able to ensure that your audience perceives every aspect of your communication in exactly the way you intended—and, even more important, avoid the mixed messages and mistrust that arise when your words and your intention cues are out of sync.

In this chapter we discuss the impact of intention cues and then get down to the business of teaching you to project cues in line with your intention and your objective.

INTENT VERSUS IMPACT

In your communications, it doesn't matter *what* your intention is if it is not clearly and accurately received and interpreted by your audience. Perception is everything when it comes to effective communication. What you are attempting to project as a speaker is only successful if it is interpreted as you intend by your audience.

A perfect example of this took place on September 11, 2001.

On the day of the terrorist attacks, President George W. Bush was in Sarasota, Florida, reading a storybook to a group of second graders when the president's chief of staff, Andy Card, approached and whispered in the president's ear that hijackers had crashed two planes into the World Trade Center in New York City. Instead of getting up and springing into action, Bush famously remained seated for nearly eight minutes, so as not to frighten the children. In an interview with *National Geographic*, Bush talked about that moment and the choices he made that day. "I made the decision not to jump up immediately and leave the classroom," he said. "I didn't want to rattle the kids. I wanted to project a sense of calm." However in a piece published in *Newsweek*, the children in the audience that day remember those moments quite differently.[3] Lazaro Dubrocq, who was seven years old at the time, saw the sudden reaction in President Bush's body language and was startled by the change. "In a heartbeat, he leaned back, and he looked flabbergasted, shocked, horrified." Another student in the audience that day, a girl named Mariah Williams, recounts the experience and what she saw in much the same way. Though the president said nothing, she could sense from the shift in his nonverbal communication that something was terribly wrong. "I don't remember the story we were reading," she says. "Was it about pigs? But I'll always remember watching his face turn red." The intention cues Bush was *attempting* to project—confidence and calm—were betrayed by the intention cues he was *actually* displaying at the moment. The nonverbal communication the schoolchildren saw during those eight minutes told his true feelings at that moment and they interpreted them accurately.

As most experts who study communication will agree, your verbal communication (that is, the words you are saying) communicates *information*, while your nonverbal communication (your body language and vocal variety) communicates *emotions* and *attitudes*. If your intention is to motivate your audience, your body language must fully support that intention. This means your audience must feel motivated by what you are saying. Similarly, if you are trying to challenge your audience with the message you are presenting and that audience does not walk away feeling challenged, the delivery of your message was not successful. Let's say you are a training manager describing an upcoming workshop that you hope your audience will be excited about. If you are not projecting or communicating excitement with your physical intention cues, the chances your message will generate excitement with your audience are low.

All speech is vain and empty unless it be accompanied by action.

—DEMOSTHENES

As human beings interacting with other human beings throughout our daily lives, we see and interpret the intention cues of others at every moment. In fact, it would be very difficult to live our lives without this innate ability to divine information and make decisions based upon what we see in front of us. Quite simply, it is one of the traits that has allowed us to survive and evolve as a species. In *Listening and Human Communication in the 21st Century*, Andrew Wolvin writes, "While recognizing that the best you can do is to approximate your partner's intentions, learning to attend to, understand, interpret, and evaluate the communication cues in your environment increases the likelihood that meaningful communication will occur."[4]

Even when a person is trying *not* to communicate information (think of how you behave in a crowded elevator), *that* is communicating a message as well. It is impossible *not* to communicate messages to others with your face and body. Through the five different areas of nonverbal behavior we discuss in this chapter, you tell countless stories, express various emotions, and share a myriad of feelings. And, just as with any good book, someone can't tell the whole story by reading a single chapter. Your audience won't interpret and understand your communication by observing only one aspect of your physical delivery; all aspects of your communication will be considered in a total bundle. Which is precisely why all your intention cues must support the pursuit of your objective: so you can avoid confusion or mixed signals.

While some of the physical messages we project to an audience are conscious and under our control (a wave, a nod, a wink), others are not. They are unconscious, often taking place without our even being aware they are happening. Yet these messages are read and interpreted by others. Cultural anthropologist Michael Wesch of Kansas State University has studied human communication for years and points out that human beings are wired to constantly take in and interpret everything they see and experience—including the *micro-expressions* of others.[5] Micro-expressions are involuntary facial movements and physical tics—a roll of the eyes, a wrinkle of the forehead, a lick of the lips—that happen without conscious thought. Such micro-expressions happen quickly—as fast as *one twenty-fifth of a second.* And even though they happen at rocket speed, they are still seen and interpreted—inevitably shaping the opinions others form about us. It is this unique ability we have to recognize and interpret the nonverbal communication of others that creates understanding and allows for empathy between human beings.

So which gender is more expressive: men or women? One such study by Vanderbilt University psychologist Ann Kring, published in the *Journal of Personality and Social Psychology*, revealed that while men and women experience the same levels of emotions, women are typically more effective at communicating how they feel. "It is incorrect to make a blanket statement that women are more emotional than men," says Kring. "It is correct to say that women show their emotions more than men."[6]

CONGRUENCE VERSUS INCONGRUENCE

In the 1960s, Albert Mehrabian, a professor of psychology at UCLA, began conducting studies exploring the relative impact of nonverbal communication and spoken words.[7] What he found in this ground-breaking (and often misinterpreted) study was that people—when determining attitudes and feelings about others—observe three different channels of communication: *verbal communication* (the actual words you are saying), *vocal communication* (how you sound while you are saying the words), and *visual communication* (what you are doing with your face and body while you are saying them). Mehrabian discovered that *congruence* in a person's communication was essential if a message was to be delivered effectively, meaning everything had to be in line, supporting the speaker's intention. If there was ever *incongruence* (or mixed signals) among the three channels, an audience would rely more heavily on what they saw (55 percent) or what they heard (38 percent) to form their opinions rather than what was actually said (7 percent). An example to show what Mehrabian meant would be a man in an argument with his wife, punching a wall with his fist while shouting, *"I'm not angry!"* While his verbal communication says one thing, the intention cues his wife is reading from his vocal and visual channels tell a different story. And because of the incongruence in the communication channels, she will most likely discount the actual words and make her judgments based on what she sees and hears.

Mehrabian's "7%–38%–55% Rule" (as it is often called) does not mean your words or content are not important (as some people who misconstrue the study would have you believe). What it shows is that for effective communication to take place, and for clear understanding to occur, all aspects of your delivery (your intention cues) must be in line. The congruence of your message requires that all channels—verbal, vocal, and visual—be absolutely in sync. If you are reprimanding your child, you can't do it with a smile. If you are praising an employee, you can't do it with a grimace or a sigh.

Stanislavski also wrote about congruence during an actor's performance, saying, "When the body transmits neither the actor's feelings to me nor how he experiences them, I see an out-of-tune, inferior instrument." He went on to offer advice on how someone could avoid incongruence: "This [congruence] makes an enormous call on our external technique, on the expressiveness of our bodily apparatus, our voice diction, intonation, handling of words, phrases, speeches, our facial expressions, plasticity of movement, way of walking . . . You must go on developing, correcting, tuning your bodies until every part of them will respond to the . . . task of . . . presenting."[8] Stanislavski spoke to actors, but his observations apply to any communicator.

CREATING A STRONG FIRST IMPRESSION

Your behavior and the ways in which you communicate with others define you. The moment you step in front of an audience, lots of judgments are made about you. Perceptions start to be created and opinions start to be formed very quickly, so it is essential that you create a strong first impression. Confident people own the space they inhabit. A lot of that strong first impression comes from body language and what your audience sees from you initially. Actors and directors understand this, which is why every entrance in a film or play is considered and executed very carefully. The moment characters appear, the audience begins to observe them and decide whether they have positive or negative feelings toward them. Think of the first appearance of a famous movie character such as James Bond, Hannibal Lector, or Pee Wee Hermann. Why do we smile when we see Pee Wee Hermann and get the creeps when we see Hannibal Lector? Because of the intention cues the actors are communicating through their delivery: the way they

I speak two languages, Body and English.

—MAE WEST

move, the way they gesture, and the way they interact with others. Sitting in that movie theater, you observe behavior and make decisions based on those observations. And your audiences at work or in social situations do the same thing with you. This is why it is important to control your physical delivery and ensure that every intention cue you initiate supports your message. And nowhere is this more important than in the opening moments of your communication.

Erica Daniels, the associate artistic director of the Tony Award–winning Steppenwolf Theatre in Chicago, has auditioned and cast thousands of actors over the years. She had this to say about creating a strong impression: "You have a very short time to create an impact with an audience, seven to ten seconds, tops. And the clock starts ticking the moment you walk into a room. If you are not 100 percent present in your communication, the authenticity is lost and we don't engage. And without engagement, you remove your listener from the moment, meaning everything you say will probably be forgotten as soon as you walk out the door."[9]

And it is no different for a person presenting a product to a group of investors, meeting a future boss for the first time, or interviewing for a new job. Researchers from New York University support Daniels's opinion. A recent study found that we make an average of *eleven major decisions* about another person's communication in the first seven seconds of meeting them.[10] This is precisely why we need to be aware of what signals we are communicating to control the perception of our audience and make it work in our favor.

In *Blink*, Malcolm Gladwell discusses the way we make snap judgments about people, using what he calls our *adaptive unconscious*. He details a fascinating study by psychologist Nalini Ambady. In the study, Ambady gave a group of students three ten-second videotapes of a collection of teachers. The videos contained no sound, just the physical intention cues (body language, gestures, and facial expressions) of the teacher. After watching the clips, Ambady had the students rate each teacher's effectiveness based on the ten silent seconds they witnessed. Next, Ambady cut the ten-second clip down to a five-second clip and had another group of students evaluate the teachers in the same way. For both groups, the teachers' ratings were the same. Even when Ambady cut the clips down to just two seconds, the judgments of the teachers' effectiveness were the same. Finally, Ambady compared the snap judgments made in her study with evaluations made about those same teachers by other students who had taken the teacher's class for an *entire semester*. What do you think she discovered? To her surprise, the perceptions about each teacher's effectiveness were essentially the same. As Gladwell states, "That's the power of our adaptive unconscious."[11] Or as the saying goes: *first impressions last*.

Bottom line? Experts suggest you have a mere seven seconds to make a lasting impact. That is not a lot of time, so it is up to you to use those initial moments effectively to shape and influence your listeners' feelings and perceptions about you and your message. Remember, it is difficult, if not impossible, to overcome a bad first impression. And in business, most people never get the chance.

Many people who take a communication or presentation skills course ask us, "Is it possible to project a confident presence if I am not confident as a communicator or not confident in my material?" The answer is simple: absolutely, it is possible. In fact, it is essential that you be able to do that with your communication. Actors often employ a technique called "Acting As If" to create their characters, and it can work for non-actors as well. If you want to project the aura of a confident executive, you need to walk and talk as if you were a confident executive. Eventually, by doing this, you will project the image you want your audience to see. Or as best-selling author Wayne Dyer maintains, in many cases, "Our intention creates our reality."[12]

EXERCISE
Snap Judgments

Here are some of the snap judgments (on a continuum from positive to negative) that an audience is likely to make in the initial moments of a communication or interaction:

Positive		Negative
Friendly	———	Unfriendly
Calm	———	Nervous
Engaging	———	Dull
Passionate	———	Disengaged
Knowledgeable	———	Uncertain
Concise	———	Long-winded
Prepared	———	Unprepared
Confident	———	Insecure
Relaxed	———	Tense
Articulate	———	Rambling
Credible	———	Dubious
Pleasant	———	Unpleasant
Humble	———	Arrogant
Approachable	———	Aloof
Well-groomed	———	Disheveled
Energetic	———	Lethargic
Aware	———	Unaware
Professional	———	Unprofessional
Organized	———	Disorganized
Genuine	———	Phony
Patient	———	Impatient
Grounded	———	Fidgety
Attentive	———	Inattentive

Think of some of the people you communicate with on a daily basis—your boss, your spouse, your mailman, or your teenager. Consider the interaction you have with them each day and the perceptions you have formed regarding their communication. Where would you place them on each continuum listed here? Or you can use various public figures: Hillary Clinton. Mahatma Gandhi. Rush Limbaugh. Woody Allen. Will Smith. Mother Teresa. Bill Maher. Nancy Grace. Robin Williams. Adolph Hitler. Mark Zuckerberg. Try to understand, in terms of their body language, *why* you placed various people in certain positions along the continuums.

Now apply this same test to your own communication. Think of a recent time you had to communicate a message to others. How do you think that audience judged you on the basis of your intention cues—how you walked and stood, your gestures and facial expressions? Try to be objective and honest; if you can't recall many details of a recent communication of yours, try to notice some of these things the next time.

• • •

We all have different bodies and different ways of expressing ourselves through movement and gesture. This is what makes our communication unique and identifiable. For actors, this is our gold and what differentiates us from other actors when competing for a role. One actor's Hamlet will not be the same as another actor's Hamlet. The same applies to you when communicating your message. It is important to put your *personal stamp* on your communication. Bring yourself to the message. Make it your own. No one is interested in watching a clone or a robot deliver a speech or presentation. The more authentic and honest you are with your body language, the more willing your audience will be to take in your message. Show them your passion *physically* and they will be more likely to consider what you have to say.

THE FIVE MAJOR AREAS OF NONVERBAL COMMUNICATION

Now that we've explored the power and importance of nonverbal communication—how strong an impression it makes, and how quickly it forms—we can get into the nitty-gritty mechanics of it. By the end of this chapter you will have a good understanding of the five main categories of nonverbal communication—posture, eye contact, facial expressions, gestures, and movement and spatiality—and the ability to read others' cues and be aware of (and modify) your own.

Posture
The position in which you hold your body as a communicator, your *posture*, has a large impact on the overall impression you create while

communicating. Anthropologist Gordon W. Hewes was the first to use the term "nonverbal communication" back in 1955. In his research, Hewes identified approximately one thousand different body postures in humans.[13]

Our posture says something to others about how we feel about ourselves and the world around us. Standing erect, but not rigid, and leaning slightly forward communicates that you are approachable, receptive, and friendly. Speaking with your back turned communicates disinterest to your audience.[14] Actors use posture to define their characters and shape an audience's perception of the character they are playing. When you wish to communicate a message, it is essential that you become aware of what your body language says to an audience, as even the smallest shift in posture can change the way audience members perceive you. According to Allan Pease, author of *The Definitive Book of Body Language*, if speakers cross their arms, an audience recalls 40 percent less of the message and has a more negative overall attitude toward the speaker.[15] In general, ineffective postures are an area where people often lose the opportunity to impress an audience.

Men acquire a particular quality by constantly acting a particular way. You become just by performing just actions, temperate by performing temperate actions, brave by performing brave actions.

—ARISTOTLE

Other weak or ineffective postures that people fall into include clasping their hands behind their back (what we call "the hostage" position), hands clasped in front of their groin (the "fig leaf"), hands stuffed into their pockets (almost never a good idea), or the "arms akimbo" position, with hands on the hips like a referee. Also, because many people hold tension or nervous energy in their extremities, they clasp or wring their hands or shuffle their feet back and forth. Another common and ineffective posture is one called the "T. rex," where speakers' elbows are seemingly melded to their sides, causing the forearms to hover above the waist (even when resting). This is caused by an innate instinct human beings have that, when we feel threatened or vulnerable, we automatically attempt to make ourselves (both our bodies and movements) as small and unnoticeable as possible.

The various postures described in this section not only limit your ability to support your delivery through expressive gesturing (you can't gesture with your hands in your pockets), they often signal discomfort or disinterest to your audience that only serves to distract their attention from the message you are attempting to deliver.

The Home Base Position A relaxed body moves much faster and more efficiently than a tense body. Adapting a relaxed posture during the delivery of your message will allow you to begin your communication from an open and neutral position, which is exactly where you want to start, otherwise the only thing your audience will see is tension and nothing else can be put across. Stanislavski often discussed the danger of tension in the body, saying, "At times of great stress it is especially necessary to achieve a complete freedom of muscles... removal of unnecessary tenseness should be developed to the point where it becomes a normal habit and a natural necessity."[16]

Imagine that you have a nice, long spine with your head extending toward the clouds and your feet pressing into the earth. To help you accomplish this, we now share with you one of the most important tools in your communication arsenal, something we call a *home base position*: a relaxed, tension-free, neutral physical posture. This projects confidence and comfort and allows your audience to focus on your message instead of any physical distractions that might take their attention away from what you are saying.

EXERCISE
Home Base Position

To experience what a strong home base position feels like, follow these steps:

1. Stand with your feet shoulder-width apart and your weight evenly distributed.

2. Make sure your knees are unlocked.
3. Center and lock your pelvis to avoid shifting and swaying.
4. Let your arms, hands, and fingers relax by your sides.
5. Hold your chest open and elevated.
6. Keep your shoulders relaxed.
7. Keep your chin parallel to the ground.
8. Focus your eyes forward.
9. Imagine you have a string coming straight out of the top of your head, and someone is gently pulling on it.

While adopting a strong home base position may initially feel odd or unnatural to you, it does not appear odd to an audience; quite the opposite: a home base position will make you appear poised and confident. Grounding yourself with a solid, neutral foundation during your delivery is critical to maintaining that aura of confidence necessary to command an audience.

To be clear: maintaining a strong home base position doesn't mean you adopt a static, unchanging posture; home base is meant to be your default, neutral body position, not an anchor weighing you down. If you wish to employ movement, please do so (as long as it follows the rules for effective movement set forth at the end of this chapter). And continue to gesture, because when the hands suddenly stop being used for emphasis by a speaker, it usually signals a lack of commitment to a point or topic (and the weakening of your intention).

Communicating While Seated While many formal presentations take place with a speaker standing, some meetings or presentations occur in less formal settings such as boardrooms, conference rooms, or offices, often due to space constraints or audience size. When communicating while seated, it is important to continue to utilize proper posture, with your spine straight, but not stiff. Don't slump or sag into your chair; this can make you appear overly casual; send your energy outward toward the person with whom you are speaking. Keep your hands above the table and modulate your gestures; don't eliminate them. And try to keep your feet firmly planted under the table to help ground your delivery.

This will help limit extraneous movement that can make you appear less than confident.

Pacifiers We all hold nervous energy in our bodies and that nervous energy shows up in various ways. When people get nervous in front of an audience, they tend to contract their bodies, trying to make themselves as small as possible. This means they are able to make very few gestures and little movement, and the behaviors they do exhibit are unconscious, nervous ones including swaying, rocking, lip licking, hand rubbing, foot shuffling, and the like.

Behaviors such as these—called *pacifiers*—are the physical manifestations of the nervous energy in your body searching for a way out. We touch one part of our body with another part of our body in an effort to soothe or calm ourselves. Or we fidget with a prop such as a pen, wedding ring, or page of notes. Unfortunately, these pacifiers also often reveal to an audience how we are truly feeling inside at any given moment. And they're distracting; because an audience's eye is drawn to movement, any ineffective action or fidgety gesture can take their focus off the message you are attempting to convey. If you are holding a pen, they are looking at the pen; if you are spinning your wedding ring, their attention is drawn to that.

To stem these behaviors, it is helpful to follow the rule that actors are taught when rehearsing for a play or movie: *don't touch a prop or piece of furniture unless you have a reason for doing so.* Try to identify any personal pacifiers that you resort to and work to *control* them. By doing so, you will help to define your audience's perception of you in a more positive way. (Using a strong home base position can also go a long way toward helping you avoid pacifiers.)

The Torso Tell The position of your torso tells your audience much about the level of interest or engagement you are showing at any given moment, and can often communicate your intentions quite clearly. If your body is pointed away from the person you are talking to, it signals that your interest possibly lies elsewhere. We call this a *torso tell*. To truly and effectively engage with the person with whom you are speaking, square your shoulders with theirs. This communicates that they have your undivided attention and you are fully engaged with the conversation. This is also important when replying to someone during a question-and-answer session. Author Janine Driver describes a technique she calls the "Belly Button Rule": imagine that you have a beam of light coming out of your belly button, and point it toward the belly button of the person you are intending to engage with your message. This concept dates back to studies done by W. T. James in the 1930s and is also supported by the work of Albert Mehrabian.[17]

Understanding the torso tell can also serve you when reading the body language of others. Next time you are in a meeting or presentation with your boss or a client, notice where the other party's torso is directed. By doing so, you might be better able to understand who holds their focus and interest in that moment.

Expressive Extremities While many people believe that the face is the most honest part of the body, Joe Navarro, a body language expert who worked as an FBI agent for twenty-five years, disagrees. In *What Every BODY Is Saying*, he writes that because we are socialized to mask our true feelings with our facial expressions, the face is often used to deceive. According to Navarro, it is actually the lower parts of the body that tend to give away true feelings or emotions. When he and other agents would interrogate crime suspects, it wasn't their faces Navarro would focus on to try and detect deception, but their legs and feet!

Eye Contact

Eye contact is the second major category of nonverbal communication. Good, steady eye contact helps facilitate the flow of communication between speaker and audience. It also signals an interest in others. In *First Impressions*, researchers Ann Demarais and Valerie White report that the average person makes eye contact approximately 45–60 percent of the time during a typical face-to-face interaction with others, but that falling below the 45 percent threshold can have negative consequences.[18] People who made less eye contact than that were thought to be superficial, less socially attractive, or less credible than those who stayed within the average range.

More important, direct eye contact gives you visual feedback—actors use it to connect with their partners in a scene; speakers use it to monitor how they are coming across to their audience. The more you stay aware of your audience and the way they are taking in your information, the more successful you will be at delivering it. If you ever want to know how you are doing during your presentation, look at the faces in your audience. Do they look excited and engaged or do they look bored and restless?

Ineffective ways to use your gaze while communicating include staring, moving your eyes from side to side, checking your watch, and looking at your feet (or the ceiling). When you avoid sustained and meaningful eye contact with your audience, you are communicating disinterest in them, and they will return the favor by declining to engage with your message. (Do be aware that while good steady eye contact is encouraged when communicating in most countries around the world, there are a few places where direct or prolonged eye contact with an audience is not as welcome, such as China, Japan, Korea, Thailand, and parts of Africa.)[19] Blinking is also a nonverbal cue to your audience. The average person blinks at a rate of eight to sixteen times per minute (except for contact lens wearers, who blink more).[20] The more nervous people are the more they tend to blink. If you can slow your blinking rate to below eight blinks per minute it can help you project to your audience that you are calm, confident, and in control.

Many people find that making eye contact during their communication makes them uncomfortable. This is completely understandable—looking someone directly in the eyes is an intimate experience, which is precisely why it can be a powerful tool if used properly during your communication.

Both too much and too little eye contact can hinder your delivery, so try to find the right balance. A good rule of thumb is to hold eye contact with someone for approximately two or three seconds, or until you complete your thought, then move on to someone else. This will ensure that your eyes don't wander and will help you better connect with your audience. When you connect with one person at a time, the rest of your listeners will feel like you are talking and connecting to them as well. So don't scan the audience in large, general sweeps; instead, pick specific people and connect with them. Talk *to* your audience and not *at* them. Finally, when beginning any communication with others, follow this one rule: don't speak until you see the whites of their eyes. Resist the urge to start speaking before you have planted yourself and connected with your audience through eye contact.

Facial Expressions

We first learn how to relate to others through facial expressions, observing and mirroring our parents, and facial expressions are an integral part of our overall communication. Think of the work of Buster Keaton, Charlie Chaplin, or Rowan Atkinson as Mr. Bean, and how they are able to tell entire stories through facial expressions alone. The face is capable of forty-three distinct muscle movements, which allows for a wide range of facial expressions.[21] How many? According to renowned psychologist Paul Ekman, humans can create over ten thousand different facial expressions, with three thousand of them being identifiable and having meaning.[22] According to Ekman, "Facial expressions, even quickly passing, signal emotional expression. The face is the mind's involuntary messenger."[23]

The more varied the facial expressions you use during your communication, the more engaging it will be for your audience—as long as your expressions clearly support your intention. Be careful when speaking to others that your face does not suddenly go blank, however. This often happens when nervousness gets the best of us and all expression suddenly drains from the face (a condition we call "stone-face syndrome," whereby your facial expressions communicate virtually nothing).

The eyebrows are another powerful tool to help you support your intention and communicate more clearly. Often underutilized and overlooked, these two small strips of hair not only protect the eyes from sweat and dust, they also aid in facial recognition and can express a variety of emotions such as fear, sadness, surprise, aggression, and attraction. Don't underestimate the power of the eyebrow; if you want to move an audience, you need to start by moving your eyebrows.

EXERCISE
Universal Expressions

In his research, Ekman found that there are seven universal facial expressions used in all cultures: happiness, sadness, anger, fear, surprise, contempt, and disgust.[24] Stand in front of a mirror and see if you can communicate those seven emotions using just your facial expressions.

Perhaps the most powerful facial expression we have at our disposal is a smile. Smiling transmits friendliness and warmth; it is a universal expression that is understood in every country on earth. People are automatically drawn to those who smile. A smile is contagious, so if you smile at your audience, they are more likely to smile back at you. If you smile frequently during your communication you will be perceived as more likable, friendly, and approachable. In fact, studies have shown that a salesperson can boost sales from 30–50 percent simply by smiling when speaking to a potential customer.[25] Smiling is especially important in the opening moments of your communication—it sets the tone.

Ekman has found in his research that humans have fifty different types of smiles, each with a different meaning and impact. For example, smiling with teeth is much more effective than smiling with a closed mouth; the latter can come across as insincere, as if you are smiling but you don't really mean it. Ekman's research also identified something else: every person possesses both a real smile and a fake smile. While a real smile expresses genuine emotions, a fake smile literally masks our true feelings. It's easy to tell the difference: a fake smile only affects the muscles around the mouth but doesn't affect the muscles that circle the eyes; with a real smile both the mouth *and* the eye muscles are fully engaged.

Certain facial expressions have a universal ability to communicate specific information about a person's emotional state. Wide eyes signal surprise, while half-mast eyes might signal skepticism or disapproval. A wrinkled nose can communicate displeasure; a furrowed brow or pursed lips might reveal a feeling of pensiveness or uncertainty. By watching for and evaluating the facial expressions of others, we can better adjust our own communication in our social and professional interactions.

Gestures

Gestures, often called "the silent language," assist in the communication of the words and ideas in your message.[26] Like a word, a gesture must have something to say and needs to clearly communicate intent to be effective. There are a staggering number—researcher M. H. Kront has identified nearly five thousand distinct hand gestures in human expression—and they express the full range of human emotion and intention.[27] In most countries, audiences appreciate and gravitate toward people who use more expansive and varied gestures during their communication (an exception is Japan, where gesturing too broadly can be seen as rude). Actors use gestures differently depending on the characters they are playing and the messages they are trying to convey. Jim Carrey uses much broader and wilder gestures as the title character in *Ace Ventura: Pet Detective* than he does in *The Truman Show*, where his character is more shy and reserved.

In almost all instances, if you neglect to gesture during your communication, you may be perceived as boring, stiff, or unanimated. A lively and animated speaking style captures an audience's attention, makes your material more interesting, and helps facilitate learning. We have a wide area of gesturing space to use—as far as our arms can reach, really—yet physical tension often limits us to a very small area just above the waist.

Expansive gestures—those that use a lot of the available space—are generally more interesting than constrictive gestures, so don't be afraid to open yourself up and use larger gestures if they support your intention and are appropriate in size in relation to your audience and setting. Think of how a single distinctive gesture can almost define a person—Adolph Hitler, Richard Nixon, and Olympic athletes Tommie Smith and John Carlos (who raised their fists in defiance at the 1968 Olympics) are just a few memorable examples.

We encourage you to use five basic types of gestures to support your communications: conventional, descriptive, emphatic, prompting, and coded.

- *Conventional gestures* have widely understood meanings that have been determined and agreed upon by a specific community or culture. Examples include waving, handshakes, and applause.
- *Descriptive gestures* are used to clarify or illustrate your words by indicating size, shape, direction, or function. Examples include gestures that would accompany phrases such as "She was about this tall," "Go straight past the bus station and take a right," and "The fish was this big."
- *Emphatic gestures* build upon a point by underscoring the emotion behind the words being spoken. Examples include shaking your fist, slamming your hand on a table, pointing at someone, or placing your hand over your heart.
- *Prompting gestures* are used to evoke a desired response from your audience. Examples include cupping your ear to ask someone to talk louder, placing a finger in front of your lips to make people be quiet, or raising your hand when asking for volunteers.
- *Coded gestures* are created by pre-established agreement among a group or between individuals. Examples include sign language, certain religious gestures, and signals between a pitcher and catcher in baseball.

Ineffective Gestures As Hamlet says to his players, "Suit the action to the word, the word to the action." That is: don't preplan your gestures or they will look phony. There are no good gestures or bad gestures, only effective gestures and ineffective gestures. As long as your gesture supports your intention, it is an effective gesture. Effective gestures appear spontaneous, arising out of the emotions of the moment (what actors call their *inner life*). Ineffective gestures are gestures that are unnatural, stiff, lazy, or fidgety, or that appear planned; they communicate nervousness, lack of confidence, and insecurity about yourself and your topic. Ineffective gestures will detract from the intention and message you are trying to communicate. Also, as a rule, avoid gestures that happen below the waist as they are generally perceived as weak by an audience. And pointing with one finger at a person (versus an object) is almost always seen as rude or offensive; when calling on someone or referring to someone, an open hand is always preferred.

Effective Gestures To be effective, a gesture should support the intention you are trying to convey with your words; it will be specific to and will appear motivated by your content. As Stanislavski wrote, "A gesture for its own sake has no place on the stage . . . superfluous gestures are the same as trash, dirt, spots . . . I reject any unmotivated gesture."[28]

Some rules of thumb:

- The extremities (hands and feet) often give away the most telling indications of how we are feeling on the inside, as we tend to exert less control over them than we do over other body parts. Be aware of this fact and use your hands and feet consciously and to your advantage.
- Gesturing with more open or splayed fingers is generally more masculine while gesturing with the fingers all together is more feminine.
- Expansive gestures can be very effective, but bigger is not always better. Your audience, your subject, your intention, and the space you are in should inform the size and expressiveness of your gestures.

Movement and Spatiality

The movement of our bodies through space as we communicate is the fifth major dimension of nonverbal communication. Desmond Morris, a zoologist and author of *Body Watching*, has done extensive studies into human behavior and identified at least thirty-six different styles of walking and variations in gait—strolling, swaggering, ambling, strutting, limping, shuffling, just to name a few—used by humans. Each style communicates our emotional or physical state.[29] How we walk and move says a lot about who we are as a person—and often reflects precisely how we see ourselves in the world, whether we're conscious of it or not. But effective movement must have purpose and be fueled by your intention. As the Broadway theater director and producer Arthur Hopkins was fond of pointing out, "The reason for walking is *destination*."[30]

When you are communicating, how near or far you are from your audience is part of your message. Your use of distance and space during communication is called *spatiality*. Movement, if used properly, can reinforce your verbal message; in a business context, it works by showing you are confident and comfortable.

Actors understand profoundly the importance of movement as a tool to enhance communication. And because actors must make each moment count, they are careful to be economical in their choices. Sean Graney, the award-winning stage director, told us this about movement: "Audiences, for the most part, see before they listen. They subconsciously watch for visual clues about the character before they digest what words are spoken. Employing movement is an effective way to quickly clarify complicated dialogue, or a highly intellectual thought, because it allows the audience to efficiently engage a little more closely with the speaker."[31] The same idea is important for anyone delivering a message. An audience likes to watch a speaker who is comfortable inhabiting space and commanding a room.

Here are some rules of thumb about movement in communication:

- Any movement employed during your communication should be direct and smooth.
- Movement toward an audience can be used to create a greater intimacy for a speaker and to command attention, actually energizing your delivery. Conversely, movement away from an audience will communicate the opposite, often creating both physical and emotional distance.
- If you choose to move, you must have a purpose for doing so. Movement is especially useful for transitions or to indicate that you are now moving on to a new point or topic.

- Beware of wandering or moving around too much as this can distract an audience, much the same way that ineffective gestures do.
- Be aware of people's personal space and try to respect it. Keep a comfortable distance between you and your audience so as not to make them feel crowded.

While effective use of movement can enhance your communication, the poor use of movement can be a negative in the eyes of your audience. New York congressman Rick Lazio, who ran against Hillary Clinton for the Senate in 2000, learned this the hard way. At one point in a televised debate between the candidates, Lazio crossed from his lectern over to Clinton's, invading her personal space. Lazio's move was intended to make him look confident, but it backfired, making him look like a bully, and voters punished him for it. Al Gore made a similar mistake in 2000 when debating George W. Bush, crossing to Bush, again in an attempt to look strong and confident. Instead, it came off as rude and awkward, an invasion of Bush's personal space.

Proxemics The study of the measurable distance between people is called *proxemics*. First introduced by anthropologist Edward T. Hall in 1966, it examines the influence two bodies have on one another in relation to the distance maintained between them.[32] When it comes to proxemics, Figure 5.1 outlines the four distinct zones that a person can use during communication: *intimate* (from 0 to about 1.5 feet), *personal* (from 1.5 to 4 feet), *social* (from 4 to 12 feet), and *public* (from 12 to 25 feet). In general, the closer you are to your audience, the easier it will be to communicate your message and achieve your objective. But don't get too close. Encroach into intimate or personal space and you could make the person with whom you are communicating uncomfortable. (Think of the "close talker" episode of *Seinfeld*, featuring a character who simply didn't understand the concept of personal space.) Make yourself aware of each zone and, depending on the intentions and objectives you have chosen for a particular communication, adjust your spatiality accordingly.

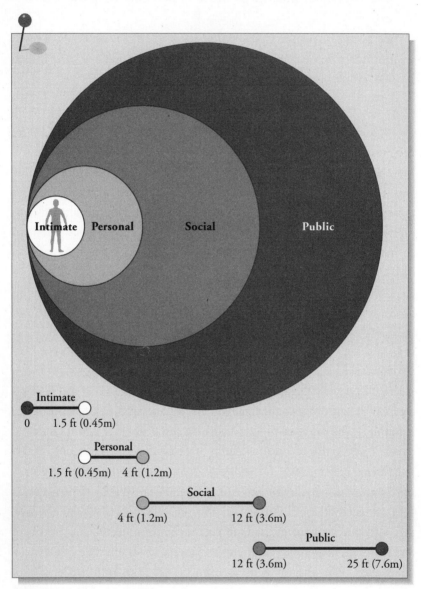

Figure 5.1   Communication Space.

Mirror Theory Stanislavski, when speaking about communication, often used the word *communion* to describe the connection between speaker and audience, musing, "Haven't you felt in real life or on the stage, in the course of mutual communion ... that something streamed out of you, some current from your eyes, from the ends of your fingers? ... What name can we give to these invisible currents which we use to communicate with one another? Some day this phenomenon will be the subject of scientific research."[33] What Stanislavski is talking about here is a phenomenon in communication we call the *mirror theory*.

Researchers have studied the connection between human beings and determined that people are wired so that when they see another person experiencing specific emotions (joy, fear, or sadness) they feel those same emotions themselves. In nature this type of mirroring phenomenon is called *isopraxism*.[34] The idea is that we routinely mirror back to someone what we are seeing, creating empathy and an emotional connection and allowing us to relate to others around us.[35]

And mirroring happens not only with emotions but with behavior as well. Often, if one person exhibits a certain behavior (yawning, smiling, avoiding eye contact), others tend to mirror those actions back to them, sometimes without even being aware that they are doing it. Why does this happen? Because specific brain cells called *mirror neurons* stimulate the exact same emotions or impulses being observed in the person doing the observing. Cognitive neuroscientist Daniel Glaser of University College London has studied these mirror neurons and the ways they affect human behavior.[36] "The brain uses everything it can to try and see the world ... to interpret the world in front of it.... What we found is... something that is absolutely fundamental to the way we see other people in the world.... The mirror system is a way you tap in to, the way that you harness, your own abilities and project them out into the world." Dr. Glaser acknowledges the particular advantage in ability actors have in the conscious use of mirroring: "What actors are expert in, is using their movements to inspire feelings in the people watching. These are the experts in the mirror system."[37]

If an actor delivers a terrifying performance onscreen, the audience will most likely react in a certain way, feeling the fear or anxiety they are witnessing right there in front of them. If the actor delivers a heart-wrenching performance as a loved one dies in their arms, it will likely elicit a very different response—a strong feeling of grief and loss. Great actors know this instinctively and they practice it consciously and artfully.

Think about how you can use mirror theory in your communication. If you are scattered and unfocused, or bored and disengaged, your audience will probably reflect that back to you in the way they take in your message—they will most likely look and feel bored and disengaged. However, if you are organized, confident, and passionate with your communication, your audience will be more likely to feel the same and mirror those emotions back to you.

The concept of mirror theory also applies to personal relationships and in building rapport with others. In *The Likeability Factor*, Tim Sanders warns, "An unfriendly first encounter can create a long, long road to establishing likeability ... random acts of unfriendliness can come back to bite you in the rear."[38]

Strive to deliver every message with passion and conviction, no matter the content, no matter the audience. Enthusiasm and excitement are contagious. People are drawn to confidence and conviction in others. The intention cues you send out during your communication are social signals that will ignite those mirror neurons in the minds of your listeners and allow them to feel precisely what you are feeling, making it easier for you to engage them, impact them, and consequently elicit the reaction you seek. Use them consistently, use them clearly, and use them wisely.

CHAPTER 6

Say It Like You Mean It
Using Your Voice to Influence

There is no index of character so sure as the voice.
—Benjamin Disraeli

The great firebrand Christopher Hitchens described the human voice as a "resonant vibration that can stir memory, produce music, evoke love, bring tears, move crowds to pity and mobs to passion." Hitchens, an intellectual and lifelong provocateur, understood the power of the vocal instrument; he used it as a weapon when he clashed with opponents in fiery political debates. When Hitchens was a small child, his mother impressed upon him that the only truly unforgivable sin was being boring. Love him or hate him, Hitchens never committed that sin. He always spoke his mind and never backed down from a fight.

But in 2010 Hitchens received some unexpected and devastating news: he had esophageal cancer. Despite the diagnosis and the months of chemotherapy treatments that followed, Hitchens continued to write and travel the world speaking to crowds on topics he was passionate about. But something changed in early 2011. As he went to hail a cab, Hitchens discovered that he had lost his voice. Literally. He tried to form the words ... nothing came out. He froze, just standing there in midtown Manhattan, helpless, wordless. The great lion had lost his roar. Hitchens later described his devastation: "Like health itself, the loss of such a thing can't be imagined until it occurs.... Deprivation of the ability to speak is more like an attack of impotence, or the amputation of part of the personality. To a great degree, in public and private, I 'was' my voice."[1]

· · ·

In technical parlance, *voice* is the capability by which all activities involving speech are performed, and its qualities include tone, volume, pitch, resonation, inflection, articulation, and pace. *Vocal variety* is the variation and blending of these qualities that creates an effective and engaging vocal presence.

As part of their training, actors spend years studying these qualities, learning to use them to enhance their delivery. In this chapter, we start by exploring why the voice is important to communication, and then get into how you can employ the various qualities of voice to influence your audience from the moment you begin speaking to your last word.

THE POWER OF THE VOICE

We use our voices to inform, persuade, and connect with other people. A person's voice can be used to express and reveal personality, and it is one of the most useful tools we have for projecting confidence, warmth, anger, humor, and more. In many ways, our vocal instrument defines us, to the point that when someone grows in confidence they are said to have "found their voice."

Your vocal dynamics—the ways in which you use your voice—are the keys to delivering your words with intention. What is important for

All I have is a voice.

—W. H. AUDEN

you as a communicator is to be able to accurately understand how people receive your vocal cues. Is your vocal delivery supporting your intention and assisting you in the pursuit of your objective? The success or failure of your endeavors can depend on how well you use your voice.

When we hear someone's voice we can discern much about them in a very short time; whether they are a man or a woman, old or young, roughly where they come from in the world, and if they are ill or in a bad mood.

Most of us are born with a voice; it settles into its adult timbre between the ages of twenty-two and twenty-five.[2] No one voice is identical to another, and no two people use their voices in exactly the same way. If you give ten actors the same line of dialogue to deliver, each will say it slightly differently, interpreting the words and their meaning (what actors call *subtext*) in their own way and making choices based on their intentions at the time. The same can be said about any person's communication. A server at an upscale restaurant is likely to speak differently to customers than to family members at home.

Even small changes in your voice can drastically alter the intention of your message and the way it is perceived by your audience.

Environment can influence your vocal delivery as well—you'll speak loudly or softly depending on the acoustics of the space you're in and the distance over which you have to project (or beyond which you don't wish to be heard). A little league game, a fancy restaurant, a library, a trading floor—each dictates a different range of vocal expression.

Just as your physical intention cues all need to be congruent for effective communication to take place, so too must your vocal cues. If what you say and how you say it project mixed messages, it will muddy the delivery of your overall message.

PARALANGUAGE

Paralanguage is a term used to categorize the nonverbal elements of communication used to convey meaning or express emotions to others—pitch, volume, resonation, articulation, inflection, and pace. All these aspects help create specific impressions with your audience or listener. Paralanguage, much like micro-expressions, can be expressed consciously or unconsciously. So what makes one person's vocal delivery more engaging or effective than another's? As it turns out, it is not one characteristic alone. According to *Time* magazine, a team of researchers from the University of Michigan studied the communication of telemarketers and found that certain vocal characteristics were far more persuasive than others when it came to interaction with customers over the phone.[3] Researchers analyzed the speed, fluency, and pitch of each telemarketer's voice. Overall, the study found that customers gave higher ratings to the telemarketers who were not overly animated, spoke at a moderate rate, and punctuated their communication with frequent short pauses.

Words mean more than what is set down on paper. It takes the human voice to infuse them with deeper meaning.

—MAYA ANGELOU

In general, listeners of both genders find the female voice more pleasing than the male voice. Research suggests that this preference starts as early as the womb for many people. According to Stanford University professor Clifford Nass, author of *The Man Who Lied to His Laptop*, this is the reason most navigation systems and recorded voices are female. "It's much easier to find a female voice that everyone likes than a male voice that everyone likes," says Nass. "It's a well-established phenomenon that the human brain is developed to like female voices."[4]

Another study that demonstrated the importance of paralanguage in a person's communication, done by psychologist Nalini Ambady and medical researcher Wendy Levinson, was detailed in Malcolm Gladwell's book *Blink*.[5] In the study, which involved insurance companies and medical malpractice lawsuits, Ambady and Levinson set out to discover whether they could correctly predict which doctors were more likely to be sued by their patients. Levinson began by recording hundreds of conversations that took place between a series of doctors and patients. While half of the doctors in the study had *never* been sued, the other half had been sued *at least twice*. Ambady then listened to the recorded conversations. For each doctor, she chose two conversations with patients and then extracted two ten-second clips of the doctors speaking from each of these conversations.

What she discovered next goes right to the power of vocal dynamics. Ambady "content-filtered" the recording snippets, taking out all identifiable words and leaving only the vocal dynamics of pitch, inflection, resonance, and pace. By doing this, she was basically removing the content of *what* the doctors were saying and focusing only on *how* they were saying it. Ambady was stunned to discover that simply by analyzing those garbled slices of a doctor's vocal landscapes, she could accurately predict which doctors had been sued by their patients and which ones had not. The doctors whose vocal dynamics were judged to sound more dominant tended to be in the sued group while the voices that sounded less dominant and more concerned tended to be in the non-sued group.

VOLUME

Volume is an aspect of speech that you as a communicator have a great degree of control over; it's also one that can be used as an effective tool to engage an audience. Though this perception varies by country or culture, volume is one of the strongest indicators of confidence—speakers with too little volume are often perceived as timid, shy, or insecure by an audience. Gigi Buffington, a voice expert who has taught at the Royal Shakespeare Company in London as well as New York University, explained it to us this way: "If you are *under* powering the voice, there will not be enough presence in the voice to engage an audience. If you are *over* powering the voice people will feel repelled or talked *at* instead of talked *to*. Ideally, you want to be what actors call 'on voice,' which is where effective communication happens."[6] Because of this, and because adequate volume allows for clarity of understanding between a speaker and an audience, in a business context it's often a good idea to project the voice.

If you are uncomfortable projecting your voice when speaking, Buffington suggests replacing the phrase "projecting the voice" with the phrase "landing the thought" to help overcome the discomfort. In general, don't be afraid to speak a little louder than you think is necessary. Professional actors learn in their training that they must *play to the back row, not the front row* with the volume of their voice. This is a good rule of thumb for anyone tasked with communicating a message. Your job is to land the thought, even with the person sitting in the very last row, so make sure that your words and message reach everyone.

PITCH

Pitch, the highness or lowness in the voice, is determined by the rate of vibration in the vocal cords. Though partly determined by the anatomy of the larynx, pitch is not entirely beyond control and is an important aspect of vocal dynamics. The human speaking voice has a range of between five and eight available notes, with the male voice generally lower than the female in pitch.[7] Varying the pitch across your available range can make your speech sound musical, conveying liveliness and a state of enthusiasm to your audience; not varying it can make it sound bland and monotonous, not worth listening to. For example, if you are signposting the topics you will be covering over the course of your meeting or presentation, it is important to build your list by using a rising pitch as you go through it. Otherwise it will sound like a grocery list, simply a series of items that all blend together in importance.

Pitch can be very expressive. The exact same words can have very different meanings depending upon how the intention you have chosen alters the pitch of your voice. To demonstrate the point, try this. Speak the word "okay," varying your pitch to match the sentiments in the following list.

- I understand.
- I'm very disappointed.
- Fantastic!

- Enough already!
- Do you understand?
- I think you are mistaken.

Notice how the slightest change in your pitch can completely alter the meaning of a single word.

Actors use what's called *monotone*—unvarying pitch in the voice—to portray someone whose communication style is boring or lacks emotion. Think of Ben Stein as the teacher in *Ferris Bueller's Day Off* ("Bueller... Bueller...?"), Billy Bob Thornton in *Sling Blade*, or Evanna Lynch as Luna Lovegood in the *Harry Potter* movies, all of whom use monotone to strip their characters' voices of strong emotion. Audiences have great difficulty staying connected and engaged to a person who speaks completely or mostly in monotone. And since you want your audience to be engaged with your message and have an emotional reaction to the words you are saying, you don't help your case if you communicate boredom or lack of passion through your voice.

EXERCISE
Eliminating Monotone

Do you use monotone? Use this exercise to find out, and to start eliminating it if you do.

STEP 1: Choose a random newspaper article and record one minute of you reading the text aloud.

STEP 2: Listen to the recording, paying special attention to the pitch variations of your voice. Does your pitch vary at all? Do you sound genuinely interested in the topic or does it simply sound like information?

STEP 3: Do a second recording, but this time read the text with the intention to *excite* your audience, as if you were reading the most enchanting fairy tale of all time to a small child.

STEP 4: As before, listen to the playback. Do you notice any difference in your pitch versus the first reading?

STEP 5: Read and record the text one last time, finding a happy medium of pitch between the first reading (mostly monotone) and the second reading (fairy tale).

STEP 6: Listen to this final recording and note your pitch. Observe how much more variety there is and how much more engaging and passionate you sound.

INFLECTION

Inflection refers to the specific pitch used at the very end of a word or phrase, with the voice sliding up or down the scale as a speaker expresses various shades of thought and feeling. Upward inflection, which takes the voice up at the end of a word or phrase, is used to express doubt, friendliness, or surprise, or to request information (it's a questioning sound). Downward inflection, which takes the pitch of the voice down, is generally used to express certainty, command, or defiance, or to indicate statements of fact. Usually an upward slide or inflection expresses a question or an uncompleted thought and a downward inflection expresses an answer or a completed thought.

Be aware that too much upward inflection in your communication can result in what linguists call *upspeak*. Studies show that younger people and women tend to resort to upspeak most frequently, often as method of avoiding interruption and seeking reassurance during their communication.[8] Upspeak can make you sound timid and unsure, while too much downward inflection can make you sound bossy and arrogant.

PACE

The creation of vocal sound is the result of a complex series of physical and emotional events that all happen at lightning speed. A study published by the National Institutes of Health found that it takes just *600 milliseconds* for the human brain to think of a word, apply the rules of grammar to it, and send it to the mouth to be spoken.[9] This astoundingly efficient system allows a human being to take an impulse from thought to word so quickly that the delay is usually imperceptible.

Pace, the rate at which a person speaks, is based on a measure of how many words are spoken per minute. Since brain and mouth can often speak faster than the situation demands, pace is under your control to a great degree, and it's a tool you can consciously and artfully use to keep an audience engaged and interested.

Is there an ideal pace, or range of pace, for effective communication? Yes, and we get to that in a moment; first, a story. Fran Capo holds the title of the fastest-talking person in the world: she can speak at a rate of more than six hundred words per minute.[10] Curt Burgess, a professor of cognitive neuroscience and psycholinguistics at the University of Rochester, studied Fran's amazing ability. In one part of his research, Burgess had Capo speed-read the Gettysburg Address, which she did in only twenty-nine seconds—nearly six times the rate at which Abraham Lincoln delivered it in 1863! When he went back and studied the recording of Capo's delivery, Burgess discovered that her rapid pace forced Capo to "normalize" her speech by eliminating almost all inflection, pitch, and pauses in her voice. She defaulted to a monotone, which requires the smallest amount of effort or energy. The lesson: when a person's speaking pace is too fast, the other qualities of the voice—such as inflection, pitch, and articulation—all tend to suffer as a result. All the vocal cues that support the intention or purpose behind the words are lost.

In almost all countries around the world, when people get up in front of others to communicate a message, they speak too fast. Nerves are a contributing factor to this common problem, as adrenaline boosts the speed. No confident or credible communicator ever feels the need to rush through a message, so take your time. Slowing down your pace is critical when driving home a point or spotlighting a specific piece of information.

So how can you practice slowing down your pace? One way to accomplish this is by focusing on your punctuation. Many people treat a period not as a period that requires a full stop to complete an idea or thought, but as a comma, a quick stop. This results in your communication all blending together like one long thought or idea instead of various specific ones.

EXERCISE
Controlling Your Pace

To practice slowing your delivery and controlling your pace, try these steps:

STEP 1: Pick a newspaper article or any random piece of text.

STEP 2: Recording your delivery, read the article or text out loud.

STEP 3: Whenever you reach a period, stop for a full two seconds and pause.

STEP 4: Listen to the recording and consider how the pauses sound as compared to how they felt during the reading itself.

STEP 5: Determine how you can incorporate more pauses into your overall communication by coding your material or paying special attention to all punctuation.

But simply slowing down to a steady pace isn't quite the answer. Speaking at the same rate throughout a presentation is another form of monotone and tends to lull an audience to sleep. Instead, find places in your presentation where you might speak a little faster and places where you might slow things down for effect or emphasis. Great actors, politicians, and preachers vary the rhythms and tempos at which they speak to keep their audience engaged and interested. Martin Luther King, in his most famous address—the "I have a dream" speech—starts at around 85 words per minute and builds to nearly 154 words per minute as passion soars in his shattering conclusion.

So the answer to the earlier question ("Is there an ideal pace for speaking?") is "It depends." According to the Academic Skills Center at Dartmouth College, if all of a person's thoughts were measurable in words per minute, you would think at a speed of around 400–500 words per minute (wpm).[11] Obviously, when you are speaking, you need to slow your pace down considerably from those numbers. Conversational speech can be up to 180–200 wpm.[12] This is too fast for delivering information during a meeting or presentation. For these types of communication, we recommend your average rate should be between 100 and 150 wpm, with 125 wpm being the target.

As it happens, most of the famous speeches throughout history fall right into that recommended range: Martin Luther King's "I have a dream" (approximately 119 wpm), Winston Churchill's "We shall fight them on the beaches" (approximately 128 wpm), John F. Kennedy's "Ask not what your country can do for you" (approximately 107 wpm), and Barack Obama's 2008 address to the Democratic National Convention (approximately 149 wpm).[13] Think of any great speech or great speaker. If you could calculate the words-per-minute ratio, it is likely it would fall right in the average range of 100 to 150.

Someone who speaks with a pace that is too fast will often be perceived as nervous or rushed, as if the message or material is not important or interesting enough to hold an audience's attention. When basketball star Shaquille O'Neal gave his 2011 retirement speech, his nerves got the best of him and he raced through his prepared remarks at a speed of 208 wpm! So noticeably hurried was his delivery that the first comment he got during the question-and-answer session that followed was from a woman who remarked, "You said a whole lot in a few minutes. . . . It's been a long time since I've heard you talk that fast!" To which the superstar sheepishly admitted, "I was nervous . . . I'm sorry."[14]

Generally, what feels like a slow pace for you as a communicator does not feel slow to your audience; people need time to grasp the information you are providing them. The best way to slow down your communication is to embrace the use of lengthy and frequent pauses. Many people (especially people from Western cultures) are afraid of silence during their speech, both in formal presentations and social settings. They fear that nothing is happening during that silence, which is simply not true. Much can happen during a beat of silence. It can allow an audience to ponder a question, consider a thought, or weigh a new option. Another misconception people have about pausing is that the silence might make them appear weak or uncertain, and they will lose their audience. This is also not the case. In most instances, a pause can make a communicator seem more confident and in control to an audience. A slower pace can captivate an audience and help draw them in. It also allows them to process and consider the information you are giving them. It's especially important if your audience is hearing this information for the very first time.

The pace at which people speak can vary by country and region, and of course by audience and setting. Just as actors will alter the pace at which they speak depending on their character (and consequently their intentions and objectives), you must be able to do the same depending on your audience and setting. Stanislavski went so far as to recommend practicing the pace of speech by using a metronome, much like a musician, always being careful to "preserve the smooth flow of words in rhythmic measures."

EXERCISE
Testing Your Pace

Read the text that follows out loud and time your reading. The passage, from the Gettysburg Address, is exactly 125 words, so if you finish much before a minute has elapsed you are probably speaking too quickly. Conversely, if you don't make it all the way to the end before the one-minute mark, you might benefit from picking up your speaking pace.

> Four score and seven years ago our fathers brought forth on this continent a new nation, conceived in Liberty, and dedicated to the proposition that all men are created equal. Now we are engaged in a great civil war, testing whether that nation, or any nation so conceived and so dedicated, can long endure. We are met on a great battlefield of that war. We have come to dedicate a portion of that field, as a final resting place for those who here gave their lives that that nation might live. It is altogether fitting and proper that we should do this. But, in a larger sense, we cannot dedicate—we cannot consecrate—we cannot hallow—this ground. The brave men, living and dead, who ...

Banish Verbal Viruses

Often you can say much more by actually saying much less. People tend to associate assertiveness, confidence, and clarity with answers or explanations that are short and to the point. When you speak too fast or ramble during your speech, you run the risk of including unnecessary fillers known as *verbal viruses*—"ah" and "um" and the like. A verbal virus is the sign of a communicator audibly thinking about the speech. They serve to buy time while the speaker figures out what to say next. As president, George W. Bush struggled with verbal viruses when taking questions from reporters during his press conferences, as does Barack Obama when he is speaking without a script. But what a verbal virus communicates to an audience is uncertainty; it makes your delivery seem sloppy. Think of how an actor like Woody Allen uses stutters and stammers in his characterizations to communicate nervousness or discomfort. And someone who resorts to verbal viruses also tends to look down or away from the person to whom they are speaking, further diminishing their ability to engage or persuade them with their message.

Other types of verbal viruses are filler words such as "you know" or "I mean" or "like." When people use fillers such as these they can end up creating one long run-on sentence that never really ends. They fear putting a period on a thought or statement, because ending a statement definitively makes a communicator accountable and responsible for the words or ideas that were just spoken. Don't be afraid of punctuation when you make a statement. Eliminating the you-knows and I-means will give your words more weight and you more credibility.

The best way to strip your communication of verbal viruses is to slow down your pace and allow yourself the time to fully form an answer before speaking. Try this: record yourself speaking about a random topic for around a minute or so. When you finish, listen to the recording and count how many verbal viruses you included. Then repeat the process again, working to reduce the number of fillers you use while speaking. By slowing down and plucking out the remaining verbal viruses, you will create a more confident and credible vocal delivery. Or as Shakespeare points out, "Mend your speech a little, lest it may mar your fortunes."

The Power of the Pause

As noted, silence can be a powerful bridge between ideas. It can help you move smoothly from one section of your presentation to the next, and it can help your audience take in and consider the words you are saying. By giving people time to process the content, you are allowing the content itself to have more of an impact. Silence is an amazing tool for a communicator—and one that is rarely used to full effect. If you have trouble believing that silence

Sometimes one creates a dynamic impression by saying something, and sometimes one creates as significant an impression by remaining silent.

—DALAI LAMA

is as important as sound in communication, think of some of the great symphonies or concertos by Mozart or Bach. These compositions are powerful because of the *combination* of the notes *and* the pauses, or rests, that together create the music.

When it comes to pauses, small is not the same as trivial. Stanislavski spoke in detail about using moments of silence for impact. He identified three different types of pauses: logical pauses, psychological pauses, and physiological pauses (which he referred to by the German expression "luftpause").[15] In a communication context, we can describe each kind of pause as follows:

- *Logical pauses.* These are moments of silence that are dictated by your material or visual aid, allowing your audience to read or absorb information.
- *Psychological pauses.* In these instances, you can use silence to evoke or provoke an emotional response from your audience, perhaps pausing for effect to highlight a specific thought or draw attention to a fact or figure.
- *Physiological pauses.* These are times during your communication where you need to stop speaking so you can take a breath or a sip of water.

For Stanislavski, the different pauses were essential for communication to be effective: "If speech without the logical pause is unintelligible, without the psychological pause it is lifeless. . . . The logical pause serves our brain, the psychological our feelings."

The overarching lesson: don't be afraid of silence during your communication. Embrace the opportunity a pause can give you to emphasize your points, letting them sink in.

Pause, along with other aspects of pacing, can add meaning and variety to your delivery and can help build suspense and anticipation in the eyes of your audience. It gives the listener a chance to hear, comprehend, and assess the information you are providing. A pause draws your audience in, so they actively participate in the construction of your message. It amplifies—by silently *underlining* for importance—the meaning of a specific fact or point. Think of a pause like a blast of silent confetti. Make your point and let the confetti fall. If helpful, *code* your presentation or manuscript by marking specific moments where a logical or psychological pause could occur for added impact.

ARTICULATION

Stanislavski often bemoaned the poor speech of actors as it related to "clarity and crispness" and the "pronunciation of words." What he is talking about here is *articulation*. Clarity of speech—your *diction*—is essential when you are communicating a message to others. Quite simply, people need to be able to understand what you are saying if they are to be able to consider your message. According to Stanislavski, a speaker "must be in possession of excellent diction and pronunciation, that he must feel not only phrases and words, but also each syllable, each letter."[16] In *Hamlet*, Shakespeare has the Danish prince advise, "Speak the speech, I pray you . . . trippingly on the tongue." This is sage advice, even hundreds of years later. Being able to speak clearly and confidently in your job and life can have a direct impact on the success you will achieve. Being able to be persuasive with your message, unsurprisingly, begins with being able to be understood by your audience. An excellent example of what we are talking about here can be seen in the rise of a former Austrian body builder who learned the hard way about the importance of speaking clearly when it came to achieving career success.

Arnold Schwarzenegger made the transition from bodybuilder to actor in the early 1970s. He got his acting break when he was cast as the lead in *Hercules in New York* (credited under the name "Arnold Strong"). When the movie was made, however, his accent was so thick that people couldn't understand what he was saying. Eventually all of his lines had to be dubbed by another actor so they could be understood. After that disappointing experience, Schwarzenegger committed himself to working on his voice and articulation, and by 1984 he had become one of the biggest box office draws in the entire world. By 2003, he was also a successful politician: governor of California, a state whose economy is the eighth-largest in the world.

The articulators—lips, jaw, tongue, and soft palate—are the structures that form words, and how you use them will determine how clear your diction is to an audience. The single biggest thing you can do to articulate clearly is, again, to slow down your speaking pace. If you are speaking too quickly you will not be able to create all the sounds necessary to fully articulate your words. Pay special attention to the sounds at the ends of words, taking the time to properly create the final sounds of a word or phrase to avoid mumbling or sounding lazy with your speech. The difference between the phrase "she lives in a nice house" and "she lives in an ice house" is a simple adjustment in articulation.

But proper articulation does not mean over-exaggerating every sound you are speaking. This will make you sound unnatural and will put an audience off. The goal with your articulation is to modify your conversational speech as needed to create the sounds required for each word, so that your audience has no trouble understanding what you are trying to say.

EXERCISE
Warming Up Your Articulators

Warming up your articulators before an important communication can help your speech. You can practice by reciting the following tongue twisters out loud and increasing your speed with each reading. Emphasize every sound, noticing how the various articulators move (lips, jaw, tongue, soft palate), as well as all of the muscles in your mouth and face.

The skunk thunk the stump stunk
Rubber baby buggy bumpers
Good blood, bad blood
The lips, the teeth, the tip of the tongue
Red leather, yellow leather
Bobby Babcock's bagpipes
Fresh fried fish, fish fried fresh
Shave a cedar shingle thin
The thirty thorny thistles thawed throughout

CHOOSE YOUR OPERATIVES

The words you emphasize, or punch, are called *operatives*. By altering your pitch, volume, or inflection when hitting a specific word, you provide that word with added weight or meaning in the eyes of your audience. Depending on the words you choose to emphasize in a particular sentence, operatives can completely change the meaning of your communication. Here are some famous movie quotes with the operative words in *italics*:

- Jack Nicholson in *A Few Good Men:* "You can't *handle* the truth!"
- Humphrey Bogart in *Casablanca:* "Here's lookin' at *you*, kid."

- Clark Gable in *Gone with the Wind:* "Frankly, my dear, I don't *give* a damn."
- Estelle Reiner in *When Harry Met Sally:* "I'll have what *she's* having."

Just imagine how the meaning and the delivery of each of these famous movie lines would have changed if the actors had chosen different operatives. Using operatives properly helps ensure that your communication is crystal clear and that your delivery supports your intention. During your preparation, it is helpful to code your material by underlining or marking the operatives you want to emphasize in your delivery. Abraham Lincoln did this with the Gettysburg Address and other speeches;[17] King George VI used it throughout his reign as well,[18] and the same technique can work for you.

PROTECT YOUR VOICE

The Roman rhetorician Quintilian wrote, "The good qualities of the voice, like those of all other faculties, are improved by attention and deteriorated by neglect." Not all qualities of the voice will be used in the same way in different settings: a one-on-one conversation for thirty minutes will take considerably less energy and effort than an eight-hour class or training session. The physical demands of projecting your voice for long periods of time or to larger audiences are much greater.

The voice needs to be prepared and warmed up before a demanding communication so that it can function properly when called upon to do so. Water is a necessary element to the proper function of the voice. When you become dehydrated, your body cuts down on mucus production, leaving you vulnerable and susceptible to injury. Your vocal folds vibrate in excess of a hundred times a second when you speak;[19] water helps to keep them lubricated so they can do their job properly. The mucus in your throat protects the vocal cords from friction, which can cause swelling, irritation, and injury, damaging your voice.

EXERCISE
Warming Up Your Voice

Shortly before you are about to begin a presentation, speech, or other prolonged communication, warm up your voice.

STEP 1: Begin by focusing on your core breath, inhaling for a count of five and exhaling for a count of five.

STEP 2: Repeat the breathing process, this time allowing the sound of a moan to be released during your exhalation, connecting the breath to the voice.

STEP 3: Starting at the center of your range, make the "ah" sound and gently cascade from the lowest pitch of your voice to the highest pitch and back to the lowest again, engaging the entire register.

STEP 4: Next, warm up the four articulators (lips, jaw, tongue, soft palate) by repeating the following phrases aloud, enunciating for crisp and clear diction:

Mumsy made me mash my mutton (lips)
Twenty tentacles tickling Ted (tongue)
Charlie chews his chocolate shoes (jaw)
Ricky's sticky yucky duckies (soft palate)

Your voice, like any other instrument, needs to be maintained and protected continually to function properly. As with anything, if you take care of your voice, it will take care of you. Stay hydrated, rest when you are ill or tired, and practice proper breathing techniques. In the end, the more comfortable your use of the various qualities of the voice, the more confident and compelling you will be as a communicator.

Everyone has a voice, and a unique one at that. As you continue to improve your personal communication, explore the qualities of the voice discussed in this chapter. Strive for variation and blending of these qualities in your speech to create an engaging and effective vocal landscape that can be used to influence and impact your audience.

CHAPTER 7

Listen to Understand
Maximizing Comprehension and Retention

The single biggest problem with communication is the illusion that it has taken place.
—George Bernard Shaw

In *The Ragged Edge of Silence*, author John Francis shares an amazing story involving the power of listening and how one decision he made completely transformed his life. It all began in 1971, when Francis—then in his twenties—witnessed two oil tankers collide under the Golden Gate Bridge and spill 500,000 gallons of oil into the San Francisco Bay. Horrified by what he saw, Francis decided to make a personal and rather unorthodox commitment to saving the planet: from that moment on, he would stop riding in motorized vehicles. Instead, everywhere he went, he walked. Because of this statement, many of those who lived in his small town questioned and challenged the motives behind his decision. Why was he doing this? Was he trying to make others feel guilty for driving cars? Everywhere Francis turned, he found himself having to justify and defend his decision. It eventually became such a source of irritation for him that on his twenty-seventh birthday, Francis decided he was going to take a break from the endless arguing and spend one full day in silence, *simply not speaking*. And so he did. For his entire birthday he went without uttering a single word. "It was a very moving experience," recalls Francis, "because for the very first time, I began listening."[1] He became so intrigued by what he experienced during that day of silence that one day turned into two days and two days turned into a week. And before he knew it, the weeks turned into months. Francis decided that he would go without speaking for one full year. But when his twenty-eighth birthday arrived, he again reassessed his decision and decided to continue his experiment and live without speaking.

That lasted for seventeen years.

For Francis, silence became a way of life. No riding and no speaking, just walking and listening and writing. He became known as "the Planetwalker" and eventually attended college. He even went on to become a professor, actually teaching classes without speaking. It was on the twentieth anniversary of Earth Day, April 22, 1990—*seventeen years after he first took his vow of silence*—that Francis finally decided to resume speaking. Over those years, Francis learned something extraordinary about himself and the way he interacted with others. Before taking his vow of silence, he had been a terrible listener. Up until then, when talking to someone, he would listen just enough to get a general idea of what they were saying and then he would stop listening, simply waiting until they were finished so he could contribute his thoughts or opinions. What he came to realize was that he was hardly listening at all and that this type of listening simply "ended communication." Through his experience, he finally learned, in profound ways, the importance of being present in the world and communicating effectively with those around him. For Francis, the key to establishing and maintaining meaningful connections with other people boiled down to one simple realization: "We really need to listen to each other."

• • •

As human beings, we spend a great deal of time communicating with others—expressing feelings, sharing thoughts, and providing information. And the sending of these messages is only half of the communication equation; the other half is receiving—listening. As a communicator, you have two main questions to consider when it comes to listening. The first is obvious: "How can I get my audience to listen to me—to receive what I say the way I want them to receive it?" Much of this book has to do with giving you the skills to maximize the chance your message will be correctly and thoroughly heard, and parts of this chapter will add to those skills as well. The second question is no less important: "How well am I listening to my audience?" The ability to listen to and read an audience is crucial in every communication—more obviously in casual contexts than in the context of a formal presentation, but no more important.

Communication is always a two-way street. As Dr. Ralph G. Nichols—often called the "Father of Listening"—says, "The most basic of all human needs is the need to understand and be understood. The best way to understand people is to listen to them."[2]

In this chapter, we discuss the importance of active listening and detail how different types of listening can affect the successful delivery of your message. We describe some of the common barriers to effective listening and analyze some bad listening habits that often hinder effective communication. Finally, we talk about the connection between listening and memory and provide a series of tips and techniques that can improve your personal skills as a listener. You cannot completely control the ways in which your message is received. But understanding how listening works—and incorporating good listening into your communication style—will help you put your message across as successfully as possible.

Being able to employ listening as a communicator shows you are comfortable with silence and confident enough to let someone else have the spotlight in a conversation. Good listening is a great way to build rapport and learn about others. Ironically, someone who is a good listener will often be perceived as a great conversationalist, even when the other person did most of the talking.

So how much time do we spend each day communicating with others? And how much of that time is spent engaged in the act of listening? A 2006 study found that the average college student spends nearly 50 percent of a day listening (as opposed to only 20 percent speaking) while involved in such activities as attending class, talking on the phone, participating in a meeting, watching television, listening to music, or chatting with friends.[3] Think about it: that means they were involved in listening up to *twelve hours a day*.

WHY LISTENING MATTERS

It has been said that we have two ears and one mouth so we can listen twice as much as we speak. The ability to listen actively during communication with others will not only have dramatic benefits for you as an individual, it can also affect the productivity and success of your entire group or organization. Good listening is essential for understanding and group cohesion. Being listened to means that you are being taken seriously, that your ideas, thoughts, and feelings matter to the other person. A person who is listened to by another will feel accepted.

The reverse is also true, of course. Poor listening has a detrimental effect on cohesion. In a corporate environment it can result in reduced productivity, misused time, and lost revenue. In interpersonal relationships, it can lead to strained friendships, eroded trust, and deflated morale. A person who is ignored will feel isolated. As the Oscar-winning actress Emma Thompson puts it, "Any problem, big or small, within a family, always seems to start with bad communication. Someone isn't listening."

Poor listening can lead to resentment, confusion, conflict, and hurt feelings on the part of the receiver of the information. This is why it is essential for all parties in communication to listen, first and foremost, with the intention to *understand* and not simply to *respond*. Think about your own experiences at work or with your family members. Would people describe you, in general, as a good listener or a poor listener? Are you a better listener with your boss than you are with your spouse?

Or vice versa? Analyze your own personal listening habits and try to pinpoint why you listen the way you do. What are the consequences of poor listening in your personal or professional interactions? What are the repercussions if information is not properly communicated or retained?

I like to listen. I have learned a great deal from listening carefully. Most people never listen.

—ERNEST HEMINGWAY

One field where good listening is of the utmost importance is medicine, as poor communication between medical professionals can literally cost lives. In a 1999 study, the Institute of Medicine found that up to ninety-eight thousand patients in the United States die each year as a result of medical errors, costing $37.6 billion a year.[4] According to Joseph G. Murphy and William F. Dunn of the American College of Chest Physicians, "The sad irony is that communication errors are probably the number one current cause of patient harm. The Joint Commission on Accreditation of Healthcare Organizations describes communication error as the cause of 60 percent to 70 percent of preventable hospital deaths."[5] One source of bad communication in medicine is the time constraints on doctors, as the dialogue between patient and doctor is often rushed and inadequate. One study found that physicians interrupt 69 percent of patient interviews within eighteen seconds of the patient beginning to speak. The result: in 77 percent of the interactions, the physician failed to identify the patient's initial reason for the visit.[6]

BARRIERS TO EFFECTIVE LISTENING

For all the benefits of good listening, people do not tend to be very good listeners. In one study, researchers found that people are distracted, preoccupied, or forgetful a full 75 percent of the time while listening to others.[7] What does this tell us? Probably that we have busy lives and a lot on our minds. There are also numerous challenges to active listening in our daily lives. Technology is often a culprit. Think of how many times you have been interrupted by a phone call or text message when you were in the middle of a conversation with someone else. Smart phones allow us to communicate in simple and efficient ways, but this technology can also have a negative impact on our interactions with others if not used properly.

Often we assume that others are always listening actively to what we are saying, but because of numerous distractions and poor listening habits, this is not always (or even usually) the case. It is important for you as a communicator to understand that every person in your audience is filtering your message through their own individual prism. Your message never follows a direct path between you and your audience—everything you say is filtered through the different attitudes, experiences, biases, and assumptions that the audience brings with them. Don't assume everyone in your audience is alert and fully attentive. You may have to address someone with indigestion who has just opened an envelope full of divorce papers. Even if this were the case, it is still up to you to get your message across.

Many communicators mistakenly assume that as long as *they* understand the message they are trying to convey they have done their job as the messenger of that communication. This is not enough—the *receiver* of information also conveys meaning to a message. The act of listening becomes a circular interaction between the sender and the receiver. Anything that gets in the way of the message being clearly transmitted is *noise*—either *internal* noise such as insecurity, high pressure, or poor preparation, or *external* noise, such as a noisy environment, poor acoustics or inadequate amplification, or a disruptive audience member.

On the audience's side—the receiving end—a myriad of distractions can interrupt the loop of effective communication: technological, factual, semantic, environmental, mental, cultural.

- *Technological distractions.* With the prevalence of virtual communication such as video conferencing and conference calls, technology will often create a barrier for effective communication even as we use it to improve and enable our communications. Poor phone connections, slow Internet speeds, and faulty equipment can make clear communication and effective listening a challenge.

- *Factual distractions.* Often listeners get so caught up in specific facts or figures that they lose sight of the overall theme of the message itself. This can also occur when people listen to a lecture and focus only on the specific notes they are taking and, as a result, miss the overall idea or message behind them.

- *Semantic distractions.* Jargon, idiomatic expressions, or unfamiliar terminology can often serve as barriers to effective listening. If someone feels baffled by words that they don't understand, they may tune out the rest of the message. Another barrier is message complexity. If your message is simply too technical or too complicated, it may cause an audience to simply give up and stop listening.

- *Environmental distractions.* Poor acoustics, color, or temperature of the room, awkward seating arrangements, obtrusive background noise, or a speaker's failure to project their voice can all make it difficult for an audience to listen to the message being presented.

- *Mental distractions.* Internal noise such as our critical inner voice or other symptoms of speech anxiety can also be barriers to effective listening. Focusing too much on the end result of the communication, only considering our own wants, or preoccupation with the status of the other person are also mental barriers that can hinder effective listening.

- *Cultural distractions.* Thick accents, idiomatic expressions, or other language barriers can also interfere with the ability to listen to and process information: the same word or gesture can have different meanings in different cultures, so awareness is key to ensuring that understanding takes place.

Awareness of all these impediments—and any others—is the first step toward correcting them. In general, a dynamic, thoughtful awareness of all the circumstances of communications is the key to success with them. And the keystone of this awareness is the practice of *active listening*.

ACTIVE LISTENING

Psychologists Carl R. Rogers and Richard E. Farson formulated the term "active listening" in 1957, putting forward the idea that listening was not a passive activity but one that requires both energy and effort.[8] They wrote, "Evidence clearly shows that ... listening is a most effective agent for individual personality change and group development.... Besides providing more information than any other activity, listening builds deep, positive relationships.... Listening is a growth experience." Rogers and Farson believed that one should not listen to what another has to say simply to agree or disagree; it is better to listen first to understand, to take in the *total meaning* of the other person's communication—this means both content and subtext, body language and emotional cues.

Chris Bond is president of the International Listening Association, an organization that has studied listening for thirty-three years. Bond told us, "Listening is the number one construct that leads to success" in most areas of life; and the reason the average person is not a very good listener is simple: they have simply never learned the skills.[9] (Actors, according to Bond, are among the best listeners—listening is an essential component of their craft.)

And how does Bond recommend we improve our listening? "First you must be aware of the listening situation that you are in.... The person you are in dialogue with may not be a good listener, so you need to adjust your own listening behaviors accordingly.... Distinguish which listening barriers you may have ... observe verbal and nonverbal cues in the listening process ... and continue to adapt and reframe messaging depending on how listening changes during the process." Clearly, though we can't change our audience's listening ability, there is plenty to work on in our own listening skills to help ensure we are communicating effectively.

There is a common misconception that hearing and listening are the same thing. They are not, and it is important to understand the difference. Hearing is a *physiological* process while listening is a *psychological* process. Put another way, hearing is when the sound reaches your

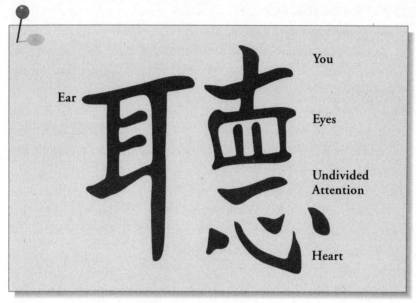

Figure 7.1   The Chinese Character for *Listening*.

ears and listening is when the sound reaches your brain. And it's even more complex than that—nonverbal cues are so integral to communication that we listen with our eyes, and with our intuition as well. In fact, the Chinese character for the word *listening* includes not just the symbols for ears but also the symbols for the eyes and the heart (Figure 7.1).

Since you can't assume you'll know how your audience will react to what you are saying, or what questions they will have, being *present* in your communication is essential. Active listening is an essential component of being present in communication.

In the early 1980s, American communication researchers Lyman Steil, Larry Barker, and Kittie Watson developed the SIER hierarchy of active listening, breaking it down into four distinct processes that needed to be followed in a particular order.[10]

STEP 1 : *Sensing*. Sensing is, basically, hearing—the purely mechanical process that happens when sound waves reach ears. There can be no listening without sensing.

STEP 2 : *Interpreting*. Once the message is received, we interpret it for understanding and assign meaning to the sounds we have received. Here is where many aspects of the message, including tone, pitch, and volume, come into play. Here we judge the intentions of the sender.

STEP 3 : *Evaluating*. Once the message is understood, we dissect and consider it to determine its validity. Does it sound credible? How should we feel about what we have heard? Should we take action as a result of hearing it?

STEP 4 : *Responding*. Once we've heard, interpreted, and evaluated the message, we must decide whether we will respond to it, and in what fashion. One option is to ignore the message and take no action. A response could be verbal or nonverbal.

Active listening involves suspending judgment until the other person has completed a whole thought or idea, giving our full attention until the speaker finishes. It also involves our remaining aware of any personal opinions or biases that may affect the way we take in the information we hear. There's a lot to active listening, but its practice has tremendous value in creating real, meaningful, mutual communication.

Information is managed in our brains by an array of complex processes, many of which have yet to be understood fully, though knowledge of the brain's function is growing very rapidly. It is common knowledge, for example, that the left side of the brain is in charge of logic, analyzing, planning, organizing, reasoning, and counting, while the right side of the brain is responsible for imagination, laughter, memory, and sensing. And different people have different learning styles, with one side often being more dominant. Therefore to fully engage your entire audience and accommodate each of their distinct learning styles, you must engage both sides of the brain with your communication. How do you do that? Use numbers and statistics to engage the left side, and stories, metaphors, and sensory descriptions to ignite the right side.

Audience members also vary widely in the capabilities they bring to the table; the gamut of barriers to listening runs all the way from physical hearing impairment through cognitively-based listening disorders to psychological and cultural biases and mood differences. Some of these you can plan for, and the better you know your audiences' potential listening barriers (and your own, don't forget), the better you can plan and the more effectively you can communicate.

For example, according to Dr. Judy Pearson, a communications scholar at North Dakota State University, men and women tend to have slightly different listening styles. Women are generally more attentive than men to things that are happening around them. This includes reading and interpreting the various nonverbal cues coming from their audience or their environment. Men tend to focus their listening on specific content or individual facts, while women are better at focusing not only on the details in any given communication but also the overall themes and big picture.[11]

THE FOUR TYPES OF LISTENING

We often listen differently depending on the audience, the environment, and the circumstances of our communication itself, and different styles of listening demand different sets of skills. You would not listen the same way to your doctor explaining your recent test results as you would to a comedian in a nightclub. There are four types of listening: comprehensive, critical, sympathetic, and selective.

Comprehensive Listening
With comprehensive listening, the goal is simply to hear and understand what a speaker is saying. Think of the time you called the customer service representative for your laptop computer and they explained how to check for connection issues and reboot your system. Other examples might involve your attending a biology class in a university lecture hall or a team listening to a project manager lay out the specifics of a new

program or plan. The goal with comprehensive listening is to absorb and retain as much information as possible.

Critical Listening

The goal of critical listening is to determine if you agree with the words being spoken by someone and whether or not the message and information being put forward sounds credible. When you listen critically you seek to make judgments on the content as well as the speaker, based almost entirely on what you hear. This kind of listening is essential during brainstorming session wrap-ups or when weighing the merits of the various alternatives or options being considered in a project or program. Or you might use it when a local politician approaches you at a bus stop to try to influence your vote.

Sympathetic Listening

Your neighbor stops by to tell you that he and his wife are getting a divorce. Your teenager discloses that she is being bullied at school. An employee expresses his disappointment over a recent performance review. With sympathetic listening you are simply there to listen and take in the information from someone who is speaking, allowing them to share their thoughts, opinions, or feelings about a topic or subject. The goal with sympathetic listening is to serve as a sounding board, showing that you are sympathetic to the words being spoken, as well as to the feelings of the person doing the speaking.

Selective Listening

Selective listening is used when numerous aural messages are going on simultaneously and the listener focuses on the one that seems most important at the time. The goal with selective listening is to block out any unnecessary sounds or noise so that you can pick up the specific information that you hope to hear and comprehend. Some examples: In the middle of a conference call, you mute your phone to discuss a deadline with a coworker who just stepped into your office; with children screaming in the background, you place a phone order for a birthday cake and balloons.

IMPROVING YOUR LISTENING SKILLS

Becoming an effective listener demands focus and practice and takes time. The main ingredient in active listening is a genuine interest in others. People can sense whether or not you are sincere and engaged with what they are saying. As we discuss at length elsewhere, your true intentions will be expressed through your vocal and visual cues. If you truly want to engage your listener, be curious about what *they* have to say. Make it your goal to truly listen and learn new things about them that you did not previously know.

Being an effective listener involves building rapport with another person. To practice it, you might start a conversation as you normally would—by finding common ground in shared interests or experiences. But let them talk. Don't interrupt or override, or interject your own anecdotes. When you say something, let it be a remark that mirrors what you just heard from them, or a question that invites them to expand on their subject. Open your mind to different ways of thinking about things, allowing yourself to be willing to see the world from the other person's perspective, truly taking in what they are saying. Remember: it is probably not a mere coincidence that the words *listen* and *silent* contain the exact same letters.

> *In order that all men may be taught to speak the truth, it is necessary that all likewise should learn to hear it.*
>
> —SAMUEL JOHNSON

Subtle changes can improve your listening skills in noticeable ways. Some techniques are fairly easy to master while others will take a little more effort. The following techniques for improving your listening skills will help you not only be a great audience member but also take in and retain information much more effectively.

- *Avoid distractions.* If possible, remove any physical barriers to listening. This might mean changing the seating arrangement, turning the thermostat up or down, closing the door, or setting ground rules. Adjust the environment to fit your needs.

- *Ask questions.* This is a great way to stay engaged and involved during your listening. Ask for clarification or confirmation when necessary.
- *Take notes.* Capturing the main points on paper will not only help you stay engaged, it will also allow you to go back and review the information afterward for better retention. As the Chinese proverb reminds us, "The palest ink is better than the best memory."
- *Use nonverbal communication.* By communicating effectively through your nonverbal cues, you can make it clear that the information the speaker is presenting is being received and understood.
- *Paraphrase what you have heard.* As you listen, try to understand the points being made by putting them into your own words. Paraphrasing will help ensure that you accurately comprehend the information being presented.
- *Be aware of personal biases and strive to set them aside.* Try to overcome your emotional reactions to words, topics, or even the presenter. Focus on what you can agree with in the other's message and use this as common ground.
- *Focus on the speaker's main idea.* You can always request specific facts and figures later. Your initial purpose as a listener should be to understand the big picture or overall theme of the sender's message. Listen for intent as well as content.
- *Give the other person your full attention.* Give the speaker the same respect and attention you would want from an audience. Too often as listeners we spend our listening time considering and crafting our responses rather than concentrating on the sender's message itself. Don't begin your evaluation until you've listened to the entire message.

Nearly everyone can benefit from working on their personal skills as a listener. Often we make mistakes with our listening that hinder our understanding of the information being presented to us. Faking attention, dismissing the subject as dull, listening only for facts, and letting emotions get in the way are just some examples of bad listening habits. Practicing active listening can help you free yourself from these and other bad habits.

EXERCISE
Active Listening

This exercise can reveal how much divided attention can take away from comprehension.

1. Sit in front of a television with a deck of playing cards.
2. Turn on the television and, with your back to the screen, listen for two minutes. While you listen, separate the deck of playing cards into four piles, dividing them by suit.
3. When the two minutes have elapsed, turn off the radio or television and put away the playing cards.
4. On a piece of paper, write down as much information as you can remember about what you heard, including the main message of the broadcast.
5. Repeat this process again. Listen to the television for two minutes, this time without the playing cards.
6. Again, write down as much information as you can remember about the information you heard, including the main message.
7. Repeat the process one last time, but this time take notes while you are listening for the two minutes. Capture as much information as you can, including the main message of the broadcast.
8. Compare the three experiences. Which one allowed you to capture and retain the most information?

Listening and Memory
Studies have shown that while people gain a large portion of their knowledge through the process of listening, the overall retention rate is not very high. According to Dr. Ralph G. Nichols, the average person

listens at around a 25 percent efficiency rate.[12] Not a very encouraging statistic. Listening and memory are intimately connected: once we hear something, our brain stores that sound and image—the message becomes ours, through our memory, and we become able to recall it or recognize it when we encounter it again. In turn, learning cannot occur without memory.

In the late nineteenth century, the German psychologist Hermann Ebbinghaus studied memory and discovered that people don't just forget facts randomly, they actually forget them at a predictable rate. Using a series of nonsense syllables, Ebbinghaus spent years trying to understand how memories fade as time passes. One of Ebbinghaus's most important discoveries was something he called the *forgetting curve* (see Figure 7.2), which showed that people actually forget things exponentially over time.

The result of his experiments, as seen on the curve pictured in the figure, showed a dramatic downward swoop, mapping the degradation of a person's ability to retain information. What does the curve mean

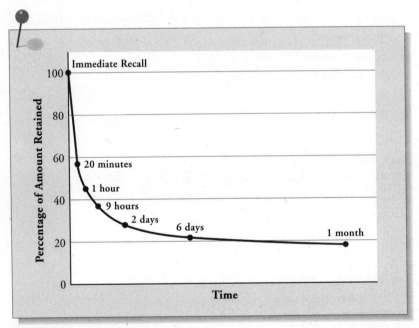

Figure 7.2 Forgetting Curve.

to you? Let's say you are attending a one-hour lecture. You go into the lecture knowing nothing about the subject, or 0 percent. At the end of the lecture, you now know 100 percent of what you know (of course, what exactly comprises that 100 percent will depend on how effectively you listened). But you don't retain information at a rate of 100 percent. Instead, what Ebbinghaus found was that in the first hour after learning information, more than half would be forgotten. After the first day, another 10 percent would disappear; and after a month, another 14 percent.[13]

So how can you improve your retention? Simply, through one of the four paths to retention: reviewing, reprocessing, repeating, or rehearsing.

What Ebbinghaus discovered in his research was that "forgetting . . . decreased with multiple relearnings" and that the more you revisit the information you have heard, the more likely you will be to move it from your short-term memory to your long-term. Put simply: you've got to do some work to make it stick.[14] By reprocessing the information through repetition or rehearsal, you are signaling to your brain that this information is important and should be remembered. This is why actors will say their lines over and over during rehearsals to memorize the words they have to deliver; by hearing them out loud over and over through the process of reviewing, repeating, and rehearsing them—and eventually adding the physical movement and gestures (reprocessing)—soon the words become second nature. This is why preparation—specifically practicing a speech or presentation *out loud*, is essential. By actually speaking and hearing the words, you will retain them more effectively, making them easier to access in your long-term memory when they are needed.

Repetition and review are also very effective rhetorical moves to make when you are the speaker. By hammering your important points more than once, revisiting them, recasting them, you signal to your listeners' brains, "Hold on to this: this is important."

Active listening is essential for the effective delivery of your message and the successful retention of the information you are providing. By understanding how your audience listens and by eliminating barriers to effective listening, you will be more successful in connecting with your listeners and communicating the benefit that you offer them. Steve Bertrand, a broadcaster for WGN Radio for nearly twenty-five years who has interviewed everyone from Stephen King to Jimmy Carter, puts the matter very well: "When listening to another person we should follow the same advice we give our children when they cross railroad tracks: stop, look, and listen. Stop to be in the moment. Don't be so preoccupied about what comes next that you miss something unexpected; get comfortable with silence. Engage the other person by looking them in the eyes. Make them feel valued in the way that you listen to them. If you do that, if you stop to be in the moment and truly give your full attention to the person who is speaking, then the third part is easy. You can't help but listen."[15]

CHAPTER 8

Think on Your Feet
Mastering Impromptu Speaking in Any Situation

Sometimes you just have to take the leap, and build your wings on the way down.
—Kobi Yamada

The idea of having to speak without preparation fills many people with dread. And chances are that most of us can recall an incident or event in our lives where we said the wrong thing or drew a blank while speaking in the moment in front of others: fumbling a math answer in high school; misspeaking during a meeting; forgetting what comes next during a presentation. *Impromptu speaking* is one of most difficult modes of communication to master: you are generally without notes or visual aids, and you must quickly organize your thoughts and communicate them in a clear and concise manner.

It is also arguably the most important, and certainly the most common (other, more formal modes include memorized speech, reading from a manuscript, and extemporaneous speaking, which is prepared in advance but delivered without notes). Answering questions during a conference call, contributing ideas during a brainstorming session, interacting with coworkers in the break room—these are everyday opportunities for impromptu speaking that carry some weight.

Improvisation is a crucial tool for an actor. Actors improvising a scene are literally making up the words they are saying in the moment, and must trust their instincts at all times—much the same way you must trust your instincts during a sales call, in a meeting with your boss, or while discussing vacation plans with your spouse. Many of the same techniques that actors use when improvising can be used in other types of communication to improve concentration, develop ideas quickly, and be assertive with thoughts or comments. In this chapter we discuss some of these techniques. We also provide a framework and guidelines for delivering effective summary statements and positioning statements when answering the most commonly asked question of all: "What do you do?"

A powerful example of impromptu speaking took place in Indianapolis, Indiana, on April 4, 1968. It was just five years after his brother had been assassinated and Robert F. Kennedy had decided to run for the presidency himself. Like his brother John, Robert Kennedy had at the time also been using an expert from the world of acting to assist him in the shaping and delivery of his message: that person was Emmy and Golden Globe Award–winning director John Frankenheimer (*The Manchurian Candidate*).

As a senator from New York, Kennedy had been the favorite for the Democratic nomination that year and had been crisscrossing the country delivering speeches on the many issues that were important to him, such as war, poverty, and racism. On this particular day he had just finished speeches at Ball State University and Notre Dame and was headed to Indianapolis for the day's final campaign stop. As he boarded his plane, however, he was informed of some terrible news: civil rights leader Martin Luther King, Jr. had just been assassinated in Memphis. A passionate champion of racial equality, Kennedy was deeply affected by the news and understood that he would need to address the tragedy in his upcoming speech in Indianapolis. His press secretary, Frank Mankiewicz, immediately began composing notes and preparing a speech. As he would later recall in an interview with C-Span, the Indianapolis speech was scheduled to be delivered in a poor area of town in front of a mainly African American audience.[1] Because of this, the police feared that the crowd might erupt in rioting when they were informed of the news, and the Indianapolis police chief warned Kennedy that he should skip the speech because they could not provide adequate security. Kennedy rejected the request to cancel the speech and headed toward the location, where a large crowd had gathered and had been waiting for over an hour to hear him speak. Without police protection, and clearly understanding the emotional reaction this devastating news would have on the assembled crowd, Kennedy decided not to speak from a prepared statement.

He knew that the message he needed to convey would have to come from the heart. He stepped to the podium, which had been mounted on a flat bed truck, and began, "I have some very sad news for all of you.... Martin Luther King was shot and was killed tonight." Kennedy spoke slowly and deliberately for approximately four minutes, and every word supported his intention of calming and soothing his audience. Kennedy even recited from memory his favorite poem by Aeschylus, and openly acknowledged the anger and bitterness his audience was most likely feeling at that moment. Drawing comparisons to his own personal experience having lost a loved one to an assassin's bullet, Kennedy encouraged the crowd to channel the emotions they were feeling in a positive direction. The result? While many other American cities burned that night, the city of Indianapolis remained calm—mainly as a result of words spoken by a single man standing on the back of a truck. Kennedy's message in Indianapolis remains one of the most powerful and resonant impromptu speeches ever delivered. Sadly, it would be only two months later that an assassin's bullet would claim Kennedy's life as well, silencing forever one of the most eloquent and passionate voices of a generation.

THE CHALLENGE OF THINKING ON YOUR FEET

Take a moment and consider how much of your communication in any given day takes place in the moment or without preparation. At breakfast you explain to your teenagers why they can't go on an overnight camping trip: impromptu speaking. At the grocery store, you run into a former classmate who asks what you have been doing since graduation: impromptu speaking. On a plane, the passenger in the seat next to you asks what type of work you do: impromptu speaking.

In actuality, most human communication happens in this fashion, with little or no time to gather thoughts, much less put together notes or an outline. With impromptu speaking you have to speak in the moment, right *here* and right *now*. And despite the fact that we all engage in it every day, it is specifically this type of communication that makes people the most anxious. The fear of misspeaking or drawing a blank makes us nervous. With good reason; thinking on your feet requires concentration and a nimble mind. Of course, not all instances of impromptu speaking are the same. There is a difference between being asked about your sprinkler system by a next-door neighbor and being grilled about diminishing profits by your board of directors. However, the challenges are the same in both scenarios, as in each you are required to think quickly and craft a message in the moment.

It usually takes me more than three weeks to prepare a good impromptu speech.

—MARK TWAIN

Actors study improvisational techniques to sharpen their concentration skills and allow them the ability to make decisions in a split second. In an environment in which anything is allowed to happen, actors must be capable of staying focused even in difficult and stressful circumstances.

Once such incident happened on Broadway in 2009 during a live performance of *A Steady Rain*, a gritty drama starring Hugh Jackman and Daniel Craig, when a phone began ringing in the audience. It continued to ring and ring until finally Jackman stopped the performance and walked to the edge of the stage. "Do you want to get that . . . we can wait," he said to the mortified audience member. The rest of the audience, who had clearly been annoyed and distracted by the inconsiderate audience member, burst into applause at Jackman's handling of the situation. With the phone finally silenced, Jackman and Craig stepped back into the scene and continued on with the performance.

When you have time to prepare for an exchange by putting together notes, building slides, or laying out an agenda—or even just taking a moment to clarify your thoughts before placing a phone call—you are engaging in what we call *proactive* communication. You know what you will be covering, have an idea what you will be saying and, in most cases, can anticipate what to expect as a result. Other interactions, however, are not planned and happen unexpectedly, such as a phone call from a customer, a run-in with an unhappy student, or a challenge from a boss. These are examples of *reactive* communication: you are not the initiator but are simply responding to what you are experiencing in the moment. While improvisation and the ability to think on your feet come into play during both proactive and reactive communication, they are especially important during reactive scenarios where you lack the luxury of foreknowledge or preparation.

Improvisation requires you to be able to make decisions—and *commit* to them—in a split second. This takes courage; the courage to put your opinions and ideas out in the world and defend them if challenged. Think of impromptu speaking like a big funnel that connects your brain to your mouth. When you are called on to speak without preparation, a myriad of thoughts and words are suddenly dumped into the funnel all at once. But all those words cannot exit the smaller end of the funnel (your mouth) at the same time; you have to make rapid decisions as to which words or phrases are going to be spoken. Being able to make those snap judgments is an essential tool—a view shared by renowned biologist Craig Venter, who, when asked what the best survival skill a person could possess was, responded, "Having good intuition and natural reaction. Most of the complex decisions that make a difference are the ones you make in a fraction of a second."[2]

But how do we make sure we can handle ourselves when speaking in the moment? Susan Messing, a veteran improviser who has performed with Second City and on Comedy Central, offers this wisdom: "In improvisation, if you have the ability to judge a moment, you are not *in* the moment." This is why it is important to return to your intention and objective, to take the focus off yourself and send it outward toward your audience. "Remember," says Messing, "it is not about *you*; your ideas are far more important than the spinach you are worried about being stuck in your teeth or whether you look fat in that dress. It's ridiculous for you to waste that energy on your insecurities when you could recommit it to what you are talking about."[3]

There are some inherent dangers with impromptu speaking, the main one being the fact that once the words exit your mouth you can't put them back in. Which is why it is often better to say less when speaking without preparation. As the maxim says, it is better to keep your mouth closed and let people think you are a fool than to open it and remove all doubt. One example of the inherent dangers of impromptu speaking took place during the 2007 Miss Teen USA Pageant, an event that happened live on network television. Contestant Caitlin Upton, Miss South Carolina, was asked the following question about U.S. geography by one of the pageant judges: "Recent polls have shown a fifth of Americans can't locate the U.S. on a world map. Why do you think that is?" As Upton began to answer, her nerves got the best of her and she froze. This is what came out of her mouth:

> I personally believe that U.S. Americans are unable to do so because, um, some people out there in our nation don't have maps and, uh, I believe that our, uh, education like such as, uh, South Africa and, uh, the Iraq and everywhere like such as, and I believe that they should, uh, our education over here in the U.S. should help the U.S., uh, should help South Africa and should help the Iraq and the Asian countries, so we will be able to build up our future.

Of course, in the Internet age, Upton's fumbled response immediately went viral, attracting nearly 3.5 million views on YouTube in a single day and becoming instant fodder for late night comedians. A few days later, Upton appeared on the *Today* show and admitted that it was her nervousness speaking on national television for the first time that caused her to botch the answer. "I was overwhelmed. I made a mistake," she said. "When the question was asked . . . I was in complete shock. . . . I only heard about one or two words of the actual question. . . . I drew a blank." During the interview, Ann Curry and Matt Lauer shared their own personal challenges speaking without preparation and even gave Upton a second chance to answer the question. This time she was ready and had obviously given her response some thought. Here was her answer the second time around:

> Personally, my friends and I, we know exactly where the United States is on a map. I don't know anyone else who doesn't. If the statistics are correct, I believe there should be more emphasis on geography in our education so people will learn how to read maps better.

Same question but two wildly different answers: The first attempt was a rambling, incoherent hodgepodge of ideas riddled with verbal viruses and delivered with deer-caught-in-the-headlights paralysis, while the second answer was clear and concise, delivered confidently. What were the differentiators? Simple: preparation, concentration, and relaxation on the part of Upton. Unfortunately, in the end, 53 million people viewed the clip of her first answer while only 4 million saw her redemptive second attempt, underscoring an important point made in earlier chapters: for better or for worse, *first impressions last.*

We are the masters of the unsaid words, but slaves to those we let slip out.

—WINSTON CHURCHILL

In his eight years as president of the United States, George W. Bush provided late night comedians with a wealth of material from his off-the-cuff stumbles, giving us such memorable gaffes as, "Families is where our nation finds hope, where wings take dream." "Rarely is the question asked . . . is our children learning?" and "Will the highways to the Internet become more few?"[4] But one particular moment of unscripted communication from George W. Bush stands out in a very different way. On September 14, three days after the terrorist attacks on the United States, Bush paid a visit to ground zero, the site of the fallen World Trade Center towers. Surrounded by volunteers and New York City firefighters, Bush was handed a bullhorn and invited to speak to the crowd gathered around him. With his arm around a firefighter, Bush began to say a few words. As he did, the crowd, unable to hear him, began shouting, "We can't hear you!" Bush paused and responded, "I can hear you, the rest of the world hears you, and the people who knocked these buildings down will hear all of us soon!" The crowd erupted in cheers at Bush's honest and decisive response. Building on the wave of emotion he suddenly felt from that audience, Bush continued, "The nation sends its love and compassion. To everybody who is here, thank you for your hard work, thank you for making the nation proud, and may God bless America!" For Bush, it was a startling and unfiltered moment of human connection. By speaking from his heart and keeping his remarks brief, Bush had turned this unscripted exchange into one of the defining moments of his eight years as president.

MASTERING IMPROMPTU SPEAKING

Knowing and following a few simple rules can help you take control of your moment in the impromptu spotlight.

- *Keep it short*. This is the reason that attorneys advise their clients to respond "no comment" when embroiled in a legal controversy. The minute you open your mouth to speak, you are providing evidence by which a listener will judge you, and again, once it's out of your mouth there's no unsaying it. When you do speak, remember that less is more, or as Shakespeare said, "Brevity is the soul of wit." Rambling on, on the other hand, can lead to embarrassment and regret.

- *Pause before you start*. In general, when responding to a question, you have approximately one or two seconds to formulate your answer. Those one to two seconds can make the difference between answering effectively or not, so use them wisely—but above all, *use them*.

- *Speak from your heart*. Be honest with your answer or response—or, as it is often said, tell the truth; it's the easiest thing to remember. Franklin Delano Roosevelt offered sage advice when it came to speaking in the moment. His recommendation? "Be sincere; be brief; be seated."

- *Choose an intention*. How do you want your listeners to feel as a result of what you are telling them—challenged, persuaded, motivated? Decide how you want them to react to the information you are providing and activate the intention that will best accomplish that.

- *Slow down*. When speaking without time to prepare, pace is your best friend. Slow down the rate of your words so you can control them and shape your message, because, once they are spoken, you can't take them back.

- *Breathe*. Don't hold your breath. Just the act of breathing will relax you and slow your pace, allowing you to properly form your ideas.

- *Frame your message before speaking*. In the one or two seconds before you open your mouth, choose three mental bullet points to serve as a roadmap for you. This will help you structure your message. As Supreme Court Justice Oliver Wendell Holmes Jr. fondly noted, "Speak clearly, if you speak at all; carve every word before you let it fall."

- *Have a strong opening and strong closing.* For a strong first impression and a strong last impression, make sure your opening starts off with some energy and your closing ends strong as well. As always, use the effects of primacy and recency to your advantage.

- *Draw from personal knowledge or experience.* When speaking off the cuff, try to stay within areas and topics that you are comfortable speaking about. The further you veer into unfamiliar subjects, the less comfortable you will be with the message.

- *Connect with your audience.* Remember to use movement and eye contact to connect with your audience. Smile. Speak *to* them and not *at* them. The more conversational your delivery sounds, the more likely they will be to listen to you.

EXERCISE
Impromptu Speaking

There is no better way to sharpen your skills as an impromptu speaker than by simply engaging in impromptu speaking. To improve upon your own abilities to think on your feet and make decisions in the moment, try this exercise.

1. Set up a video camera.
2. Write the following words on individual slips of paper:

   - Vacation   - Cooking   - Books
   - Politics   - Astronomy   - Planets
   - Family   - Sports   - Photosynthesis

3. Place the slips of paper in an envelope.

4. Draw each of the slips, one at a time, and speak about the topic without preparation. Keep all responses succinct (under one minute) to avoid rambling. Record.

5. Watch the playback and note your body language, vocal variety, and gestures. Notice the difference in delivery between the topics that you enjoyed and those that were more of a challenge for you.

TACKLING THE "WHAT DO YOU DO?" QUESTION

Imagine you're invited to a social event—a picnic, a wedding, a class reunion. Picture yourself entering the room and think about what happens as you begin to mingle and meet people. In a situation like this, what is the first question that people generally ask when they meet you? After learning your name, the first question that most people will pose is: "What do you do for a living?" Why do they ask this particular question? It's simple, really. Aside from being an effective icebreaker, in many ways, your job defines who you are in the eyes of other people. It provides a window inside you and information about how you spend your days. If you say you are a coal miner, people will probably begin to form different opinions about you than they would if you said you were a seamstress or a personal trainer.

By leading off with a compelling description of your occupation, you can generate interest in the mind of the other person to hear more or learn about you in greater detail. But the sad truth is that most people are not very good when it comes to answering this particular question, often selling themselves (and their company) short by assuming that others could not possibly be interested in their occupation. If your response to the "What do you do?" question is, "My job is pretty boring," you are probably right to assume that your audience will not be impressed by or interested in what you do—in fact, you've just ensured they won't be. In truth, if you don't take advantage of the "What do you do?" question, you are missing a fantastic opportunity.

Now imagine this. You are flying to an industry conference that has attracted all the major business leaders in your particular sector. And on your way to the conference, you find yourself on the airplane sitting next to the CEO of one such company—someone you have been attempting to do business with for years. As the plane takes off, this CEO notices the logo on your shirt, smiles, and asks, "So what do you do?" You suddenly have your chance. This is the opportunity you have been dreaming about for years, your one shot to pitch your company to this CEO and pique his interest and generate additional questions.

If this situation arose for you, what would you say to this CEO? How would you say it? In fact, take a moment right now and, *without preparation*, answer the question, "What do you do?" Record your response and listen to it back. Consider not only what you said but also how you said it. What reaction would your words elicit in that CEO?

This chapter provides two tools to help tackle the "What do you do?" question: a summary statement and a positioning statement.

Creating a Summary Statement

A *summary statement* is a brief yet comprehensive summary of who you are and what you do. The description should be clear and concise, but no longer than one or two sentences, tops. Use a summary statement when you don't have a lot of time or are unfamiliar with the person to whom you are introducing yourself. If you have already introduced yourself, you don't need to include your name in your summary statement. If the other person does not know your name, it is a good idea to include it as you make your introduction. An effective summary statement should contain the following information: name (yours and your company's); what you do (both you and your company).

The goal with a summary statement is not to provide all the information you want the other person to know—it's to generate enough interest that the listener wants to know more. Because your objective is to hook the other person in and evoke additional questions, your delivery must support an intention to excite or impress. Aside from providing answers to the who and what questions, your summary statement should also include a specific fact or detail that will assist you in rousing interest in your listener. Here are three sets of summary statements for a pharmaceutical salesman, a college student, and a policeman—for each, there's an ineffective summary statement and an effective one.

Ineffective Summary Statements

SALESMAN: "I'm in sales."
STUDENT: "I'm a student."
POLICEMAN: "I'm a cop."

Effective Summary Statements

SALESMAN: "I'm a senior sales rep for a pharmaceutical company called KostTech."
STUDENT: "I'm a freshman at Princeton studying chemical engineering."
POLICE OFFICER: "I'm a twenty-five-year veteran of the Chicago police department."

You can imagine how differently they would be received by another person. The first answers have "just the facts," with no details that would compel a listener to want to hear more. The second answers contain details that could interest the listener, possibly leading to additional questions.

Take a moment and try to come up with a personal summary statement for yourself. Think about how you could describe who you are and what you do in a way that would generate additional questions from a listener. Then distill it down to one or two compelling sentences. Once you've come up with your summary statement, share it with your boss or a coworker to get their feedback as to whether or not it is clear and consistent.

When someone you've just met asks you the "What do you do?" question and they respond favorably to your summary statement—they appear genuinely interested or ask for additional details—this is good news. You've earned an opening to deliver a version of your positioning statement.

Crafting Your Positioning Statement

A *positioning statement* is a short, compelling description of your company, product, or service—*and its benefit*—that can be communicated in a few sentences. Like a summary statement, a positioning statement should say what your name is (yours and your company's) and what you do (both you and your company). To this, it adds a focused and compelling case for what benefit you provide.

Your positioning statement should also establish credibility—your own and your company's—and might also include mention of your target audience, the industry or category, and key competitors, as well as why your company stands out as superior or remarkable. With an effective positioning statement, you are continuing to refine the overall impression your audience is forming of you and your company. Because of that, every further interaction will be judged by how well what you say matches up with what they heard in both your summary and your positioning statements. So feel free to tout the benefits your company or product can provide but limit the hyperbole—don't oversell. Be specific but avoid excessive jargon unless the listener is an industry insider and would understand such terminology.

When it comes to crafting a positioning statement—which is commonly known as an elevator pitch—there is no one correct path. One size does not fit all—this is, after all, a statement that captures your unique worth within your industry or field. You also don't want your elevator pitch to sound memorized or rehearsed, even though it should be carefully prepared in advance, and rehearsed often enough that it rolls off your tongue. And you are not simply repeating a tagline or your corporate mission statement, which is apt to be too general and filled with buzzwords to capture a listener's attention. The positioning statement is crafted to be delivered from one person to another, in conversation.

The delivery of your positioning statement should be relaxed and conversational, focusing on your intention (to excite or impress) and your objective (to initiate or further a business relationship). Think of your positioning statement as an opportunity to shine a light on your company or product and drive home all of the great things it has to offer. Keep the delivery conversational but enthusiastic, and as always, don't be afraid to use passion and emotion in your delivery. Passion is contagious and people respond to it.

So how can you make a positioning statement sound natural and conversational? In his book—aptly titled *So What?*—Mark Magnacca provides a simple formula for responding to the "What do you do?"

question effectively.[5] It involves two very simple phrases that you can use as a springboard and framing device for your positioning statement:

"Do you know how ... (*problem or concern*)?"

"Well, what I [or we] do is ... (*solution to their problem or concern*)."

Returning to the previous examples—the salesman, the student, and the police officer—here are positioning statements using Magnacca's structure:

SALESMAN: "I'm a senior sales rep for a pharmaceutical company called KostTech. Do you know how a large percentage of the population suffers from diabetes? Well, what we do at KostTech is develop the test strips and insulin pumps that make the process of monitoring their diabetes simpler and less painful.

STUDENT: "I'm a freshman at Princeton studying chemical engineering. Do you know how the world has begun to move away from fossil fuels and toward more clean energy sources? Well, what I plan to do after completing my degree is find a job with one of the companies at the forefront of exploring these alternative sources."

POLICE OFFICER: "I'm a twenty-five-year veteran of the Chicago police department. Do you know how families want to feel protected and secure in their homes? Well, what I do is patrol the neighborhoods to make sure that laws are being obeyed so people can feel safe."

EXERCISE
Your Positioning Statement

Using what you've just learned about positioning statements, create one for yourself that is clear, concise, and compelling. Identify the benefit you are providing and make sure you are clearly communicating it to your listener. Once you have finished crafting your positioning statement, ask your coworkers to do the same. Try out your positioning statements on each other. Continue to refine and sharpen yours until your delivery sounds natural and conversational.

Many people mistakenly believe that a positioning statement is something that is only needed for people who work in sales. Not true. Every person at every company—from the custodian to the CEO—should be able to communicate in a clear and concise manner exactly what they do and the benefits they provide. Why? Because you never know who you are going to meet and what that person can do for you. In this type of situation, you become the face of your company—an ambassador of sorts. Why not be prepared so you can capitalize on the moment? The person with whom you are speaking just might hold the key to a future opportunity.

CHAPTER 9

Stay Focused and On Track

Handling Questions and Controlling Your Audience

Expect the best, plan for the worst, and prepare to be surprised.
—Denis Waitley

When communicating a message to others, you are responsible for the flow and feel of that message's delivery. And because no two audiences are exactly the same, you have to be quick on your feet and ready for anything. Hostile audience members, malfunctioning equipment, personality clashes, and inattentive participants can all threaten to derail the successful delivery of your message.

In the current technological age, a myriad of distractions—phone calls, e-mail, and text messages—can pull your audience's attention away from you. "Interruption is the enemy of productivity," warns *Rework* author Jason Fried. The problem results from something he refers to as our "communication addiction."[1] And what are the end results of these constant interruptions? The loss of progress and profits for your product or company. Just how distracted are we as a culture? According to Basex, a business research company in New York City, distractions such as unnecessary texts, e-mail messages, and phone calls can consume as much as eight hours of an average employee's work week and can reduce overall productivity and innovation to the tune of $650 billion dollars a year.[2] Something to think about next time you decide to update your Facebook status during your weekly conference call.

As discussed in preceding chapters, when you are delivering a message it is your job to engage your audience and limit distractions. To do this, you need a strong intention to stay in control.

Make sure you have finished speaking before your audience has finished listening.

—DOROTHY SARNOFF

Actors understand that remaining focused and on track during a performance is key to keeping an audience engaged. In Shakespeare's time, this was no small feat. While Shakespeare did not have to contend with instant messaging or cell phones going off during performances of his plays, he had other challenges. For one, most performances during the Elizabethan period took place during the daytime hours in open courtyards with up to three thousand people in attendance. That's a large crowd to manage. And on top of that, nearly a thousand of those audience members had to stand for the full duration of the performance! And since attending the theater was not the only leisure activity enjoyed by the public in Shakespeare's time, he and his actors were forced to compete for audiences with other forms of popular entertainment of the day—cockfighting, bear baiting, and public executions. Tough competition. And if an Elizabethan audience was not happy with what they were seeing on stage, they were not afraid to express their displeasure by shouting insults or hurling items at the actors. Fortunately most people who have to present material or deliver a message today don't have to worry about flying tomatoes, but they do have to deal with other types of challenges that Shakespeare could never have even imagined.

In this chapter we offer up some tips on how to manage your time when presenting material to others, how to handle challenging questions and audiences, and how to keep your meeting or presentation moving forward by setting ground rules, managing conflict effectively, and staying focused on your message and its intention from start to finish.

In September 2008, the American economy was in freefall. As the financial industry teetered on the brink of collapse, Congress wanted answers: What happened? What caused the problem? Who was to blame for the mess that the country now found itself in? To get these answers, Congress ordered the heads of all the leading financial industries and government regulatory agencies to come to Washington to testify before the banking committee. Because Treasury Secretary Hank Paulson was on an official trip to China, his deputy, Robert Steel, was chosen to take his place. In *Too Big to Fail*, Andrew Ross Sorkin details how Steel secretly prepared to testify before the committee and the impact it had on his performance.[3]

Robert Steel was a confident and polished speaker with a vast amount of experience and expertise in financial institutions and the markets. But Steel knew that for this particular appearance and hearing, the stakes were high. And it would be anything but pleasant. Congress was angry and wanted a scapegoat, someone to make the villain, and this televised hearing offered the perfect opportunity to play the heavy. Steel's objective going in to this hearing was clear: to ensure that the finger of blame did not get pointed at the Treasury Department. To do that, Steel knew he would need to be prepared. So to get ready for the hearing, Steel enlisted the help of his staff members in an exercise called "murder board." First developed by the U.S. military, murder boards are commonly used in business and politics to help people get ready before a big meeting, interview, or debate. One sets up a simulated environment and has colleagues role-play actual audience members who will ask the likely gotcha questions. The murder board would not only allow Steel to anticipate what questions might be asked, it would give him the opportunity to try out different answers until he found the right one. The underlying idea: better to give the wrong answer in front of the murder board *and fix it* than to blow the answer in front of the actual committee.

So round after round they went. Hour after hour, the staffers peppered Steel with questions, sharpening and refining his responses and delivery so he would appear relaxed and credible in front of the committee. Through it all, Steel knew that one specific question was almost guaranteed to be asked—a question involving the role the government had played in the run-up to the collapse of the investment bank Bear Stearns. This was a difficult question, and Steel knew that to answer it incorrectly could have devastating effects. So, in front of his murder board, Steel tried out different variations on his answer, getting feedback each time from his staffers until his response was succinct and he was comfortable with it.

The hour arrived and Steel headed to Capitol Hill. When he entered the hearing room, it was already packed with people, the crowd buzzing with excitement. Steel took his seat in front of the committee and the hearing began. Chairman Christopher Dodd offered a scathing opening statement and began firing questions. And just as Steel and his staffers had anticipated, the Bear Stearns question was asked. His preparation in front of the murder board served him well. Calmly and deliberately, Steel answered the question. His body language was relaxed and his pace was measured, as if this were just another question in a series. His delivery gave no indication that the answer had been meticulously planned and crafted ahead of time, and all that came across to an audience of millions was this: a government official answering a very difficult question with poise and purpose.

DISTRACTED AUDIENCES

As the great actor Sir Ralph Richardson once said, "Acting is merely the art of keeping a large group of people from coughing." Engaging with and controlling an audience, as anyone who has ever had to run a meeting or deliver a presentation knows, can be a challenging proposition. An audience takes on a personality of its own and, depending on the circumstances, this can pose distinct challenges.

Not least of these is the omnipresence of distraction. Quite simply, the age of YouTube, Twitter, and e-mail has wreaked havoc on the modern person's attention span. As Peter Jensen at the National Institute of Mental Health has concluded, being exposed to this constant stream of information results in the "development of brain systems that scan and shift attention at the expense of those that focus attention."[4] And these distractions are costly. An article by Tony Schwartz and Catherine McCarthy in *Harvard Business Review* discussed the cost, revealing that "a temporary shift in attention from one task to another ... increases the amount of time necessary to finish the primary task by as much as 25%."[5]

In a time when nearly everyone has access to instant information through a computer or smart phone, it is no surprise that we find modern audiences unable to focus when listening to others. According to Paul Atchley, a researcher from the University of Kansas, "That desire to stay connected is extremely powerful because it taps directly into your brain's reward system."[6] And technology is clearly affecting the ways in which we communicate and interact with others. Says Michael Rich, an associate professor at Harvard Medical School, with the new technologies available to the modern child, "Their brains are rewarded not for staying on task but for jumping to the next thing. The worry is we're raising a generation of kids in front of screens whose brains are going to be wired differently."[7] Much of this is due to how we process information and how we have adapted to the era of high-speed information. And this has been happening for a long time. Almost thirty years ago, Bob Pittman, the creative force behind MTV, spoke about modern attention spans in the *New York Times*, noting that viewers brought up in the modern media age "can watch [television], do their homework and listen to music at the same time. What kids can't do today is follow things too long. They get bored and distracted, their minds wander. If information is presented to them in tight fragments that don't necessarily follow each other, kids can comprehend that."[8]

You are always fighting for your audience's attention.

—SYDNEY POLLACK

In truth, the objective that a film maker or politician has—to engage an audience with a chosen message—is the same one you have. You've got to engage an audience and capture their attention, not an easy task. We all face obstacles, whether we are relating a story, pitching a product, or delivering a keynote address—we are always fighting to keep an audience engaged with our message. This is why a strong objective and intention—knowing what you want and how you are going to get it—are such essential tools to ensure true engagement.

Even apart from the electronic distractions that permeate our lives, we are still very easily distracted. Why? According to research done by psychologists Matthew Killingsworth and Daniel Gilbert of Harvard University, the reason is simple: "Our mental lives are pervaded, to a remarkable degree, by the non-present." What Killingsworth and Gilbert discovered in their research was that people's minds wander about 46.9 percent of the time.[9] It is a challenge for us to simply give our undivided attention to another person without being distracted by something—anything—other than the topic at hand: *What time do the kids get done with soccer practice? I wonder if my wife called the plumber to fix that leaky faucet? What should I have for lunch today?*

RED FLAGS AND WARNING SIGNS

Here are some of the telltale signs that your audience may not be engaged with your message:

- Asking irrelevant questions
- Being silent
- Not maintaining eye contact
- Fidgeting
- Checking their watches
- Yawning
- Reading ahead
- Doodling
- Crossing their arms
- Whispering among themselves

So how much time do you have when delivering your message before you start to lose the attention of an average audience? Not much, as it turns out. According to Gloria Mark, an informatics professor at the University of California, Irvine, the average worker's attention span lasts only about *three minutes* before they feel the impulse to set aside whatever they are doing and begin a new activity.[10] Three minutes! But if the three-minute attention span is typical for someone executing a task, what is it for a person listening to a presentation or speech? How long do you have to engage your listeners before they get the itch to check their BlackBerry or chat up their neighbor? Not much more, it turns out. Joan Middendorf and Alan Kalish of Indiana University studied attention spans in college classrooms and reported, "Adult learners can keep tuned into a lecture for no more than 15 to 20 minutes at a time [and] . . . as the lecture proceeded the attention span became shorter and often fell to three or four minutes towards the end." And which portion of the lecture impacted students the most? "Students recalled the most information from the first five minutes of the presentation."[11] This means the concept of primacy (see Figure 3.1) is in full effect, and, additionally, the longer you continue to speak, the harder it will be for your audience to remain attentive for anything other than short bursts of information here and there. As researcher P. J. Fensham observed, "During the falls [in attention] the student has, in effect, phased out of attending to the information flow."[12] In other words, the speaker's *in*tention is no longer strong enough to keep that person's *a*ttention.

CONTROLLING YOUR AUDIENCE

As we established earlier, engagement begins with a compelling message, and this requires a strong intention supporting your words. Full engagement is impossible without it. So how can you make sure that your audience is with you? For starters, make every meeting or presentation you facilitate or deliver a *dialogue,* not a *monologue.* Look at your audience. Read their faces. Observe their body language. Be *present.* Don't speak into a void; look people in the eyes and direct your message to specific *individuals.* Stay connected with your audience and read the nonverbal cues they are providing you. Stanislavski was a vocal proponent of people remaining finely attuned to one another's nonverbal signals: "There are people gifted by nature with powers of observation . . . [but] average people have no conception of how to observe the facial expression, the look of the eye, the tone of the voice, in order to comprehend the state of mind of the person with whom they talk." Stanislavski believed these skills were essential for effective communication and encouraged his actors to continue to sharpen and refine them through "work, time, desire to succeed, and systematic practice."[13]

Create a Pattern Interrupt

Think about how the energy in the room drops when a group returns from lunch and proceeds to slip into a food coma. Or how the energy flags with an audience the closer you get to the end of the day. As noted, and as Middendorf and Kalish stress in their findings, the burden of engaging an audience lies with the person speaking to "do something to keep their . . . attention." It is up to you to find some way to combat participant fatigue when attention or energy levels begin dropping.

The most effective way to accomplish this is to create a *pattern interrupt* (or "change-up")—something you do or say that is designed to break behavior patterns or habits that can lull your audience into a state of complacency. Screenwriters do this when they introduce a new character or throw in a plot twist that sends the action of the story careening in a new direction. Surprise your audience with something interesting or unexpected at frequent intervals throughout. Shift gears. Change direction. Be creative. Schedule brief breaks to give people a chance to make a phone call or visit the bathroom and return refreshed and ready to re-engage with your message. Engaging your audience directly through participation or interaction can be an excellent way to include a pattern interrupt. As Middendorf and Kalish explain, making your communication more interactive can yield valuable results. "Many of our colleagues . . . report that when they intersperse mini-lectures with active engagement . . . for as brief a time as two to five minutes, students seem re-energized for the next fifteen to twenty minute mini-lecture."[14]

Here are some ways to creatively shake things up during the delivery of your message:

- Change speakers.
- Solicit feedback or opinions.
- Introduce a new visual aid.
- Tell a story or anecdote.
- Change topics.
- Ask a direct or rhetorical question.
- Divide the audience into groups.
- Incorporate physical activity.

Manage Conflict

As the Irish proverb says, "If you want to draw a crowd, pick a fight." Conflict sells. Just turn on your television or radio and witness the arguments and outrage that fill the airwaves on a daily basis. When people communicate ideas or opinions, you can count on others to offer opposing or competing ideas. Often it is the loudest or most aggressive voices that dominate the discourse and enjoy the most attention. But, as *The Daily Show* host Jon Stewart warns, "If we amplify everything, we hear nothing." It is for this reason that you, as the presenter or facilitator, need to stay in control by moderating arguments, maintaining civility, and making clarity out of noise. Conflict management is based on the idea that, while conflicts cannot be avoided entirely, they can often be managed to improve communication and allow a group or individuals to work toward positive outcomes.

Conflicts that arise when you are running a meeting or facilitating a discussion between two or more people can run the gamut from calmly expressed differences of opinion to full-blown arguments. As the German writer Johann Wolfgang von Goethe said, "Every word that is uttered evokes the idea of its opposite." In other words, when one view is expressed, the odds are good that people will almost reflexively think about other, competing aspects of the topic. And with that comes conflict as the two ideas are placed side by side for judgment or further discussion.

Not all conflict is bad. It can be a healthy and natural part of communication that, when managed, can improve people's ability to work together. When you are serving as the leader or facilitator, you must try to resolve any conflicts that arise in a way that also helps participants understand how the conflict arose in the first place and how they were able to resolve it.

Researchers Kenneth W. Thomas and Ralph H. Kilmann studied how people deal with conflict and discovered that there were basically two dimensions along which to measure behavior during a conflict situation: *assertiveness* and *cooperativeness*.[15] Assertiveness relates to how people attempt to satisfy their own needs, while cooperativeness relates to how they attempt to satisfy the needs of someone else. These two dimensions of behavior define five basic ways that people manage conflict:

- *Avoiding:* Goal is to postpone the conflict by ignoring it or changing the subject.
- *Accommodating:* Goal is to yield or surrender one's own needs.
- *Collaborating:* Goal is to work together to find a win-win for both parties.
- *Competing:* Goal is to win at the expense of the other.
- *Compromising:* Goal is to find a middle ground or reach agreement.

We discuss assertiveness in the next chapter, but each of these five methods of dealing with conflict relates to the two dimensions—assertiveness and cooperativeness—to varying degrees, as referenced in the Thomas-Kilmann Conflict Mode Instrument (TKI; see Figure 9.1).[16]

We are all capable of using all five of these conflict-managing modes, but each of us tends to be better at certain modes than others—thus we use them more frequently. When you find yourself in conflict with others, which is your go-to method of managing conflict? Do you tend to avoid conflicts? Are you a good collaborator? Do you tend to

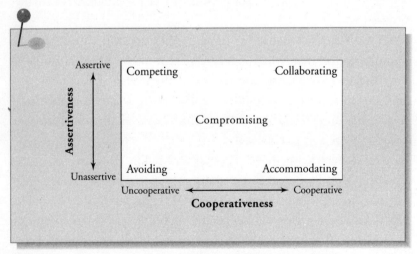

Figure 9.1   Thomas-Kilmann Conflict Mode Instrument (TKI).

compromise when confronted by a person with an opposing view, or do you take the opportunity to assert yourself and compete? What about other people in your life? Which methods do they tend to use?

As a presenter or facilitator, it's essential you have a clear grasp of these modes of conflict handling. Why? The way you are able to manage conflict within a group will ultimately affect that group's ability to solve problems, be creative, and move forward to accommodate the different interests and demands placed upon it. Staying in control of a meeting where emotions or passions are running high, and where conflict is emerging, is never an easy task. But if it is your job to maintain control of the meeting and keep the group moving forward toward a common objective, it is your job to intervene and address the behavior. An *intervention* is any action meant to address behavior and improve a group's ability to successfully work together toward a common goal. A great tool to assist you in dealing with conflict is a step-by-step process shown in the *Conflict-Resolution Chain* (Figure 9.2).

Here's how it works:

Step One—*Observe:* As a speaker or facilitator, it is up to you to observe the behavior and interactions taking place at all times during your meeting or presentation. Watch not only the body language of the people in your audience but also how they react and relate to the other people in the room.

Step Two—*Understand:* As you take in the conversation and the various nonverbal cues and signals coming from the members of your audience, try to infer meaning from them and understand their

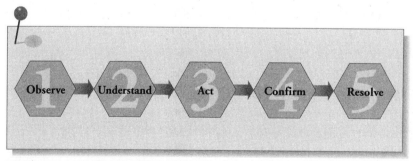

Figure 9.2   Conflict-Resolution Chain.

feelings not only toward the topic but also toward the others in the room.

Step Three—*Act:* If you notice a conflict arising or one of the ground rules not being followed, this is the point where you will need to intervene and take action. You are responsible for the flow and feel of the meeting or presentation. If something is happening in your audience that either changes the group dynamic in a negative way or interrupts the forward flow of your message, it is up to you to step in and take control.

Step Four—*Confirm:* Once you step in to intervene on behaviors taking place within the group, you need to confirm with the group or individual that the inference you made in your initial observations is indeed correct. Point out which ground rules were not being followed or which comment was insulting to another participant and try to get agreement from others in the room that what happened is not productive or helpful.

Step Five—*Resolve:* Before moving on, make sure that the problem is resolved and also help the group understand how it was resolved (following ground rules, respecting others, contributing ideas, and so on).

CAPTURING (AND KEEPING) YOUR AUDIENCE'S ATTENTION

Earlier in this chapter we touched on some of the challenges you face when communicating with others, and on how very difficult it can be to hold your listeners' attention. Here are some techniques to use to engage your audience from the opening moments of your message to the close.

Connect Early

Try to arrive early for your presentation or meeting so that you can greet your audience and build rapport as people come in. Smile, shake their hands, and learn their names. Thank them for coming. This is your first impression: perceptions are being formed the moment you walk in the door. Your audience first begins making judgments about you, whether conscious or not, now. Start off strong by showing you are open, friendly, and approachable.

Be in the Moment

Actors, who often perform the same play up to eight shows per week, have to deliver each performance as if they are doing it for the first time. That means saying every line for the first time and making every entrance for the first time; they can't simply repeat the same performance they delivered the night before. It's a new audience, so a new performance is required every time. That is what makes theater exciting: the chance to witness drama live and in the moment. Don't slip into "auto-pilot" (what actors call "phoning it in").

As Stanislavski said, "A constant supply of spontaneity is the only way to keep a role fresh, on the move. The unexpected is often the most effective lever."[17] A speaker in a corporate environment should do the same, creating the same feeling in the audience, a sense that the unexpected could happen at any moment. Don't ever get so caught up in the words you are speaking or the material you are presenting that you end up sounding rehearsed or robotic. This is where a strong intention can help you. Think of a salesperson who is tasked with delivering the same presentation over and over again to different audiences, or an engineer who has to demo the same software product from client to client. As Susan Messing told us, "The day you decide to phone it in, that's the day you could have made a $250K sale. It doesn't matter what kind of mood you're in—good, bad, or indifferent—you've got to project your energy forward and out. You have something to *share*. If you are excited about what you are communicating, others will be excited. Joy is contagious; so is apathy."[18]

Set Ground Rules

Ground rules are guidelines for individual and team behavior. They are important tools for you to use in order to keep your message on track and your meeting under control. It can be helpful to write down the ground rules and post them in advance for the benefit of the group. Ground rules can be adjusted to accommodate specific situations, but the entire group should agree upon specific ground rules at the start. When the group has ownership over the rules, people will be less inclined to violate them. Possible ground rules:

- Cell phones and e-mail stay turned off until meeting is over.
- One person speaks at a time.
- Crosstalk and side conversations are limited.
- Active participation is expected from all.
- Questions and topics must stick to the agenda.
- Meeting will start and finish on time.

Ground rules get more difficult to set the higher your audience rises in status. It is much easier to set ground rules for peers or direct reports than it is for superiors or other senior leaders. A junior high math teacher should have no problem requiring a class to shut off their cell phones. But a pharmaceutical sales rep presenting a new product to a dozen doctors (and potential customers) might have a little more difficulty making a similar request. To get agreement on the setting of ground rules, it is important to return to the benefit to the audience. What is in it for them? What do they get by giving you their undivided attention? Perhaps the benefit is an understanding of how much money this product will save them or how much time they will save their workers as a result of instituting this policy. Or maybe it is even simpler than that. Maybe by silencing their cell phones, they will let you deliver your message more quickly and get them back to work sooner. As with almost all communication, by clearly stating the benefit to your audience, you will be more likely to engage them with your message.

Take Frequent Breaks

Build in breaks when necessary to give participants a chance to refresh themselves. As Chris Bond says, "With the boom of technology in this new wired world . . . we're almost *wanting* distractions and *needing* distractions." So, knowing people get distracted, how does he recommend we keep them with us? One way that works is to "Bring the distractions into the conversation . . . Twitter, Facebook, literally bring them into the dialogue. Make that distraction part of the dialogue."[19] For example, if cell phones are a distraction in a college classroom, instead of banning students from using them during class, set up specific breaks for students to check messages. If you do this, they won't be worried about what they are missing—knowing they will be able to check their phones at various intervals. This way, they can focus on what you are saying at the moment and give you their undivided attention. If you notice students talking among themselves, solicit an opinion or seek an answer from them to keep them engaged with the topic at hand.

When it comes to meetings or longer presentations, in our experience, ninety minutes is the longest you should go before giving people a break. The simple physiology of the human body requires a break. Also, after ninety minutes, we've found that an audience's ability to retain information diminishes significantly. People need an opportunity to refresh and reset.

Blank Your Screen

The "b" key on your computer keyboard is another tool that is vastly underutilized in the business world. When using PowerPoint in full-screen slide show mode, it is often helpful to draw your audience's focus away from the slide and bring it back to you as the speaker, to answer a question, share an anecdote, or elaborate on a point. To do this, simply press the "b" key on your keyboard to make the screen go blank. This signals to your audience that you want their focus to shift from the slide to you and, specifically, what you have to say. When you have completed your thought and are ready to shift the audience's attention back to the visual aid, press the "b" key again and the slide will reappear.

Honor the Time

Never go longer than your scheduled speaking time. Once you have passed your allotted speaking time, your audience's attention span tends to drop very quickly. In essence, by going over time, you are breaking the agreement you set up with your audience and you run the risk of their resenting you as a result.

HANDLING QUESTIONS EFFECTIVELY

The ability to answer questions in a confident and compelling manner is essential to establishing or maintaining credibility in the eyes of your audience. If you nail the delivery of the message but can't answer the questions effectively, all your audience will remember is that you were unable to answer questions to their satisfaction. The way you respond to your audience during this interaction is every bit as important as how you delivered the actual presentation itself.

In nearly all cases, people value information that they *request* more than information that is presented to them. Answering questions is a form of both reactive communication and impromptu speaking—you are simply reacting to the questions right there in the moment. Questions that come from superiors, team members, or clients can range from softball questions with simple answers to more difficult questions that require thoughtful consideration. As we've discussed, one bungled answer during your communication can torpedo the effective delivery of your message.

Focus on the Question and the Questioner

When you're asked a question, let a second or two pass before responding. Take a breath before offering a response. This will allow you to absorb the tone and spirit of the question and consider your answer carefully. As you begin to answer the question, use your spatiality and movement: take a step toward the person who asked the question. This closes the distance between the two of you and creates intimacy. It shows you are confident as a speaker and also suggests an interest in the question and the questioner. Square off your torso and aim that belly button toward them to indicate your attention and interest.

Use Checkbacks

As a facilitator, you must stay attuned to the needs of your audience and should be prepared to field questions during the delivery of your message. Effective communication should include frequent dialogue between facilitator and audience. If an audience member asks a relevant question and you give an answer, it is helpful to conclude your answer with a *checkback* to confirm the questioner's understanding and comprehension of the information that you just provided. A checkback can be verbal ("Did I answer your question, Tom?") or nonverbal (observing Tom nodding in agreement), but it should always serve the same purpose: to ensure that you have answered a question to the participant's satisfaction. Checkbacks are excellent tools to confirm that the information being discussed is reaching its intended target effectively.

Create a Bridge

Often, when confronted by a difficult question that you are unprepared or unwilling to answer, a technique called *bridging* can help you stay in control of your message and maintain your credibility. This technique allows you to deflect attempts to derail your message by allowing you to move from a difficult subject back to an aspect of the message you want to communicate. To bridge between topics, employ the following phrase: "I can't speak to (*topic you don't want to discuss*), but what I can tell you is (*info about topic you do want to discuss*)."

By creating a bridge, you shift the focus away from a topic you do *not* want to talk about and toward one that you are more comfortable discussing. Use a bridge when a question involves a topic or subject that is out of your scope or is something you are not prepared or at liberty to discuss.

Maintain a Confident Presence

As noted, the human body is a billboard that constantly gives off intention cues to an audience that reveal how the speaker is feeling. Because of this, control your facial expressions and body language, even when confronted with a difficult question—perhaps especially then. To do this, return to your intention for your answer and the reaction you want to elicit from the person asking the question. Use a strong home base position to appear solid and steady.

Reflect and Answer Carefully

Pause before speaking and carefully consider what you are about to say. Remember: once the words come out, you can't put them back in. You will be accountable for your answer, so give yourself a second or two to formulate a response. Slow down your pace as you answer, too, to give yourself more time to answer thoughtfully.

Defer an Answer Until Later

If you don't know the answer to the question being asked, it is better to defer the answer than to make something up that could be wrong. It will destroy your credibility if you are perceived as bluffing. Don't be afraid to ask for time to research a question that may be out of your scope or would require you to take some time to investigate more fully. It is also important to establish a timeline as to when the questioner or audience can expect the answer or information (as always: the sooner the better).

Be Succinct

When handling difficult questions, keep your answers succinct. Period. As Albert Einstein was fond of saying, "Everything should be made as simple as possible, but not simpler."[20] If you can answer the question with a simple yes-or-no response, do it. The longer you speak or the more detail you go into, the more likely you will be to misspeak, ramble, contradict yourself, or venture into areas you are not prepared to address. Many communicators fail to be concise with their communication and end up repeating themselves or going on and on when they should have simply ended or moved on (this meandering phenomenon is something we call "taking a walk in the woods").

Defer to an Expert

If you don't know the answer to the question posed and there is someone in the meeting or presentation who might be able to answer the question more effectively, engage them in the discussion and solicit their expertise.

Repeat the Question

If you need more than a couple of seconds to gather your thoughts before answering, you can repeat the question back to the person asking it. This works best when speaking to larger groups, especially if the people sitting in the back may not have heard the question. Use this technique sparingly to avoid the appearance of simply stalling whenever you are confronted with a tough question.

Facilitate a Discussion

Throw the question out to the rest of the group and let it generate thoughts and opinions. This keeps your audience engaged and involved. Facilitate the discussion and try to bring the group to some sort of consensus around the answer to the original question that was asked.

Rephrase Hostile Questions in Neutral Terms

If a question is overly emotional or accusatory, it is often helpful to rephrase it in less hostile terms before answering. Begin your answer by saying, "So this question has to do with ..." Choose words that are more neutral and less negative, accusatory, or demanding. Remain calm and composed and answer respectfully. Also, beware of answering hypothetical questions, as they can often be traps, asked by someone with a hidden agenda.

Use Connector Statements

It is easy to feel thrown off when confronted by a difficult or hostile question, and this is when verbal viruses show up. By beginning your answer with a stammer or stutter, you create the perception that you are uncertain about what you are saying, causing you to lose credibility in the eyes of your audience. Instead, use a *connector statement* in place of a filler or verbal virus:

I appreciate your question ...
I've asked myself that same question before ...
It's interesting that you bring this up ...
This is a topic that's very important to me ...
Good question. I'd be happy to answer it ...
I'm glad you asked that question. Let's discuss this ...
You've raised a very interesting point here ...
I can certainly understand why you would ask that question ...

Incorporating an appropriate connector statement will allow you to gather your thoughts and appear more empathetic and credible to your audience.

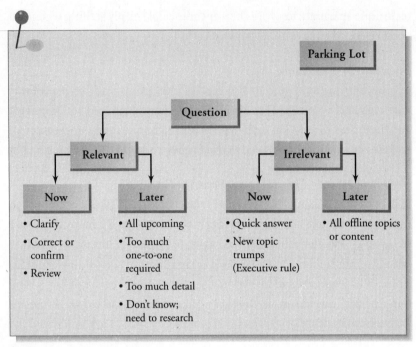

Figure 9.3   Relevancy Tree.

Use the Relevancy Tree

To help keep your meetings and presentations on track, you can use a tool we have developed called the *relevancy tree* (Figure 9.3). As a presenter or facilitator, you must be ready for any question your audience throws at you and know how to handle it in an instant. By following the steps in the relevancy tree, you will be able to quickly determine which questions are relevant and which are irrelevant, as well as which need to be addressed right away and which would be better deflected or deferred until a later time. Don't fall into the trap of feeling the need to answer every question that is asked by your audience. Remember, it is your presentation and you control the flow. Set up a sheet of paper or flip chart labeled "parking lot" at the beginning of the meeting or presentation and set the expectation that any non-agenda questions or comments will be "parked" in the parking lot and answered later (make it part of your ground rules).

To feed a question through the relevancy tree, ask both: Is it relevant or not relevant? And should it be answered now or later?

- Questions that you deem relevant and should (or can) answer now will be any question that is meant to clarify, correct, or confirm information that has already been addressed. Also, if a question is relevant and requires a brief review, it should be handled now as well.
- Questions that you deem relevant and can be answered later would involve any topics that will be discussed later, anything that requires too much detail or is only relevant to one person, and questions that you can't answer and need to research.
- Irrelevant questions that can be dealt with now are any questions that can be answered with a quick response (one word or sentence) or off-topic questions that are asked by a client or senior leader.
- Irrelevant questions that should be dealt with later are any questions that can be taken offline or parked in a parking lot, to be answered at the conclusion of the meeting or presentation.

PREPARE BY MURDER BOARD

As discussed earlier in this chapter, the process of "murder boarding" is used in business before an important meeting, interview, or presentation, or by politicians before a debate to prepare for any difficult questions that might arise. It is helpful to prepare this way before a sales call or meeting to consider any challenges, skepticism, or pushback that you may experience from your actual audience. Think of interruptions such as these:

What makes you better than your competitors?
It's too expensive.
We're perfectly happy with the company we use now.
It's a "nice to have" and not a "need to have."
What makes this a priority right now?

The idea with this method of preparation is that you treat your murder board like a laboratory where you can tinker and experiment with each of your answers and refine your delivery until you feel comfortable that you can handle them in front of your actual audience.

EXERCISE
Murder Board

Before a tough presentation or meeting, gather together one or more team members to practice, using a murder board of your own.

1. On individual slips of paper, write down the most difficult questions you anticipate being asked by your audience.
2. Put the questions in an envelope.
3. Have a team member pull a slip and ask the tough question.
4. Answer the question and record your response.
5. Encourage team members to ask any follow-up questions that your actual audience is likely to ask, and answer these as well.
6. Continue the process with all remaining questions.
7. When you have answered all questions, watch the playback and analyze both your vocal and physical delivery as well as the actual answers given.

No matter what audience you are presenting to or what material you are there to provide, staying in control and managing the various personalities in the room is always a challenge. To be most effective when doing this, employ the tools discussed in this chapter and use your vocal and physical intention cues to let your audience know that you are always in control. Don't concentrate so much on your material that you forget about your audience, and heed the warning of sixteenth-century English philosopher Francis Bacon, who said, "A sudden bold and unexpected question doth many times surprise a man and lay him open." Be prepared for the unexpected; remain steady, even under fire, and use intention to stay in control and on message at all times.

CHAPTER 10

Assert Yourself

Gaining Commitment, Providing Feedback, and Delivering Difficult News

If passion drives you, let reason hold the reins.
—Benjamin Franklin

We all *want something* as a result of our persuasive communication—a teenager wants to stay out past the parental curfew, a coach wants the team to stop making mistakes, an insurance sales rep wants you to renew your policy—and none of these things can be accomplished without assertiveness. Identifying an objective and knowing what you want is usually the easy part, but as the cartoonist Walt Kelly once put it: "It is not enough for things to be planned, they still have to be done; for the intention to become a reality, energy has to be launched into operation."[1] Translation: you must use a strong intention and be assertive with your delivery if you hope to persuade someone to see things your way.

In this chapter, we provide techniques on how to be assertive in various communication scenarios, including when presenting to senior leaders or providing feedback or criticism. This chapter will also help you analyze your personal assertiveness and show you how it can be tuned effectively to get what you want.

Melissa Haney was a Canadian learning specialist working in the United Arab Emirates when she agreed to do a favor for her neighbor. The neighbor had recently hired a young woman from the Philippines to be her nanny, and since a fair amount of paperwork was required to secure the woman a labor card, papers needed to be dropped off at the Filipino consulate.

When Melissa arrived at the consulate she entered and noticed a small room filled with cots and mattresses. The room was packed full of young Filipino women. When Melissa inquired why these women were there, she was shocked to learn that they were being housed in the consulate because they had no place to go. And their situation was a common one: once the women had been hired, their bosses immediately took their passport and labor card to deter them from stealing or performing poorly on the job. Without their documents, however, the women found themselves in a vulnerable position—in danger of being deported or arrested. With no place to turn, they had fled to the consulate, seeking refuge.

As Melissa got to know some of the women, she learned that many had been abused by their employers and some had been thrown out with nothing but the clothes on their backs. One woman showed Melissa the marks on her arms where her boss had burned her with an iron. The small bunk area where the women slept was meant to hold up to fifty people—it currently housed nearly three hundred. And since few of the women spoke Arabic, their inability to communicate made it nearly impossible to explain their situation to Emirati officials. To complicate matters, as Melissa discovered, by the time most of these women reached the refuge of the consulate, they were so broken and frightened that they were unable to stand up for themselves and plead their case.

As someone who taught communication and used it to empower people on a daily basis, Melissa made it her personal mission to communicate on behalf of these women and help them. Melissa began to ask questions and gather information from each woman to help understand her circumstances and build a case. Next, she began to engage the Emirati officials themselves—the very men who held the keys to these women's freedom. Being in a traditional Muslim country, Melissa knew she had to be aware of how she—a Western woman—spoke to these officials and how she used her body language. She was always sure to be assertive but respectful, keeping her volume low and her gestures contained, as she presented the case for each woman she was trying to help. Whenever possible, she connected with each official on a personal level; listening to their objections and concerns and learning personal tidbits about them. As time went on, Melissa would ask about the officials' wives and their children, gradually building rapport. Sometimes she would even notice them smile when they saw her enter their office. She knew that was a sign that her efforts were slowly paying off. As the weeks passed, Melissa passionately and patiently acted as an advocate for these women. And eventually her efforts yielded results.

Within a few months, Melissa had successfully negotiated for a half-dozen of the women to be allowed to retrieve their passports and return to their families in the Philippines. Others received a new labor card and were allowed to continue to work as legal visitors in the UAE. In this instance, Melissa used her communication to persuade and gain commitment in a scenario where the ability to communicate and negotiate assertively literally meant the difference between freedom and a life trapped in legal limbo.

GETTING WHAT YOU WANT

Being assertive offers many benefits, perhaps the most important of which is the way it prevents others from taking advantage of you. You show that you are not afraid to express your thoughts or feelings without equivocation. You create more honest relationships, build self-confidence, and improve decision-making skills that, in turn, will help you earn respect from those around you.

And which gender tends to communicate more assertively? One recent study found that when it comes to negotiating, men are four times more likely to initiate a negotiation than women.[2] Another study, conducted by researchers at several business schools, including Columbia University, found that one reason women get overlooked in the workplace is that men are better at talking up their accomplishments—oftentimes embellishing or exaggerating in the process. Says author Vickie Milazzo, "That doesn't mean men lie during job interviews or performance reviews, but it does mean they exhibit a lot more confidence in workplace situations. They're not afraid to sing their own praises."[3]

According to a 1999 article written by economist Deirdre McCloskey in the *American Economic Review*, an estimated 28 percent of the GNP in the United States involves commercial persuasion of some form or fashion—law, religion, psychology, or marketing.[4] That equals more than $4 trillion last year alone generated by commercial persuasion—simply *selling*.

Think about how much of your day is spent promoting ideas, selling things, or convincing other people. As someone who seeks to persuade with your communication, it is your job to make a listener care about what you care about—this means understanding your objective and then approaching it with a specific intention. As always, it is not your audience's job to be persuaded; it is up to you to be persuasive with your message and delivery. And you do this by pursuing an objective that makes clear to your listeners precisely how you are going to solve their problem or ease their pain (provide a useful service, demonstrate a necessary skill, offer a helpful product, or the like).

THE PERSUASION EQUATION

Perhaps the easiest way to illustrate how intention is used in the process of gaining commitment is to imagine a little boy and a cookie jar. Let's say you are the parent of this child. He asks you if he can have a cookie and you say no. What happens? Does the child smile, place the lid back on the jar, and go back to what he was doing? Unlikely. If he is like most other children, he has an objective he is pursuing ("Get that cookie!") and he is not going to give up until he has achieved it. After that first "no," the child will likely ask the question again, but in a different way. You will notice a bit more urgency as he moves closer to you, frowning and flashing puppy-dog eyes to show you how sad your decision has made him. And did you notice the slight whiny quality in the voice that was not there before? These are all intention cues he is employing to make you change your mind. And when he asks a third time and you say no, he pulls out all the stops—stomping feet, crying, screaming, throwing toys. What the boy in this example clearly shows us is that when we are pursuing an objective, as circumstances dictate, our delivery must change if we hope to get what we want in the end.

While most of us don't have the luxury of simply throwing temper tantrums to get what we want, we can employ intention in much the same way the boy did when trying to get that cookie. To convince people that your idea is the best, your product the most efficient, or your service the most reliable, you have to choose different intentions to inform your delivery. Knowing *what* you want is the easy part. The used car salesman wants to sell that car. The pharmaceutical rep wants to get that referral. The crossing guard wants pedestrians to obey the hand signals. Where people fall short in their communication is in the delivery of the intention itself, which can comprise a great deal of sustained work.

Take the example of a politician. Knowing that cameras are likely capturing every speech and appearance they make, politicians are aware of their public persona and work to project an appealing and confident presence at all times. The public wants leaders to appear confident and credible as well as open and honest, as we often project the image of ourselves onto our leaders. But in recent years, in order to garner votes, politicians also need something else, what writer Benjamin Toff calls the "Reality Show Rule."[5] "It used to be asked which candidate you'd rather have beers with, but that was a simpler era," says Toff. "Today, there's a better yardstick we might use: Could he or she win America's Next Top Pol?" He details how today's politicians are required to communicate well in so many different mediums—town halls, debates, radio, television, Twitter, YouTube, talk shows—they almost need to "follow the playbook of the genuinely popular reality-show star: Be driven without being inhuman, confident without being too off-putting, distinctive but not a freak show." And others agree that the ability to communicate is essential in the era of modern politics. As political analysts have noted, Ronald Reagan was not the first president to be an able communicator—but after him, the best communicators have been the ones who have won.

So what makes a person persuasive? What separates a good sales rep from a bad one? Why do we gravitate toward one politician but feel that another is disingenuous or a phony? Why do we enjoy the company of one neighbor and go out of our way to avoid another? In his 1997 paper "The Roots of Popularity," psychologist and author John Kinnell wrote, "Likeability was the greatest predictor of popularity and social acceptance in a group for adults, more important than wealth, status or physical attractiveness."[6] Simply put, we are more likely to associate with someone we find pleasant, engaging, and interesting. We want to buy something from someone we trust and feel a connection to. Likeable people are more successful in business and life. Think about the factors that determine a person's likeability:

- Empathy
- Sincerity
- Openness
- Interest in others
- Ability to listen
- Relevance

Now think about how you interact with others on a daily basis. In general, do people tend to gravitate toward you or do they find you abrasive or unapproachable? Think of a recent encounter where you met someone for the first time. Try to picture what that initial interaction looked like through the eyes of the other person. Revisit the conversation—from greeting to good-bye—and try to determine how your personal likeability would score based on the six factors in the list.

If we want to gain commitment from other people or otherwise influence them with our communication, being likeable helps. But it's not the only element we need. In his treatise *Rhetoric*, Aristotle wrote

*Some cause happiness
wherever they go; others
whenever they go.*

—OSCAR WILDE

extensively about the art of influence
and identified three basic *appeals* (or
means of persuasion) that a speaker
could use to persuade or influence
others. These became known as Aristotle's Rhetorical Triangle: Ethos,
Pathos, and Logos (Figure 10.1).[7] Aristotle argued that each of the
three appeals has a direct influence on the success or failure of a person's
communication.

- *Ethos* involves an ethical appeal that speaks to the sincerity and
trustworthiness of the person speaking. Does this politician seem honest?
Does my potential business partner seem like a good person? Does my
date appear genuinely interested in what I am saying? To be open to
persuasion, an audience needs to feel that a speaker has good intentions
and is being honest with regard to the words being said. It was Aristotle's
contention that an audience wanted to feel that someone was, at the
core, ethical and decent as a person, and that the words that were being

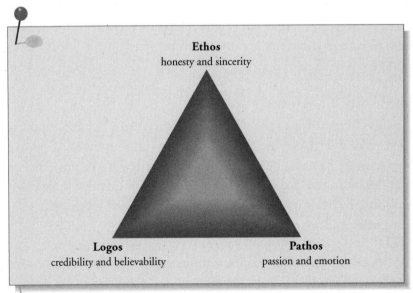

Figure 10.1   Aristotle's Rhetorical Triangle.

spoken were truthful. To engage and persuade effectively, a speaker first needed to be perceived as genuine and reliable in the eyes of the audience. In *The Foundations of Personality*, psychologist Abraham Myerson says, "We resent what we call 'insincerity' because we fear being fooled. . . . There is no blow quite so severe as the sudden realization that we have mistaken the opinion of others, we have been 'fooled.' "[8]

- *Pathos* is an appeal to the passions and emotions of an audience. Does the graphic designer seem pleased with the design on the table? Does the person we are interviewing appear excited by the prospect of working at this company? Does the nurse seem happy to be helping me? Aristotle believed that emotions had the power to modify judgment and influence behavior, and so, in order to persuade, a speaker had to arouse an audience's higher emotions (that is, love, hope, pity) as well as their lower emotions (that is, greed, lust, revenge). Or as Ronald Reagan said, "When you can't make them see the light, make them feel the heat."[9] One way to do this is through the use of simile or metaphor. The more effectively a speaker can touch or move an audience emotionally, the more successful the effort at persuasion will be. Human beings are drawn to people who appear passionate about what they are saying. As the German philosopher Georg Wilhelm Friedrich Hegel once stated, "The motive power that puts [ideas] in operation, and gives them determinate existence, is the need, instinct, inclination and *passion* of man."[10]

- *Logos* is the appeal to logic; it goes to the relevance and accuracy of the actual words being spoken by someone. Does this doctor's diagnosis sound reasonable? Does my accountant's financial findings seem plausible? Does the teacher's assessment of my son's progress make sense? Aristotle believed that a speaker had to be perceived as credible by an audience in order to persuade them, and that the speaker accomplished this by providing evidence, facts, and claims that were reasonable and accurate.

It was Aristotle's contention that these three appeals, when present together, created an ideal environment for a person to be able to persuade an audience with a message. But before speakers can do this, they first have to know what they want from their audience or where they want to move them. They need a goal or something for which they can fight—an intention informed by their objective. Stanislavski describes effective communication as "Energy heated by emotion, charged with will, directed by intellect [that] ... manifests itself in ... action, full of feeling, content and purpose."[11]

FINDING YOUR SIGNATURE STYLE

Incorporating Aristotle's principles and an actor's techniques, each of us is capable of evolving our own personal style of persuasiveness. We develop our different communication styles based on our specific life experiences. This is what makes us each unique. Jesse Jackson spent many years as a minister, and that is reflected in the way he speaks. Bill Clinton grew up poor in the South, and that colors his ability to connect with ordinary citizens. John McCain survived years of torture as a prisoner of war, and we see that in his combative communication style. Each of these different styles works to persuade an audience.

While people tend to stick to the same communication style over time, different circumstances will require different intentions, so it is important to learn some flexibility. Actors are expert at adapting their style even as they maintain their personal integrity—bringing their whole, authentic self to every performance they deliver, but also adjusting their portrayals depending on the character they are embodying and the circumstances they find themselves in. Leonardo DiCaprio communicates one way as the young lover in *Titanic* and another as the government informant in *The Departed*. Actors learn early on that they always need to create a specific perception in the eyes of an audience to get them to react the way they want.

Consider your own personal communication style. Think about the last time you had to deliver feedback or give an opinion to a coworker or friend. How do you think you were perceived? Would people categorize you as patient or impatient? What about your style as a negotiator? Do you usually get what you want or are you more likely to just give in or compromise? In meetings, do you voice your opinions or remain silent?

When people pile extra work on you do you say yes even when your plate is full? Are you quick to judge or condemn others? Are people in your life more likely to engage you or avoid talking to you?

Characteristics of a Passive Communicator

- Rarely asks questions
- Never challenges the ideas of others
- Doesn't contribute ideas
- Spends the majority of time listening
- Uses low volume when speaking
- Is happy with others taking credit
- Uses constrictive gestures and body language
- Avoids direct or sustained eye contact

Characteristics of an Assertive Communicator

- Asks questions when appropriate
- Isn't afraid to challenge the ideas of others
- Is comfortable contributing own ideas
- Consistently listens in an active fashion
- Uses appropriate volume when speaking
- Uses active gestures and body language
- Uses direct eye contact

Characteristics of an Aggressive Communicator

- Is inflexible when working with others
- Constantly interrupts others
- Tends to dominate discussions
- Violates others' personal space
- Doesn't listen to others
- Uses louder-than-usual volume when speaking
- Uses intimidating gestures and body language
- Uses direct and sustained eye contact

Try to honestly assess your overall style, referring to the three lists of characteristics, and place yourself on the continuum in Figure 10.2,

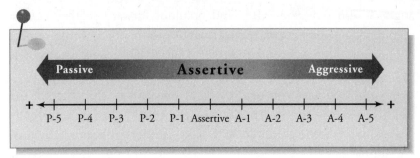

Figure 10.2   Assertiveness Spectrum.

which runs from passive to aggressive, with assertiveness occupying the middle of the continuum. Think of your interactions with the different people in your life: your boss, your spouse, your children, and others. Where do you place yourself with each of these examples? Where would you place your family members or friends on the continuum? How about your coworkers or boss?

Is it ever effective to be either passive or aggressive with your communication? Of course, if the circumstance and intention require it. Let's say you made a mistake that caused a project to run over budget. When discussing this situation and its consequences with your boss, you will likely be more passive and apologetic, using your voice and body to support that intention. But if you are leaving a restaurant and you notice a man trying to break into your car, neither passive nor assertive communication will do. As you confront this person, your physical and vocal cues would change: the volume of your voice would rise and your body would probably expand as you approached the would-be thief. Your intention in this scenario—to *confront* or *challenge* the thief—requires being aggressive with your body language and voice.

As these examples show, different circumstances will require different objectives and intentions. However, the usual goal is assertive communication because, in general, people don't want to interact with someone whose communication is predominately passive or aggressive. When you communicate assertively, you are making space for your own thoughts, ideas, and needs without squashing those of the other person. This stance not only relieves your own stress and helps control anger, it also puts your ideas and opinions forward so they can be considered by others. Assertiveness can deepen trust and foster respect within relationships, both business and social, by keeping all channels of communication open between parties.

If you find that you tend to be at one end or the other of the assertiveness spectrum—that is, you are usually passive or usually aggressive—here are some ways to be more assertive with your individual communication:

Use "I" statements. To truly show assertiveness, it is helpful to use "I" statements as much as possible. "I disagree" sounds less accusatory than "You're wrong." By using "I" statements, you are very clearly making your thoughts, feelings, and opinions known to others.

Speak up. People cannot be expected to read your mind; therefore, if you have ideas or opinions that you feel should be seriously considered, share them. If you want something, ask for it; if you need assistance, make a request. This means using your voice effectively, commanding attention so that you can clearly articulate your position.

Challenge respectfully. If you have a strong and differing opinion about something that is being discussed, raise those concerns openly. State your objections unequivocally and explain the reasons why you disagree. Make your point or state your request confidently, without apology or vacillation, but also without attacking those who differ from you.

Learn to say no. If a request is not feasible or realistic, it is perfectly acceptable to say no. Acknowledge the person making the request and give a brief and truthful explanation as to why you are saying no. If it is possible to find a compromise or fulfill the request under different circumstances, share those options or offer alternatives.

Be firm but not rigid. Be open to the ideas of others and listen actively, but be firm in the delivery of your own. Be willing to defend your idea or push for your request; be empathetic but don't give in too easily or without clearly defending your position.

Get comfortable with conflict. A certain amount of creative conflict can be healthy when a group is brainstorming or trying to reach a consensus. Challenge others if you feel you have better ideas or options to contribute. This does not mean being disagreeable just for the sake of disagreeing. Play devil's advocate; ask questions and explore ideas from all angles.

Use body language. As with anything else, your physical cues must support your intention. If your intention is to persuade or excite, your facial expressions and body language must clearly communicate this. An assertive intention must be supported by an assertive delivery. Use appropriate gestures to express your passion for the ideas or positions you are putting forward.

Look others in the eye. You can't be assertive if you don't make eye contact with the people you are talking to. By looking them in the eye and holding their gaze, you will signal that you are serious and committed to the ideas you are putting forward. When interacting with others, whether you are negotiating, giving criticism, or providing information, it is important to clearly understand how others perceive you.

If the way people see you is not the way you would like to be seen, you can change their perception by adjusting your intention cues and delivery. Do you need to listen more and talk less? Should you be more conscious of your nonverbal habits such as sighs or eye rolling? Should your eye contact be more direct or less direct? What is the essence of *you*? And how can you adjust the ways in which you communicate with others to project a more positive and persuasive presence? To have a positive impact on others, you first need to understand how you are perceived and how you communicate. Bring yourself to the party and let your individuality inform your communication. Or as Stanislavski put it, "Always act in your own person ... you can never get away from yourself."[12]

GAINING COMMITMENT

The final stage of persuasive communication often involves gaining commitment—coming to an agreement, getting buy-in, closing a deal, arriving at consensus. This process needs to be handled carefully and done thoroughly. According to Janine Driver in *You Say More Than You Think*, "Up to 90% of success in selling depends on your skills for establishing rapport with your prospect or customer."[13] All successful negotiations trade in trust and credibility, and the way you communicate with others throughout the process will help determine how successful you are in the end. If you have not properly established trust and credibility early on, and if you have not developed and maintained the relationship with care, you will have a difficult time gaining the commitment you seek. Gaining commitment too quickly or without a proper foundation of trust only creates the illusion of success. Making the commitment hold or pay off in the long term is the real test. When convincing or persuading, you are not only selling your message, you are selling yourself as the messenger. As Annette Simmons points out in *The Story Factor*, "When you fail to influence, it is often because people filter your words through negative suspicions about your intentions."[14] In every interaction, remember the three elements of Aristotle's triangle. To be persuasive you must bring your passion, your sincerity, and your credibility—all in one complete package.

> *You don't lead by pointing and telling people some place to go. You lead by going to that place and making a case.*
>
> —KEN KESEY

If you are attempting to gain commitment as a result of your communication, here are some effective approaches:

Tout the benefits. Don't be shy about providing concrete and specific details about how your program or plan could have a positive effect on productivity or the bottom line. Don't assume your audience is already aware of this information. And don't be afraid of the word *no*. A no is not a final curtain; it is a pause in the action and a redirection. Let the closing of one door be the opening of another.

Uncover their needs. Spend as much time as necessary gathering information. Analyze your audience ahead of time so you clearly understand their goals and expectations for your meeting or presentation. By being aware of past buying patterns, previous vendors, and present pain points, you will be more prepared to meet their needs and give them what they want. The more you can make your unknowns known, the more prepared you will be to deliver your message.

Ask questions effectively. In a situation where you are attempting to persuade, questions not only build rapport but also serve to confirm understanding and uncover information. Asking a close-ended question such as "How long were you at your last job?" is effective when all you want is a short, specific answer. Open-ended questions cannot be answered with a simple yes or no; they are designed to encourage a more detailed response, to reveal the feelings, opinions, or knowledge of the other person. Open-ended questions often begin with "How," "Why," or "Tell me about . . ."

Suggest alternatives. If you notice sudden resistance to or lack of interest in an aspect of your program or proposal, don't hesitate to shift gears and offer an alternative that might meet the client's needs more effectively. People generally appreciate being given choices, so offer one or more opportunities to consider various possibilities before making a final decision. As you prepare for your meeting or presentation, identify the various options available to you and be ready with backup plans or alternate ideas.

Listen actively. This means listening with your eyes as well as your ears. Listen not only to what the client or customer is saying but also to the way they are saying it. Also, pay attention to what they are *not* saying. Stay attuned to the signals coming from the other party and adjust your intention as necessary. If you sense apprehension, your intention should be to reassure the other person. If you sense indecisiveness, your intention should be to build excitement.

Don't oversell. People do not like to feel that they are being sold to, so be careful about going overboard with your pitch or proposal. Avoid the hard sell at all costs. Don't rush your delivery and don't oversell; it is always better to under promise and over deliver than the opposite. Be sincere with what you can offer and factual about when you can deliver it. And when it comes to cost, be upfront. Clearly state the *benefit* you can provide to your audience and drive it home through your intention.

Use trial closes. An effective way to gauge a listener's level of interest in what you are proposing is to attempt a *trial close*. A trial close is a question meant to determine how close you are to an agreement. Trial closes could involve asking, "What would it take to get a commitment from you on this project?" or "Do you think this is something we will be able to initiate in the next two weeks?" As you feel the process getting closer to commitment, float a trial close to your client to test your assumptions about the possibility of an agreement.

Bring the passion. People are drawn to others who are passionate and excited, so make sure your body language and voice communicate passion about your program or product. Be sincere, be engaged, and be *present* in your presentation.

Ask for a commitment. As with anyone who is attempting to persuade or influence an audience, at a certain point, you need to be prepared to ask for commitment. As the great hockey player Wayne Gretzky once said, "You miss every shot you don't take."[15] So don't be afraid to ask for the sale or push for buy-in once you've made your case and earned the right to do so. Be assertive in your "ask." This is not the time to hesitate, waver, or retreat from your intention.

GETTING BUY-IN FROM SENIOR LEADERSHIP

All audiences are not created equal, and those that are higher in status or influence than you can often present distinct challenges. Seeking buy-in from senior leadership can often test even the most skilled communicator. High-level executives often have limited time and tunnel vision, which can make them particularly challenging audiences.

To present successfully to senior leaders, remember these tips:

Know the personalities involved. Does this group like information to be communicated through visual aids? Does a particular client prefer to consider information for a few days before making a decision or do they usually just go with their gut instinct and say yes or no on the spot? Is price likely to be the deciding factor or are other factors more important? Seek out information by asking questions of others who have dealt with these executives so you know what to expect.

Let them know what you want up front. If they want to know the price and that is at the end of your presentation, give it to them right away and then spend the rest of your presentation explaining why it is a great investment or purchase.

Stay within your area of expertise. You are the expert on what you are prepared to present, so don't stray too far away from topics or material with which you are familiar. If a question or comment comes up that you can't answer knowledgeably straight off, acknowledge the question, offer to do some further research, and assure your audience that you will share your findings with them when you have done so.

Offer choices and alternatives. While developing your material, put together some options and alternatives to your various points. That way, if you experience resistance, you have something else ready to offer as another choice.

Be flexible with your presentation or message. When you're dealing with senior leaders or influential clients, a new topic may arise that supersedes the topic that you are speaking about currently. It's up to you to stay nimble as a presenter and be able to shift to a different area or a different topic to accommodate the executive or client's request, provided you are sufficiently knowledgeable in the new subject. Listen for subtext or subtle clues in the responses you are receiving from audience members and adjust your intention and delivery accordingly.

PROVIDING FEEDBACK

Whether you are the parent of a teenager or the manager of a shipping company, you will need to provide feedback or criticism to another person from time to time. People cannot grow and learn without feedback and coaching. Stanislavski stressed the importance of constructive criticism and honest feedback for actors. "Fear your admirers!" he warned. "Learn in time to hear, understand and love the cruel truth about yourselves."[16] Unfortunately, most people are not very good at providing feedback unless it is positive.

But being able to clearly and concisely deliver feedback in a work context is an essential skill for a manager, supervisor, or team lead. It is also vital in a marriage and when raising children. People want to feel appreciated and valued as part of a family or organization, and the way you communicate feedback to them will help achieve that. Without timely and well-founded feedback people can become resentful and irritable. Teamwork and morale can suffer. Poorly delivered feedback—incomplete, abusive, or sporadic—can have bad results, too. On the flip side, when feedback is handled well by a leader or manager, it can result in higher employee satisfaction.

Anyone who manages people, leads a team, or runs a business understands the importance of delivering feedback or criticism to others. Feedback, when delivered effectively, can celebrate success and motivate the uninspired. In all instances, providing feedback (whether it is positive or negative) is always done to accomplish the same goal: to improve performance. Whether your audience is an individual, a team, a client, or an entire workforce, constant and thorough feedback is necessary for individuals to grow and prosper. If feedback is neglected, or worse yet, delivered ineffectively, it can be counterproductive, and performance may suffer instead of improve.

A 2004 poll of five thousand adult workers in the United States found that only 43 percent were happy with their current bosses.[17] And it is safe to assume this number is so low at least partly because the bosses are such poor communicators. According to a Gallup poll, "a bad relationship with the boss" was the number one reason people gave for quitting their job.[18] What the poll found, emphatically, is that "employees leave supervisors, not companies." The ability to provide honest, constructive opinions about another person's performance is an essential skill required of an effective communicator. And, as with all communication, intention is a vital tool for putting the message across successfully. Here's a story about how intention comes into play when providing feedback to others:

Mujib Shaikh grew up in Mumbai, India, and at the age of eighteen, he joined the armed forces. During his time as a soldier, he learned discipline and how to follow orders. Years later, when he left the army to join the corporate world, Mujib brought along with him the discipline and work ethic that had served him so well as a soldier, and he quickly climbed the corporate ladder. But he also brought with him another habit he had developed as a soldier, this one not so helpful: he rarely smiled. Even Mujib's wife complained to him about how serious he always looked, and his team members found him to be intimidating and unapproachable as a manager. Generally a happy and fun-loving person, Mujib was genuinely puzzled by this reaction to him.

One day Mujib called one of his subordinates into his office. She was an exemplary employee and the management team had decided to reward her with a much-deserved promotion. She entered his office and took a seat and Mujib began to speak. After only a few sentences, the woman suddenly burst into tears! Shocked, Mujib asked her what was wrong. When pressed, the employee confessed that the look she saw on Mujib's face when she entered his office seemed so stern and serious, she was certain she was about to be fired. Though Mujib's intention was to commend the employee, his facial expression actually ended up communicating the exact opposite effect.

The lesson? An intention needs to solicit an emotional response, but you want it to be the *correct* emotional response. You can't afford to have your communication be misinterpreted by an audience, and this may be especially so when giving feedback, due to the potential for the receiver to feel hurt or defensive. Before you begin, try to pinpoint what emotional reaction you would like your audience to have as a result of hearing your message. Do you want them to leave feeling happy, challenged, inspired, confident? Choosing your intention and focusing on it will hone the delivery of your feedback.

Mike Quade, the former manager of the Chicago Cubs, discussed his thoughts on providing feedback to his team in an interview with *Chicago* magazine, saying, "You have to have the communicative skills to get through to people. The communication is what's most important—relating to your guys and getting them to buy into something. Part of that process is being flexible. I might have one thing I want to communicate but have to communicate it three different ways to three different people."[19] If you are tasked with delivering bad news to someone you know to be defensive, you will need to be aware of your intention cues and perhaps be a bit more assertive with your delivery. If another person reacts emotionally, you may need to soften your delivery to prevent the person from overreacting or bursting into tears.

Certainly, no one likes to deliver bad news. It is an uncomfortable situation for both the sender and the receiver of the message. The playwright Noel Coward once remarked, "I love criticism, just so long as it is unqualified praise."[20] Unfortunately for Mr. Coward and the rest of us, not all feedback is positive—but being able to deliver difficult news or offer constructive criticism is something that communicators must be comfortable doing. Whether informing someone that they are being terminated, delivering a negative financial statement, or explaining why an employee will not be getting a raise, delivering the information in a meaningful and compassionate way will help make this challenging communication easier for all parties involved.

One of the most important things you can do is hear criticism of yourself and embrace it.

—LEONARDO DICAPRIO

But even the best communicators can struggle when delivering negative or unpleasant news to others. Mistakes are common when we initiate these difficult types of conversations. Because emotions are often involved, these mistakes may not only cause damage to morale and reputations, they may also erode trust and increase anxiety within a family or organization. The following tips can help you put critical feedback across fairly and constructively:

State feedback in clear and absolute terms. Be very clear with the criticism or feedback so there is no confusion or opportunity for your message to be misinterpreted or misconstrued. Let the other person know that these points are not up for debate. These are facts that need to be addressed and that is why you are there.

Address only the issues at hand. Resist the urge to lump other issues or concerns into the same conversation. Stick to the points you are there to discuss and only those. If the other person starts to bring up unrelated topics, steer the conversation back to the business at hand.

Keep feedback professional and not personal. Make the feedback or criticism about the person's performance or abilities and not about their personality or character. This will help to take the emotional charge out of the conversation.

Ensure the feedback is timely. Don't wait until it is too late to provide criticism to the person. Try to deliver the feedback so that the other person has a sufficient amount of time to improve upon the areas being discussed.

Maintain consistent eye contact. As discussed, you can't be assertive without making eye contact with the other person. The information you are providing may be hard for someone to hear. Have the courtesy to look them in the eye while you are providing it.

Monitor body language. Keep an eye on the other person's body language for any intention cues that show how they are feeling about the information you have just delivered. Remember, a person's face and body are billboards giving off a myriad of specific messages. Make sure you are reading them.

Anticipate comments and questions. After hearing criticism or feedback, people will often have questions or comments regarding the information that has just been shared. Be prepared for and open to that. Once you have delivered the feedback, allow the person to share thoughts or ask questions about it; let them speak. Don't interrupt until they have completed their thought, otherwise you run the risk of appearing defensive or uncaring.

Use examples and anecdotes to build connections. If possible, use stories or anecdotes to show empathy and help describe a path forward. Personal stories are even better, especially if there is a core theme that relates to the person's current situation.

Offer support and guidance. End your communication by offering help or guidance to the person. If there is a possible path forward, help put together a plan for improvement. To quote Abraham Lincoln, "He has a right to criticize, who has a heart to help."

Stay in control. You are creating a lasting impression in the eyes of the other person. They are looking to you, so be assertive; control the interaction from start to finish to ensure that the perception you are creating in that person will elicit the reaction you seek.

If you are uncomfortable providing criticism or delivering difficult news, a three-step process called the "sandwich technique" can help. The sandwich technique works like this: you start with a positive statement—a very quick bit of honest praise or good news—up front; then you move on to the main criticism or challenge you are there to discuss. Once you have delivered the main message, you end with another brief statement that is either positive or complimentary. By sandwiching your critical feedback between two positive statements, you soften the blow for your listener and provide a useful structure for the message itself. If you do choose to use positive statements before and after your feedback or criticism, be sincere about what you are saying; after all, this goes to your credibility. Also, keep the positive remarks short and direct (remember primacy and recency, which can work against you in this instance if you are not careful); resist spending too much time on small talk before getting to the challenge or criticism. Otherwise it will look like you are stalling or uncomfortable addressing the subject at hand. When you get to the criticism, do your best to be assertive, honest, and forthcoming. People will more readily accept bad news if the messenger is clear and candid.

DELIVERING BAD NEWS

The company is being downsized. There will be no salary increases this year. The project won't be completed on time. All of these situations are bad news to someone, but as professionals, we often have these types of messages to impart. No one likes to deliver news that is negative in nature; it is difficult for both the sender and the receiver of the information. Think of the bad news you have had to deliver in the past week. How did you feel having to deliver it? And how did the person receiving it react? As Lee Iacocca, the former CEO of Chrysler, advises, "Communication has to start with telling the truth, even when it's painful."[21]

Whether the topic is a termination, a negative financial statement, or the lack of a raise, an assertive yet compassionate delivery will help make this challenging communication easier for all parties involved. This is not to say such conversations can ever be made easy—especially since they often involve a person's livelihood, and strong emotions will be involved.

Here are some guidelines for delivering difficult news effectively:

Be direct. Don't make the mistake of spending too much time on small talk before delivering your difficult news. Use the feedback sandwich if that is helpful, but get to the meat promptly. Greet the audience, whether it's one person or many, thank them for coming in to speak with you, and get to it. Otherwise it will look like you are stalling or afraid to address the subject at hand.

Provide context. Employees will want to know who made the decision, why it was made, and what led up to it. Take the time to clearly explain the details so that there is no confusion as to what led to this decision being made.

Time it right. As Colin Powell once said, "Bad news is not like wine; it doesn't get better with age."[22] Many people make it harder than necessary to deliver difficult news because they wait too long to do it. If you screwed up, admit it. If your calculations were off, own up to it. Don't delay the inevitable and don't dole out bad news in dribs and drabs. Be honest and forthcoming. People will more readily accept bad news if the messenger is upfront and candid.

Don't make assumptions. You can't know just how an employee or client will handle the bad news. People are all different, and the way they process bad news is different as well. Consider the personalities involved as well as the various reactions they could have, stay open during the conversation, and listen actively.

Be prepared for questions. Before you deliver the difficult news, take some time to anticipate what questions might be asked. Why did you do it that way? How could you let this happen? Whose fault is this? These are all questions that are likely to arise. Think about how you will handle each of these questions ahead of time.

Look the person in the eye. While it can certainly be a challenge to maintain eye contact with a person while giving them bad news, it is an essential element for this type of communication. If you avoid eye contact you will appear less than confident and could be perceived as not being completely truthful.

Watch your body language. Be conscious of what your body language is conveying and make sure your cues support your intention, whether that intention is to reprimand, challenge, reassure, or motivate. By controlling your intention cues, you will be able to project an assertive and confident presence.

Don't minimize the event. Try to understand the emotions that someone is experiencing as a result of hearing the news that you have just given them. Because they are reading your body language as you deliver it, be careful not to appear too casual or flippant.

Show empathy. If this news were being delivered to you, what reaction would you have? What emotions would you be feeling? Considering these questions will give rise to empathy, and your listener will pick up on it. Be conscious of what your voice and body language might be conveying and make sure they support your intention at all times. As the nineteenth-century historian Joel Tyler Headley advised, "Like a fine actor, [a speaker] must study the hearts of others ... if he would awaken sympathy."[23]

Do it in person. While it is sometimes easier to simply compose an e-mail and deliver bad news to an employee electronically, this is not an effective way to handle this type of communication. Being assertive means sitting down with the person face-to-face to share the news and discuss the situation.

Don't let emotions get in the way. It is important that you remain calm and collected during the delivery of difficult news, even if the other person becomes angry or emotional. Resist the urge to strike back or be insulting. Simply present the facts in a clear and honest way. This will help strip the exchange of emotional heat.

Apologize. If you have made a mistake that has caused the problem being discussed, own it. Take responsibility. Offer a sincere apology and assure the other party that a problem such as this will not happen again. Detail specifically how you are going to correct the situation or what steps you are going take to prevent it from happening again in the future.

Whether delivering bad news, attempting to gain commitment, or offering your honest opinion to a friend or coworker, doing it in an assertive manner will not only help you solidify trust with that person, it will give you credibility. Whether your intention is to reprimand or commend, to apologize or reassure, make sure your verbal and nonverbal cues are congruent and clear as you pursue your given objective.

Conclusion

Work makes the journeyman.
—Johann Wolfgang von Goethe

Finishing this book, like completing a great training or workshop, is not an event—it is the beginning of a process. You are now aware of the individual building blocks that make up effective communication; going forward, it is up to you to put those tools and techniques to work for you. As we have emphasized throughout this book, retention is the key to improving your personal communication, so review, rehearse, reprocess, and repeat these techniques and methods as much as possible. As any actor, athlete, or musician understands, the minute you stop honing your skills, you begin to regress. Without frequent practice, trumpet players lose their lip, pitchers lose their fastball, and actors lose their ability to think on their feet. The same holds true for anyone who has to communicate regularly with others. Don't get lazy or complacent; it is easy to let bad habits slip back into your communication style. It's up to you to make sure you don't abandon the building blocks discussed in the preceding pages. Never settle. Good enough rarely is. Harness the power of intention to actively pursue objectives in every communication you deliver.

Take the time to implement a personal action plan for yourself that will allow you to continue refining your skills. Sharpen these techniques through *doing*. Create a workspace for yourself as Demosthenes did with his stone bunker. Find a preparation partner and agree to give each other encouragement and honest feedback. Be open to criticism. Drill. Videotape yourself. Analyze your communications. Monitor your progress and make sure you are continuing to use these tools and techniques as you continue your individual journey. When it comes to improving your communication, don't focus on perfection—focus on progress. The goal is to strive for 100 percent awareness as a communicator.

The information you've learned in *The Pin Drop Principle* will not take you to the end of the journey toward becoming a more engaging and influential communicator; it will only supply you with the tools for a stellar beginning. Where you go from here is completely up to you. We wish you the best of luck. Get out there and be amazing.

Notes

Introduction

1. "Meetings in America: A Study of Trends, Costs and Attitudes Toward Business Travel, Teleconferencing, and Their Impact on Productivity," A network MCI Conferencing White Paper, INFOCOMM, 1998; available online: https://e-meetings.verizonbusiness.com/global/en/meetingsinamerica/uswhitepaper.php; access date: January 9, 2012.
2. "Meetings in America."
3. *Us Magazine*, January 31, 2011.
4. Erving Goffman, *The Presentation of Self in Everyday Life* (Garden City, NJ: Doubleday Anchor, 1959), p. xi.
5. Lou Cannon, *President Reagan: The Role of a Lifetime* (New York: Public Affairs, 1991), p. 20.
6. Cannon, *President Reagan*, p. 35.
7. James Hunt, Richard Osborn, and John Schermerhorn, *Organizational Behavior* (Hoboken, NJ: Wiley, 2002), p. 190.
8. Interview on *The Colbert Report*, October 4, 2011.
9. Ken Howard, *Act Natural: How to Speak to Any Audience* (New York: Random House, 2003), pp. 6–9.

Chapter 1

1. Constantin Stanislavski, *An Actor Prepares* (New York: Theatre Arts, 1936).
2. Constantin Stanislavski, *An Actor's Handbook* (New York: Theatre Arts, 1963), p. 103.
3. Stanislavski, *An Actor Prepares*, p. 137.
4. Peter Guber, *Tell to Win* (New York: Crown Business, 2011), p. 174.
5. Daniel J. Siegel, *The Mindful Brain: Reflection and Attunement in the Cultivation of Well-Being* (New York: Norton, 2007), p. 276.
6. Siegel, *The Mindful Brain*, p. 206.
7. Uta Hagen, *Respect for Acting* (New York: Macmillan, 1973), p. 71.

Chapter 2

1. Robert Dickman and Richard Maxwell, *The Elements of Persuasion* (New York: HarperBusiness, 2007), p. 125.
2. Dickman and Maxwell, *The Elements of Persuasion*, p. 5.
3. William R. Cupach and Brian H. Spitzberg, *The Dark Side of Relationships II* (New York: Routledge, 2010), p. 63.
4. Jason Hensel, "Once Upon a Time," *One + Magazine*, February 2010, p. 80.
5. Greg J. Stephens, Lauren J. Silbert, and Uri Hasson, "Speaker-Listener Neural Coupling Underlies Successful Communication" (*Proceedings of the National Academy of Sciences of the United States of America*, June 18, 2010).
6. Kelley Griffith, *Writing Essays About Literature* (Boston: Wadsworth, Cengage Learning, 2002), p. 52.
7. Gene Wilder, *Kiss Me Like a Stranger: My Search for Love and Art* (New York: St. Martin's Press, 2005), p. 127.
8. Dickman and Maxwell, *The Elements of Persuasion*, p. 46.
9. David Ball, *Backwards and Forwards* (Carbondale: Southern Illinois University Press, 1983), p. 34.
10. Richard Corliss, "Super 8: Just as Great as You Hoped It Would Be," *Time*, June 2, 2011.
11. Terry M. Levy, *Handbook of Attachment Interventions* (San Diego, CA: Academic Press, 2000), p. 77.
12. Mayo Clinic Staff, "Stress Relief from Laughter? Yes, No Joke," Mayo Clinic, July 23, 2010; available online: www.mayoclinic.com/health/stress-relief/SR00034; access date: January 9, 2012.
13. Cameron Lynne Macdonald and Marek Korczynski, *Service Work: Critical Perspectives* (New York: Routledge, 2009), p. 25.

14. Sarah Kay, "How I Got the Courage to Tell My Story," cnn.com, May 1, 2011; available online: http://articles.cnn.com/2011-05-01/opinion/kay .spoken.poetry_1_stories-anansi-word-poetry?_s=PM:OPINION; access date: January 9, 2012.

Chapter 3

1. Garry Wills, *Lincoln at Gettysburg: The Words That Remade America* (New York: Simon & Schuster, 1992), p. 36.
2. Stephen Sondheim, "Master of the Musical," comments at Academy of Achievement, Los Angeles, July 5, 2005.
3. James C. Humes, *Speak Like Churchill, Stand Like Lincoln* (New York: Three Rivers Press, 2002), p. 26.
4. David Sousa, *How the Brain Learns*, 4th ed. (London: Corwin Press, 2011), p. 95.
5. Roy Peter Clark, *Writing Tools* (New York: Little, Brown, 2006), p. 101.
6. Kathleen Parker, "Something Different This Way Comes," *Newsweek*, June 19, 2011.
7. Evan Thomas, "Learning from LBJ," *Newsweek*, March 25, 2010.
8. Peter Burrows, Ira Sager, and Andy Reinhardt, "Back to the Future at Apple," *Businessweek*, May 25, 1998.
9. Peter Archer, *The Quotable Intellectual* (Avon, MA: Adams Media, 2010), p. 209.
10. George A. Miller, "The Magic Number Seven, Plus or Minus Two: Some Limits on Our Capacity for Processing Information," *Psychological Review*, 63, no. 2 (1956): 81–97.
11. TED: Ideas Worth Spreading, "Helen Fisher Tells Us Why We Love + Cheat," February 2006; available online: www.ted.com/talks/helen _fisher_tells_us_why_we_love_cheat.html; access date: January 9, 2012.

Chapter 4

1. Josh Levine, *Jerry Seinfeld: Much Ado About Nothing* (Toronto: ECW Press, 1993).
2. Lybi Ma, "Fighting Stage Fright," *Psychology Today*, December 6, 2005.
3. Malcolm Gladwell, *Outliers* (New York: Little, Brown, 2008), p. 40.
4. *Talking Funny*, HBO Studio Productions; Director: John Moffitt; April 20, 2011.
5. Constantin Stanislavski, *An Actor's Handbook* (New York: Theatre Arts Books, 1963), p. 70.

6.   Ma, "Fighting Stage Fright."

7.   "Proust Questionnaire," *Vanity Fair*, April 2011.

8.   Robert Dickman and Richard Maxwell, *The Elements of Persuasion* (New York: HarperBusiness, 2007), p. 30.

9.   Uta Hagen, *Respect for Acting* (New York: Macmillan, 1973), p. 202.

10. Alice Park, "The Two Faces of Anxiety," *Newsweek*, December 5, 2011, p. 59.

11. Park, "The Two Faces of Anxiety," p. 65.

12. Michael J. Mosley and Nicholas Rossiter, producers, *The Human Face*, BBC Warner, Wednesdays, March 7–28, 2001.

13. Park, "The Two Faces of Anxiety," p. 62.

14. Hans Selye, "Confusion and Controversy in the Stress Field," *Journal of Human Stress* 1, no. 2 (1975): 37–44.

15. Casey Schwartz, "High on Anxiety," *Newsweek*, February 6, 2011.

16. Schwartz, "High on Anxiety."

17. Matthew Belloni and Stephen Galloway, "Hollywood Actresses Recount Career Challenges," *Hollywood Reporter*, January 2, 2011.

18. Nick Summers, "Why Winners Win at . . . ," *Newsweek*, June 11, 2011.

19. Stephen Cope, *The Wisdom of Yoga: A Seeker's Guide to Extraordinary Living* (New York: Bantam Books, 2006), p. 213.

20. Chuck Thompson, "You're Breathing All Wrong," *Men's Health*, June 18, 2009.

21. Jacqueline Stenson, "Exercise May Make You a Better Worker," MSNBC.com, July 12, 2005.

22. Ben Court, "27 Ways to Power Up Your Brain," *Men's Health*, December 2011, p. 122.

23. Rex B. Kline, Principles and Practice of Structural Equation Modeling, 3rd Ed. (New York: Guilford Press, 2011), p. 3.

Chapter 5

1.   David Greenberg, "Rewinding the Kennedy-Nixon Debates," *Slate*, September 24, 2010.

2.   Allan Pease and Barbara Pease, *The Definitive Book of Body Language* (New York: Bantam Dell, 2006), p. 10.

3.   Tim Padgett, "The Interrupted Reading: The Kids with George W. Bush on 9/11," *Time*, May 3, 2011.

4.   Andrew D. Wolvin, *Listening and Human Communication in the 21st Century* (Oxford, UK: Wiley-Blackwell, 2010), p. 143.

5.   Peter Guber, *Tell to Win* (New York: Crown Business, 2011), p. 243.

6. Ann M. Kring and Albert H. Gordon, "Sex Differences in Emotion: Expression, Experience, and Physiology," *Journal of Personality and Social Psychology*, 74, no. 3 (1998): 686–703.

7. Albert Mehrabian, *Silent Messages* (Belmont, CA: Wadsworth, 1972).

8. Constantin Stanislavski, *Building a Character* (New York: Routledge/ Theatre Arts Books, 1949), p. 276.

9. Erica Daniels, interview with G. Riley Mills, September 2011.

10. Carol Kinsey Goman, "Seven Seconds to Make a First Impression," *Forbes*, February 13, 2011.

11. Malcolm Gladwell, *Blink* (New York: Little, Brown, 2005), p. 13.

12. Deanna Davis, *The Law of Attraction in Action* (New York: Perigee/ Penguin, 2008), p. 17.

13. Gordon W. Hewes, "World Distribution of Certain Postural Habits," *American Anthropologist*, 57, no. 2 (1955): 231.

14. Ewan Ingleby, Dawn Joyce, and Sharon Powell, *Learning to Teach in the Lifelong Learning Sector* (London: Continuum International, 2010), p. 78.

15. Dustin Goot, "Baffled by Body Language?" *Happen*, n.d.; available online: www.match.com/magazine/article/7587/; access date: January 9, 2012.

16. Constantin Stanislavski, *An Actor Prepares* (New York: Theatre Arts, Inc., 1936), p. 107.

17. Janine Driver, *You Say More Than You Think* (New York: Crown, 2010), p. 66.

18. Ann Demarais and Valerie White, *First Impressions: What You Don't Know About How Others See You* (New York: Bantam Dell, 2005), p. 62.

19. Stefan H. Verstappen, *Chinese Business Etiquette: The Practical Pocket Guide* (Stone Bridge Press, 2008), p. 64; Harry Mills, *Artful Persuasion: How to Command Attention, Change Minds, and Influence People* (New York: AMACOM, 2000), p. 47; George Henderson, Dorscine Spigner-Littles, and Virginia H. Milhouse, *A Practitioner's Guide to Understanding Indigenous and Foreign Cultures* (Springfield, IL: Charles C. Thomas, 2006), p. 178.

20. William F. Morrison, *The Savvy Negotiator* (New York: Praeger, 2006), p. 104.

21. Judy Foreman, "A Conversation with Paul Ekman: The 43 Facial Muscles That Reveal Even the Most Fleeting Emotions," *New York Times*, August 5, 2003.

22. Paul Ekman, *Emotions Revealed* (New York: Henry Holt, 2003), p. 14. See also Gladwell, *Blink*, p. 201.

23. Tim Sanders, *The Likeability Factor* (New York: Three Rivers Press, 2005), p. 175.

24. Ekman, *Emotions Revealed*, p. 58.

25. Michael J. Mosley and Nicholas Rossiter, producers, *The Human Face*, BBC Warner, March 7–28, 2001.

26. Edward T. Hall, *The Silent Language* (New York: Anchor Books, 1959), back cover.

27. Roger Axtell, *Gestures: The DO's and TABOOS of Body Language Around the World* (Hoboken, NJ: Wiley, 1998), p. 7.

28. Constantin Stanislavski, *An Actor's Handbook* (New York: Theatre Arts, 1963), p. 66.

29. Desmond Marvin Morris, *Body Watching* (New York: Crown, 1985), pp. 229–236.

30. Uta Hagen, *Respect for Acting* (New York: Macmillan, 1973), p. 69.

31. Sean Graney, interview with G. Riley Mills, August 2011.

32. Edward T. Hall, *The Hidden Dimension* (New York: Doubleday, 1966), pp. 116–124.

33. Stanislavski, *An Actor's Handbook*, p. 39.

34. David Givens, *Love Signals* (New York: St. Martin's Press, 2005).

35. Eliza Ridgeway, "When a Woman Should Act Like a Man," CNN, April 5, 2011.

36. Peter Tyson, "Monkey Do, Monkey See," *NOVA*, January 1, 2005.

37. Julia Cort, "Mirror Neurons," *NOVA*, aired January 25, 2005, on PBS.

38. Sanders, *The Likeability Factor*, p. 102.

Chapter 6

1. Christopher Hitchens, "Unspoken Truths," *Vanity Fair*, June 2011.

2. Jenevora Williams, "The Developing Voice," 2006; available online: www.vocalprocess.co.uk/resources/Developing_Voice_presentation.pdf; access date: January 7, 2012.

3. Meredith Melnick, "Want to Be Heard? Try Changing the Way You Talk," *Time*, May 20, 2011.

4. Quoted in B. Griggs, "Why Computer Voices Are Mostly Female," CNN.com, October 21, 2011.

5. Malcolm Gladwell, *Blink* (New York: Little, Brown, 2005), pp. 42–43.

6. Gigi Buffington, interview with G. Riley Mills, October 2011.

7. Richard Payne, *The Vocal Skills Pocketbook* (UK: Management Pocketbooks, 2004), p. 45.

8. Christopher Peterson, "The Good Life," *Psychology Today*, December 31, 2010.

9. Michelle Price, "Close to the Speed of Light: How Fast Are You Trading?" *Financial News*, April 18, 2011.

10. Termite Art Productions, *More Than Human*, Discovery Channel, February 2006.

11. Ralph G. Nichols, "What Can Be Done About Listening?" *Supervisor's Notebook* 22, no. 1, Spring 1960.

12. Payne, *The Vocal Skills Pocketbook*, p. 52.

13. The authors calculated the approximate speaking rates by randomly choosing five one-minute samplings from each speech and then averaging the wpm for each, taking out pauses for applause.

14. Video of the speech is online at www.youtube.com/watch?v= VQmzTjcDqo8; access date: January 7, 2012.

15. Constantin Stanislavski, *Building a Character* (New York: Routledge/ Theatre Arts Books, 1949), p. 140.

16. Constantin Stanislavski, *An Actor's Handbook* (New York: Theatre Arts, 1963), p. 128.

17. Garry Wills, *Lincoln at Gettysburg: The Words That Remade America* (New York: Simon & Schuster, 1992), p. 194; Douglas L. Wilson, "Lincoln the Persuader," *American Scholar*, Autumn 2006).

18. Mark Logue and Peter Conradi, *The King's Speech* (New York: Sterling, 2010), p. 7.

19. Lucian Sulica, M.D., Voice Medicine, New York City. http://www .voicemedicine.com/normal_voice_functioning.htm.

Chapter 7

1. John Francis, *The Ragged Edge of Silence* (Washington, DC: National Geographic), 2011.

2. The International Listening Association quotes Nichols's statement at www.listen.org/Quotations; access date: January 9, 2012.

3. Laura A. Janusik and Andrew D. Wolvin, "24 Hours in a Day: A Listening Update to the Time Studies," paper presented at the annual meeting of the International Listening Association, Salem, Oregon, 2009.

4. Linda T. Kohn, Janet M. Corrigan, and Molla S. Donaldson, *To Err Is Human* (Washington, DC: National Academies Press, 2000), pp. 1–2.

5. Joseph G. Murphy and William F. Dunn, "Medical Errors and Poor Communication," *Chest*, 138 (2010): 1292–1293.

6. Andrew D. Wolvin, *Listening and Human Communication in the 21st Century* (Oxford, UK: Wiley-Blackwell, 2010), p. 77.

7. Kay Lindahl and Amy Schnapper, *The Sacred Art of Listening: Forty Reflections for Cultivating a Spiritual Practice* (Woodstock, VT: Skylight Paths, 2002), p. 89.

8. Ruth G. Newman, Marie A. Danziger, and Mark Cohen, *Communicating in Business Today* (Lexington, MA: D. C. Heath, 1987).

9. Chris Bond, interview with G. Riley Mills, August 2011.

10. Thomas N. Ingram, Raymond W. LaForge, Ramon A. Avila, Charles H. Schwepker, and Michael R. Williams, *Professional Selling: A Trust-Based Approach*, 4th ed. (South-Western College, 2007), p. 119.

11. Judy Pearson, e-mail communication with G. Riley Mills, September 2011.

12. Ralph Nichols, "Listening Is a 10 Part Skill," *Nation's Business*, 45, no. 4 (1957).

13. Joshua Foer, *Moonwalking with Einstein: The Art and Science of Remembering Everything* (New York: Penguin Press, 2011), p. 23.

14. Endel Tulving and Fergus I. M. Craik, *The Oxford Handbook of Memory* (New York: Oxford University Press, 2000), p. 5.

15. Steve Bertrand, interview with G. Riley Mills, August 2011.

Chapter 8

1. Brian Lamb, "Q&A with Frank Mankiewicz," C-SPAN, August 19, 2009; available online: www.c-spanvideo.org/program/288472-1; access date: January 9, 2012.

2. Will Cockrell, "Survival Skills: Craig Venter" (interview), *Men's Journal*, May 20, 2011.

3. Susan Messing, interview with G. Riley Mills, September 2011.

4. These quotes are from a poem compiled from statements made by George W. Bush; available online: www.snopes.com/politics/bush/piehigher.asp; access date: January 7, 2012.

5. Mark Magnacca, *So What? How to Communicate What Really Matters to Your Audience* (Upper Saddle River, NJ: Pearson Education FT Press, 2009), p. 90.

Chapter 9

1. Jason Fried and David Heinemeier-Hansson, *Rework* (New York: Crown Business, 2010), pp. 104–105.

2. Steve Lohr, "Is Information Overload a $650 Billion Drag on the Economy?" *New York Times*, December 20, 2007.

3. Andrew Ross Sorkin, *Too Big to Fail* (New York: Penguin, 2009), p. 66.

4. Mary Fitzgibbons, Michael Mahon, and Amy Maus, *The Care Team Approach: A Problem-Solving Process for Effective School Change* (Washington, DC: National Catholic Education Association, 2008), p. 8.

5. Tony Schwartz and Catherine McCarthy, "Manage Your Energy, Not Your Time," *Harvard Business Review*, October 2007, p. 6.

6. "Ask Men's Health," *Men's Health*, December 2011, p. 26.

7. Matt Richtel, "Growing Up Digital, Wired for Distraction," *New York Times*, November 21, 2010.

8. Kay Dickinson, *Movie Music: The Film Reader* (New York: Routledge, 2003).

9. Matthew A. Killingsworth and Daniel T. Gilbert, "A Wandering Mind Is an Unhappy Mind," *Science*, 330, no. 6006 (2010), 932.

10. Gloria Mark, Victor M. Gonzalez, and Justin Harris, "No Task Left Behind? Examining the Nature of Fragmented Work" (Irvine: University of California, 2005), p. 321.

11. Joan Middendorf and Alan Kalish, "The Change-Up in Lectures," The National Teaching and Learning Forum 5, no. 2 (1996); available online: www.ntlf.com/html/pi/9601/backup/article1.htm; access date: January 9, 2012.

12. Middendorf and Kalish, "The Change-Up in Lectures," p. 2.

13. Constantin Stanislavski, *An Actor's Handbook* (New York: Theatre Arts, 1963), p. 104.

14. Middendorf and Kalish, "The Change-Up in Lectures," p. 2.

15. Kevin R. Thomas and Ralph H. Kilmann, *Thomas-Kilmann Conflict Mode Instrument* (Tuxedo, NY: Xicom, 1974).

16. Thomas and Kilmann, *Thomas-Kilmann Conflict Mode Instrument*.

17. Stanislavski, *An Actor's Handbook*, p. 182.

18. Susan Messing, interview with G. Riley Mills, September 2011.

19. Chris Bond, interview with G. Riley Mills, September 2011.

20. Robert B. Cialdini, *Influence: The Psychology of Persuasion*, rev. ed. (New York: HarperBusiness, 2006), p. 1.

Chapter 10

1. Jeff Youngs, *The RESET Button: How to Move Your Business Forward When There Is No Going Back* (Santa Monica, CA: Youngs Communication, 2010), p. 99.

2. Linda Babcock and Sara Laschever, *Women Don't Ask* (Princeton, NJ: Princeton University Press, 2003), p. 3.

3. Vickie Milazzo, "Do Men Exaggerate Their Work Accomplishments More Than Women?" *Cypress Times*, January 15, 2012.

4. Robert Dickman and Richard Maxwell, *The Elements of Persuasion* (New York: HarperBusiness, 2007), p. 3.

5. Benjamin Toff, "The Snooki Standard," *New York Magazine*, March 6, 2011.

6. Tim Sanders, *The Likeability Factor* (New York: Three Rivers Press, 2005), p. 90.

7. Jeanne Fahnestock and Marie Secor, *A Rhetoric of Argument: Brief Edition* (3rd Ed.) (New York: McGraw-Hill, 2004) p. 19.

8. Sanders, *The Likeability Factor*, p. 127.

9. Iain Murray, "Make 'em Feel the Heat," *National Review*, September 15, 2009.

10. Georg Wilhelm Friedrich Hegel, *The Philosophy of History* (New York: Dover, 1956), p. 22; original publication 1837.

11. Constantin Stanislavski, *An Actor's Handbook* (New York: Theatre Arts, 1963), p. 110.

12. Stanislavski, *An Actor's Handbook*, p. 91.

13. Janine Driver, *You Say More Than You Think* (New York: Crown, 2010), p. 53.

14. Annette Simmons, *The Story Factor* (New York: Basic Books, 2001), p. 118.

15. Brian Tracy, *Create Your Own Future* (Hoboken, NJ: Wiley, 2002), p. 167.

16. Stanislavski, *An Actor's Handbook*, p. 125.

17. Stephen J. Rossetti, "Post Crisis Morale Among Priests," *America*, September 13, 2004.

18. Willow Lawson, "Good Boss, Bad Boss," *Psychology Today*, November 1, 2005.

19. Noah Isackson, "The Wisdom of Coaches," *Chicago Magazine*, April 2011.

20. Colin Jarman, *The Book of Poisonous Quotes* (Chicago: Contemporary Books, 1993), p. 7.

21. Lee Iacocca, *Where Have All the Leaders Gone?* (New York: Scribner, 2007), p. 7.

22. Bradley G. Richardson, *Career Comeback* (New York: Broadway Books, 2004), p. 100.

23. Joel Tyler Headley, *The Handbook of Oratory* (Cornell, NY: Cornell University Library, 1901), p. 283.

Glossary of Terms

Acting As If—A technique used in acting or life that takes advantage of your natural mental and emotional responses to posture and behavior to impose a feeling of confidence or security

Active Listening—A concept pioneered by psychologists Carl R. Rogers and Richard E. Farson that puts forward the idea that listening is not a passive activity but requires energy and effort

Adaptive Unconscious—A set of mental processes influencing judgment and decision making

Articulation—The formation of clear and distinct sounds in speech

Attention Span—The length of time a person can devote to an activity before their mind wanders

Beat—A term first coined by Constantin Stanislavski that signified a transition for an actor from one moment or intention to the next

Belly Button Rule—A term coined by author Janine Driver stating that the direction a person's belly button faces can reflect their attitude and reveal their emotional state

Benefit—Something advantageous or positive that an audience will achieve or receive as a result of hearing your message

Body Language—*Nonverbal communication* such as gestures, postures, and facial expressions that help support a person's intention

Bottler—Someone whose nervous energy manifests itself in stiffness, stillness, or lack of gestures

Bridge—A rhetorical device to allow someone to move smoothly from one topic to another

Burner—Someone whose nervous energy manifests itself in excessive or extraneous movement and gesturing

Butterflies—Tremors felt in the stomach region due to nervousness

Button—A device used to signal to an audience that you have completed a topic or thought and are about to move on to something new

Callback—A rhetorical device in which a speaker revisits a previously discussed fact or subject for emphasis

Checkback—A technique used by a speaker when answering a question to confirm that the answer given is satisfactory to the person who asked it

Climax—The highest point of tension in a story; the major turning point in the plot

Close-Ended Question—A question that can be answered with a simple yes-or-no answer, or with one specific piece of information

Coding—The act of marking your material with specific notations to remind you of various actions to take or techniques to employ—and where to use them—during your communication

Cognitive Nervousness—Anxiety relating to or involving thinking, reasoning, or remembering

Communication—The process of sending and receiving messages with attached meaning

Conflict-Resolution Chain—A tool for a facilitator to employ to effectively manage conflict within a group

Congruence—The state in which all aspects of voice and body language perfectly support a communicator's intention

Connector Statement—A phrase used to connect an answer to the question asked

Core Breathing—The low belly breath used by actors and singers for maximum support; also called *diaphragmatic breathing*

Core Theme—The main idea or concept of your message, distilled down to a single phrase or headline

Creative Visualization—The art of using mental imagery and affirmation to produce positive changes in your performance or life

Critical Inner Voice—Any negative thoughts or insecurities that can distract or cause anxiousness in a speaker

C-Suite—The senior group of officers in a business organization who have the word "chief" in their titles

Devil's Advocate—One who argues against a cause or position, not as a committed opponent but simply for the sake of argument or to determine the validity of the cause or position itself

Distress—Negative stress; threat stress that causes strain, anxiety, or suffering

Engagement—A connection with an audience that finds them in a willing state of attentiveness during your communication

Eustress—Positive stress; challenge stress that is healthy or provides fulfillment

Exposition—The basic information (who, what, when, where) an audience needs to know to be able to follow a story

Extemporaneous Speaking—The delivery mode used by speakers that reduces content or material to slides, notes, or bullet points from which the speaker makes up the narrative commentary on the spot

External Noise—Distractions caused by a noisy environment, poor acoustics, inadequate amplification, or disruptive audience members

Falling Action—The short series of events in a story immediately following the climax and just before the final resolution is reached

Forgetting Curve—The concept developed by German psychologist Hermann Ebbinghaus that discusses the decline in retention of information in individuals

Gesture—Any movement of the hand, arm, body, head, or face that communicates a specific idea, opinion, or emotion

Glossophobia—Greek term for stage fright or speech anxiety

Ground Rules—Guidelines for individual and team behavior

Home Base Position—The relaxed, open body position that serves as a communicator's physical neutral when not moving or gesturing

Hook—A device used at the beginning of a presentation to capture an audience's attention and compel them to continue listening

Idiomatic Expression—An expression whose meaning is not predictable from the usual meanings of its constituent elements (such as *kick the bucket* or *cut the waffle*)

Impromptu Speaking—A delivery mode in which someone is called upon to speak without preparation or notes

Inciting Incident—The event in a story that serves as a trigger to set the initial events or action in motion

Incongruence—The state of someone's delivery in which mixed messages are being communicated, a result of an intention not being properly supported

Inflection—The specific pitch in the voice (up or down) used at the end of a word or phrase

Intention—An aim that guides action, informing all aspects of a person's physical and vocal delivery

Intention Cues—Any aspect of a person's vocal or physical communication that conveys meaning to an audience or listener

Internal Noise—Negative thoughts that can distract a speaker or interfere with the effective delivery of a message

Intervention—Any action taken by a speaker that is meant to improve group behavior or processes

Isopraxism—The idea that an audience will mirror back whatever emotion or behavior a speaker projects; see also, *mirror theory*

Jargon—Words or expressions that are used by a particular profession or group and are difficult for others to understand

Listening—The process of receiving, constructing meaning from, and responding to spoken or nonverbal messages

Logical Pause—A moment of silence dictated by your material or visual aid that allows your audience to read or absorb information

Master Closing—The five points that need to be established at the conclusion of a meeting or presentation

Master Introduction—The five points that need to be established at the outset of a meeting or presentation

Metaphor—A figure of speech in which a word or phrase is applied to an object or action to which it is not literally applicable

Micro-Expressions—The involuntary facial movements and physical tics that occur without our even being aware of them

Mirror Theory—The idea that people pick up on whatever emotion or intention a speaker projects and both feel and project back that emotion; see also, *isopraxism*

Monotone—A succession of sounds or words without change in pitch

Murder Board—A technique, first developed by the U.S. military, by which a group or committee simulates worst-case scenarios during the preparation process for a meeting, interview, or presentation

Muscle Memory—The consolidation of a specific activity or motor task into memory through the use of repetition or practice

Nonverbal Communication—Any aspects of communication—aside from the actual words spoken—that send messages or convey meaning to a listener

Objective—A goal you hope to accomplish with your communication

Open-Ended Question—A question that cannot be answered with a single word or a yes or no and requires more information or detail

Operative—A specific word or phrase given special emphasis or importance

Pace—The rate, based on words per minute spoken, at which a person speaks

Pacifier—Any nervous behavior or activity displayed by a speaker that communicates discomfort or nervousness

Paralanguage—Nonverbal vocal nuances in communication that may add meaning to language

Parking Lot—A time-management tool that allows a speaker to defer irrelevant questions until the end of a meeting or presentation

Pattern Interrupt—Any action or behavior that breaks a pattern in an effort to maintain the attention of an audience

Performance-Based Communication—Utilizing time-honored performance techniques from the acting world to enhance one's personal communication

Personal Stamp—The uniqueness and individuality a speaker or actor brings to a presentation or performance

Physiological Pause—A silence during your communication that requires you to stop speaking so you can take a breath or a sip of water

Pitch—The highness or lowness in the voice determined by the rate of vibration in the vocal cords

Positioning Statement—A short, compelling description about your company, product, or service and the benefit it can provide to the listener; sometimes called an *elevator pitch*

Posture—The position of a person's body when standing or sitting

Primacy—The state of being first in order (with *recency*, one of the two parts of a presentation most likely to stay with the audience)

Proactive Communication—An interaction that has been preplanned or prepared such as a meeting or presentation

Proxemics—A term first introduced by anthropologist Edward T. Hall that involves the nature, degree, and effect of the spatial separation individuals naturally maintain and of how this separation relates to environmental and cultural factors

Psychological Pause—A silence during your communication used to evoke or provoke an emotional response from your audience

Reactive Communication—An interaction that is unexpected and requires you to respond in the moment without preparation or planning, such as answering a question or confronting an accusation

Recency—The state of being last in order (with *primacy*, one of the two parts of a presentation most likely to stay with the audience)

Relevancy Tree—A time-management tool that allows a speaker to properly handle both relevant and irrelevant questions without getting sidetracked

Resolution—The final element of a story where all loose ends are tied up and any outstanding questions are answered

Resonation—The prolongation and intensification of sound produced by transmission of its vibrations in the various body cavities (chest, mouth, nasal cavity, skull, throat)

Rising Action—The events in a story that follow the inciting incident and build to the climax

Rule of Three—A concept in writing that suggests that content or messages delivered in threes is generally more satisfying and effective than content delivered in other numbers

Serial Position Effect—A memory-related term coined by Hermann Ebbinghaus that refers to the tendency to recall information presented first and last (like in a list) better than information presented in the middle

7%–38%–55% Rule—Refers to the research by Albert Mehrabian that studied congruence in communication and how an audience decides their feelings toward a speaker

Signpost—A rhetorical tool whereby a speaker provides a series of items in specific ascending or descending order

Simile—A figure of speech that directly compares two different things, usually by employing the words "like" or "as"

Soft Palate—The soft tissue constituting the back of the roof of the mouth

Spatiality—The way in which a speaker uses space, movement, and distance when communicating a message to others

Spotlight—A rhetorical tool whereby a speaker provides added emphasis or importance to a specific fact or item

Statute of Six—A guideline for creating slides that says you should have no more than six word slides in a row, no more than six bullet points per slide, and no more than six words per bullet point; additionally, an audience should be able to understand the meaning or essence of a slide in six seconds or less

Stone-Face Syndrome—A condition whereby a speaker's facial expressions communicate virtually nothing, usually a result of nervousness or anxiety

Subtext—The implicit or underlying meaning of a person's verbal communication, or *the words beneath the words*

Summary Statement—A short, compelling description that establishes who you are and what you do

Super-Objective—The overall goal you hope to achieve with your communication

Teaser—A rhetorical tool whereby a speaker mentions something that is upcoming in an effort to arouse interest

Torso Tell—A concept that the direction your torso is facing signals interest and intent

Trial Close—A question, usually in a selling scenario, meant to determine how close the parties are to an agreement

Tricolon—A rhetorical term for a series of three parallel words, phrases, or clauses

Upspeak—The tendency to make your voice rise at the end of sentences so that statements sound like questions

Verbal Virus—Verbal fillers (such as *ah*, *um*, or *I mean*) that show up in speech and communicate uncertainty to an audience or listener

Vocal Dynamics—The ways in which you use the various qualities of the voice (pitch, tone, resonation, inflection, articulation, volume, and pace)

Vocal Variety—The effective variation of vocal qualities achieved through combining and varying pitch, tone, resonation, inflection, articulation, volume, and pace

Acknowledgments

To quote the great Chris Van Allsburg from his 1986 Caldecott Medal acceptance speech, "Conceiving something is only part of the creative process; giving life to the conception is the other half." *The Pin Drop Principle* was not created in a void. Every tool and technique detailed in these pages was tested and refined over time in various Pinnacle trainings and workshops across the globe. Because of that, we would like to gratefully acknowledge the contributions of our core group of Pinnacle trainers and team members, many of whom have been with us from the very beginning: Brad Lawrence, Jay Collins, Jo Mills, Jay Schwartz, Gerri Leon, Brian McNeany, Tim Kasper, Rob Lynch, Geetanjali Khatri, Jason Denuszek, Frey Hoffman, Clare Hallinan, Surabhi Thirumalai, Laura Shatkus, Cindy Tegtmeyer, DawnMarie Vestevich, Chris Gausselin, and John Garnett. Your commitment, dedication, and input have been invaluable in creating and developing the methodology that has led to the writing of *The Pin Drop Principle*.

To our families—in particular, our wives, Celeste and Jo, our children, Rider, Hunter, Sadie, and Sawyer, and our parents and in-laws—thank you for the infinite patience and understanding that you have shown as we shaped and formed this book over the past seven years, often spending extended periods of time working out of town or overseas.

To our various teachers and mentors throughout the years—specifically Judy Jamieson, Rob Nelson, Warren Stowell, Steve Farley, J. Mark Reisetter, Chip Stevens, Greg Porcaro, Paul Kampf, Shawn Cole, and Don Ilko—thank you for giving so generously of your time and talent, and for sharing your knowledge and insights as we embarked on our various plots and plans. You have truly taught us the value of imagination and its ability to empower others.

We'd also like to thank our agent, the amazing Eric Lupfer at William Morris/Endeavor, for championing this project from the start, as well as our brilliant editor Genoveva Llosa, the staff at Jossey-Bass/Wiley—especially John Maas and Mary Garrett—our developmental editor, Clancy Drake, and our fantastic copyeditor, Hilary Powers. We are humbled by the invaluable guidance you have provided in shaping this book throughout the entire process. Thanks for giving us a home.

Finally, we wish to thank our various clients across the globe—from Los Angeles to London, from Minneapolis to Mumbai—and specifically, Aarti Gupta, Tom Schencker, Bill Joiner, Archana Arcott, Eloise Haverland, Greg Willmore, Joie Settle, Satya Mishra, Larry Frazier, and Susan St. Amant. We are grateful for the privilege you have given us to work with you. By graciously allowing us into your organizations, you have become more than business partners; you have become part of the fabric of the Pinnacle organization. We are continually awed and inspired by the talent and openness we are privileged to witness on a daily basis as part of our work together. Without you, this book would not have been possible.

About the Authors

David Lewis is cofounder and CEO of Pinnacle Performance Company, a global training firm that has revolutionized presentation and communication skills training based on the time-honored performance-delivery techniques favored by professional actors. He has guest-lectured on and taught the principles of the award-winning Pinnacle Method to audiences all over the world.

In 2004 David cofounded Last Line Endeavors, a film development and production company that produced the award-winning feature film *Brothers Three: An American Gothic*, starring John Heard, Patrick Wilson, and Neal McDonough. As a professional actor and member of the Screen Actors Guild, David has amassed a number of credits both on stage and on camera.

Prior to launching Pinnacle, David established a strong résumé in the corporate world, holding executive-level sales and marketing positions at both Fortune 500 companies and hi-tech and Internet start-ups, where he was responsible for building and developing new product sales and sales forces.

David is a graduate of Cornell University and lives in Chicago with his wife and two children. A baseball enthusiast, he looks forward to the day when the Chicago Cubs win a World Series.

G. Riley Mills is the cofounder and COO of Pinnacle Performance Company and has taught effective communication to executives and CEOs across the globe. He has guest-lectured or delivered keynotes at the Cox School of Business, Southern Methodist University, Valparaiso University, Singapore Management University, Moorhead State University, and Joliet Junior College.

As a writer, Mills has twice been awarded the Joseph Jefferson Citation (Chicago's Tony Award) for Best New Work. His first book, *Sawdust and Spangles* (written with Grammy-nominated musician Ralph Covert), won a 2007 NAPPA Honor Award; their follow-up book, *A Nutty Nutcracker Christmas*, was profiled in *USA Today*. In 2012, their acclaimed musical, *The Hundred Dresses*, premiered off Broadway at the Atlantic Theatre Company in New York City.

As a professional actor, Mills last appeared at Steppenwolf Theatre in Chicago. Television credits include episodes of *ER*, *Early Edition*, and *Missing Persons*. Film credits include lead roles in *The Home Coming* (World Wide Pictures) and *35 Miles from Normal*, which premiered at the 1997 Sundance Film Festival. A member of the Screen Actors Guild, Mills recently cofounded a not-for-profit company called The Bookwallah Organization, whose sole mission is to collect storybooks and set up libraries in orphanages around the world (www.bookwallah.org). He lives with his family in Chicago.

ABOUT PINNACLE PERFORMANCE COMPANY

Founded by professional actors and Fortune 500 executives, Pinnacle Performance Company delivers its Performance-Based Communication training to business professionals all over the world, meshing time-honored performance-delivery techniques with essential business communication skills needed to succeed and influence at every level of the corporate arena. Building on its award-winning methodology (the Pinnacle Method), Pinnacle uses customized, interactive simulations and a detailed focus on delivery to help participants become more confident, credible, and compelling communicators. For more information about our company and offerings, please log on to www.pinper.com.

For additional material and bonus content not included in *The Pin Drop Principle*, go to pinper.com/resources.

Index

U

Up in the Air, 89
Upspeak, 126
Upton, Caitlin, 162–163

V

Venter, Craig, 161
Verbal communication: importance of congruence of, 24–25, 97–98; information transmitted by, 95. *See also* Voice
Verbal viruses, 131
Villains, in presentations, 52–53
Vocal communication. *See* Voice
Vocal dynamics, 120, 123
Vocal variety, 120
Voice, 119–137; articulation of, 133–135; congruence of, 24–25, 97–98; defined, 120; importance of, 119–120; inflection of, 126; nonverbal qualities of (paralanguage), 121–123; for operatives, 135–136; pace of, 126–133, 227n13; pitch of, 124–125; power of, 120–121; protecting, 136–137; volume of, 123–124
Volkonski, S. M., 79
Volume, 123–124

W

Waitley, Denis, 173
Ware, Eugene, 90
Warm-up exercises: for articulators, 135, 137; to combat stage fright, 87–88; for voice shortly before presentation, 137
Water: to combat stage fright, 88; to protect voice, 136
Watson, Kittie, 147
Welch, Jack, 3
Wesch, Michael, 96
West, Mae, 98
"What do you do?" question, 166–171
What Every BODY Is Saying (Navarro), 107
White, Valerie, 107
Whitman, Meg, 3
Wilde, Oscar, 201
Wilder, Gene, 40–41
Williams, Mariah, 94–95
Winfrey, Oprah, 3, 7
Winston, Sally, 82
Wolvin, Andrew, 95–96
Writing Tools (Clark), 55

Y

You Say More Than You Think (Driver), 207